Students
Helping
Students

Students
Helping
Students

A Guide for Peer Educators on College Campuses

Second Edition

Fred B. Newton, Steven C. Ender
Foreword by John N. Gardner

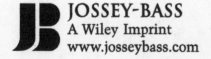
JOSSEY-BASS
A Wiley Imprint
www.josseybass.com

Published by Jossey-Bass

A Wiley Imprint

989 Market Street, San Francisco, CA 94103-1741—www.josseybass.com

Readers should be aware that Internet Web sites offered as citations and/or sources for further information may have changed or disappeared between the time this was written and when it is read.

Jossey-Bass books and products are available through most bookstores. To contact Jossey-Bass directly call our Customer Care Department within the U.S. at 800-956-7739, outside the U.S. at 317-572-3986, or fax 317-572-4002.

Jossey-Bass also publishes its books in a variety of electronic formats. Some content that appears in print may not be available in electronic books.

Library of Congress Cataloging-in-Publication Data

Newton, Fred B.
   Students helping students : a guide for peer educators on college campuses / Fred B. Newton, Steven C. Ender ; foreword by John N. Gardener. - 2nd ed.
      p. cm. - (The Jossey-Bass higher and adult education series)
   Includes bibliographical references and index.
   ISBN 978-0-470-45209-7 (pbk.)
1. Peer counseling of students   2. Peer-group tutoring of students.
I. Ender, Steven C.   II. Title.
   LB1027.5.N727 2010
   371.4′047–dc22

                                                                2010009694

THE JOSSEY-BASS
HIGHER AND ADULT
EDUCATION SERIES

CONTENTS

LIST OF FIGURES AND TABLES

Figures

Tables

FOREWORD

In my four decades as a higher educator the full realization of "students helping students" has been dawning on me gradually, but powerfully and persuasively. And now, in what my friend Betty Siegel calls the "wintering into wisdom" phase of my life, I can safely posit that I believe the most important generic strategy that colleges and universities can adopt to increase student success is one that greatly increases intentional efforts for "students helping students." How did I come upon this position?

For me, this epiphany began when I was in college. I wrote about this in November of 2009 in a blog entitled "Power to the Peers." I insert this now in this foreword to Fred Newton's and Steven Ender's important second edition of *Students Helping Students* to serve as my foundational introductory comments on this important work.

> Power to the Peers!
>
> The ring of the header above has to reveal that I am a child of the 60s with its evocation of "power to the people." I confess: I am. That was the period in which I acquired my idealism which drives me still. I was inspired by President Kennedy, Martin Luther King, the early feminist thinkers and leaders, the Civil Rights and Women's Rights movements and the anti-war movement, in which I participated after I completed my own tour of military service, honorably and with gratitude. Anyway, to the point of this blog: students have always had power.

Decades of good research has determined that the single greatest influence on college student decision making during the college years is the influence of other students. This is one of those things like the students working in college phenomena. We can't beat it. Why not join it? This is to say, once you recognize the enormous influence of students on students, the logical conclusion should be we need to try to influence this by putting the students we want to influence other students into positions of influence to do just that.

Inspired by uses of "peer mentors" in first-year seminars that I saw at such places as Baldwin-Wallace College (Ohio) and Kean University of New Jersey, I decided in 1991, when I was the Executive Director of University 101 at the University of South Carolina, to personally be the first 101 instructor to use a "peer mentor" as a test case. It was a wonderful experience. I am indebted to my peer leader, Ms. Lisa Huttinger, for giving me and my students such a wonderful experience. And then I became even more indebted to my Co-director of University 101, Professor Dan Berman for picking up the ball and creating our powerful peer leader program at USC. Today, over 175 sections of the course annually have a peer leader.

I say "even more indebted" because my colleague, Dan Berman, had been a sophomore at Marietta College in 1961, when I was a floundering first-year student also at Marietta. And it was his spontaneous and generous reaching out to influence me, by showing me how to take lecture notes, and select really engaging professors, that I attribute more than anything else to getting me off academic probation. I often think were it not for my own "peer leader" I would never have been able to stay in college, and then go on to help other college students. So, by all means: Power to the peers!

Newton and Ender have provided us with a new manual that can tell both us and our students everything we needed to know about why students should be empowered to help students by being placed in official positions of institutional influence, and then how to influence students positively and realize concomitant personal growth and learnings themselves. This work reaffirms my own learnings on my journey that has led me to conclude that an intentional strategy for students helping students should be the foundation of institutionalized efforts to improve student success.

As indicated in my blog above, this learning journey for me began with my own college experience with that life transforming, serendipitous encounter with an upperclass student who literally "saved" me, a failing first-year student.

It was later, in my senior year in college, that I learned the next two lessons about students helping students. The first came when a fellow student shared with me an all time best-seller book, Erich Fromm's *The Art of Loving*. Reading the manuscript of *Students Helping Students* reminds me of this lesson because of the pedagogical emphasis that Newton and Ender put on the idea that students must first know themselves before they can fulfill their potential to help others, particularly their strengths and weaknesses, and how those are revealed in interactional contexts with other students. Comparably, Fromm argued influentially that before any person (e.g., college student) can "love" another, she or he must first have attained sufficient self-esteem to have developed the capacity for self-love and respect.

My second lesson that senior year was my experience as a student government leader, the founding chair of a student judicial system that aspired to root out academic dishonesty and raise academic standards. This was, I sincerely believed, in the name of students helping students. And I found that of all my experiences in college, this was by far the most powerful. Student government interactions gave me a relatively risk-free laboratory to apply most all the skills I had been learning in my liberal arts courses: critical thinking, problem solving, persuasive writing and speaking, and more.

Several years later, I really had the opportunity to see an analog to "students helping students" when I had the good fortune to be drafted during my own graduate school education, into the U.S. armed forces. It was during the military that I saw as I never had before the learning and personal growth value that derives from giving the lowest-status members of the organization (young, entering troops = first-year students) *responsibility*. I saw the transformative power of giving and taking responsibility, literally responsibility for the lives of others and millions of dollars worth of property. And after my military service, that is exactly what I have seen for students whom we place in official positions of authority to help other students: responsibility is the most powerful teacher.

I have to ask, but don't have time in this brief foreword to answer: why don't we give students more responsibility? *Students Helping Students* gives us plenty of answers for why and how we should. One fine thinker I discovered on my own professional journey is my namesake but no relation, Phillip Gardner, who leads the Collegiate Employment Research Institute at Michigan State University. Phillip Gardner is a foremost researcher on what happens to recent college graduates in positions of employment. He has even studied why some recent college graduates lose their first job after college. The most common reason: "failure to take initiative." I believe that if we included more deliberate learning experiences for students from "students helping students" that we could produce more graduates who definitely know how to take initiative.

Another very influential thinker, and practitioner, that I have discovered in my career is a scholar and teacher whom I fondly refer to as the "guru of service learning": Professor of English Edward Zlotkowski of Bentley University. It was Edward and his writing and speaking about the transformative educational influence of service learning who really got me to realize that the root of this influence on student development must rest in what Zlotkowski calls "reflection." This is identical to the case that Newton and Ender make for an essential component of peer leader training to be what they call "reflection." This argues for the necessity of having students reflect on their own learnings from the challenges they have faced in college and how those have been connected to personal learning, growth, and change. That reflection process becomes inextricably connected to the introspection process that the authors also argue is an essential part of the peer leader training component. I believe that the more we teach, encourage, insist, that students practice reflection and introspection, the higher their level of engagement will be in their remaining college courses and career.

I had been in my career for over twenty years, working on the so-called "first-year experience" reform movement, when I launched another Don Quixote crusade for what I called "the senior year experience," which was also the title of a 1998 Jossey-Bass book. In the process of editing that work I discovered another fine scholar, Professor Ed Holton of Louisiana State University. Holton enlightened me by his persuasive analysis of how the cultures of most postcollege work environments are different from, and in many ways not compatible with, the cultures of most colleges and universities, which prepare students to enter those postcollege environments. In college students are not required to exercise nearly the same levels and extent of responsibility that they must exhibit immediately after college. In college they are told precisely what they must do, when, and how. This is frequently not the case in the world of employment, where there is much more ambiguity and space for personal differences in initiative. *Students Helping Students* appeals to me because I think we educators must do a better job of giving students more meaningful responsibilities, through helping and leading others, before they leave college for the real world of work. In that sense, college could also become the "real world of work."

As I write this foreword, I do so living near a small North Carolina town, Swannanoa, which is the location of one of the very few remaining "work colleges," as they are known in American higher education: Warren Wilson College. Here the students do virtually everything to keep the college operating and fellow students nourished: they grow and prepare the food, maintain the grounds and physical plant, and far more. Each student has an academic and a work curriculum and both are regarded as equally important. There is a chief academic officer and a "dean of work." This is the ultimate attainment of "students helping students." It occurs to me that a fallout from the Great Recession may be to encourage more institutions to return to more of the practices of the work college, an environment where *all* students help *all* students. Just think of the combined cost savings and learning outcomes with real-life transfer values. *Students Helping Students* could show the way.

Well, this is surely enough of my reflection and introspection on why colleges ought to invest more intentional educational energies into placing more students in more positions of authority to help other students; and why we should provide the intentional training and support to accomplish this. I am persuaded that this could truly leverage and increase student success. Students helping students is a process to fulfill the potential for college as both a time and context for students to explore and develop their potential for helping themselves, others, our communities, and society. Now you just need to experience Fred Newton's and Steven Ender's *Students Helping Students* for yourself.

The use of this book by our students could truly be individually and institutionally life transformative. Best wishes on your own higher education journey of which students helping students is such a fundamental part.

John N. Gardner

PREFACE

The world was still celebrating the new millennium when *Students Helping Students* was released in the first edition. We were anticipating that higher education was entering an exciting era of new technology, increasingly diverse students, and expanded opportunities for connecting people with common interests all across the globe. We knew that peer educators were going to be an important part of our colleges and universities entering the new age. Who would be better prepared to deal with change and adjust to new challenges than those in the generation of change?

During the past ten years many milestones have occurred: the tragedy of 9/11 and the shock of vulnerability, followed by war in Iraq and Afghanistan. Mark Zuckerman introduced Facebook and within months millions of students joined the new social networking club. Our libraries became 90 percent accessible from a student's room two thousand miles away during a semester abroad. Tuition costs more than doubled at many institutions, an African American became president, tragic violent events occurred on major college campuses, and student demographics grew to represent more diversity than at any time in history. As we predicted, the decade was filled with change, even if we did not anticipate the specific changes that occurred.

Has change also taken place with peer educator roles and responsibilities on campus? The first task of our revision was to investigate the changes taking place for students serving in helping and educating roles with their fellow students. Data were readily accessible from our own campus, from colleagues around the country, and from students, the Internet, and current journals. A Google search turned up over 500 descriptions of peer education programs in nearly every service or academic unit possible on a college campus. A colleague working in Residence Life indicated that over 10 percent of residents served in peer educator positions. At another institution an estimate was made that over 30 percent of the students had actively participated in service projects during an academic year. Three trends were identified: the proliferation of peer educators in a wide range of service duties; the expansion of service delivery methods to include not only direct contacts but also electronic blogs and social networking and interactive Web sites; and the growth of peer leadership into social consciousness movements, such as matters of campus safety, advocacy for sound ecology, and responsible community. These trends are discussed further in Chapter One.

ADDITIONS AND IMPROVEMENTS TO THIS EDITION

Updating for current trends and reporting new information and research were major reasons for revision. Feedback and experience from the first edition indicated that we could make some key improvements. Students today are active learners wanting more examples of real situations and more engagement through activities; also, conceptual maps are helpful when there is a need to explain the big picture. This edition has included many new examples, mostly collected from students in peer educator classes who have offered their stories as a part of training. A number of activities have been added as well so that you, the reader, can make your own story part of the learning. Each chapter now contains figures and graphs that illustrate many of the key points in that section of the book. We want the experience offered in the book to be engaging and an enjoyable part of your training. Another addition is a new chapter that provides several examples of peer educator programs in a variety of service areas. These are used as illustrations of the breadth of possibilities for peer educator service.

USE OF THE BOOK

Students Helping Students may function as a training manual and also as a resource guide for those in preservice or in-service preparation as peer educators. We have found that it may also be used as part of training for leadership classes training for service learning, or for paraprofessional or entry level staff training in staff positions that do not have formal specialized training in a social service or student service field.

The book is designed to utilize what is described as a *reflection* model, at work when you see the terms *what, so what,* and *now what.* You will go through the steps of explaining the basic principles of a concept *(what),* reflecting upon what this means to you and the situation of concern *(so what),* and anticipating how to apply and utilize the *what* in a real life situation *(now what).* Each chapter provides opportunity to go through this reflection process.

STRUCTURE OF THE BOOK

The book comprises eleven chapters. The first four provide the core helping foundation and personal knowledge that we believe are necessary for later skill development. As we have said, competent helping people first know themselves and the personal strengths and weaknesses they bring to the helping relationship. With this concept in mind, the first four chapters require you to be somewhat introspective in regard to yourself, the world around you, and your communication skills as a helping person.

In Chapter One, "Peer Educators on the College Campus," we present an overview of the role you are taking up. We review the extent to which peer interventions are used on college campuses and how peer programs have been effective. We introduce the model of training and ask you to reflect upon how this experience will impact your own life.

As a peer educator, you will be assisting other students who are facing personal challenges of all types. In Chapter Two, "Student Maturation and the Impact of Peers," we explore the types of personal changes and challenges most college-aged students experience. We explore the concept of challenge-and-response dynamics as it relates to and stimulates personal change. In this chapter, we encourage you to reflect on your own development and maturation level, assess your strengths, and consider strategies to improve areas that you note for improvement.

Chapter Three, "Enhancing Cultural Proficiency," is extremely important to the understanding of culture and diversity of cultures and their impact on our interactions and very existence. We are a multicultural society to which people bring their various worldviews. It is important that we know and understand ourselves as cultural beings in order to understand and respect the many issues of diversity.

In Chapter Four, "Interpersonal Communication Skills: Creating the Helping Interaction," we explore the significance of effective listening and responding skills, emphasizing both verbal and nonverbal communication patterns. Core helping areas of empathy, respect, and warmth are defined. Basic responses in helping interactions are explained with specific examples.

Most important, you will learn that helping others with personal concerns is accomplished by being a competent, empathic, nonjudgmental listener.

In Chapter Five, "Problem Solving with Individuals," we cover the topic of assisting others through the use of active problem-solving approaches. We also present the integration of communication skills with a problem-solving model, as well as other specific problem-solving techniques.

We present an overview of how groups develop and function in Chapter Six, "Understanding Group Process." In this chapter we challenge you to heighten your awareness and subsequent attention to group communication patterns, normative behavior, decision processes, cohesion, and individual coordination toward group task. Attention to group process is a major ingredient in improving the functioning level of a group.

In Chapter Seven, "Leading Groups Effectively," we look at the necessary characteristics of being an effective leader, as well as covering the very practical nuts and bolts of conducting productive group meetings and making group presentations. We also explore skills and methods for organizing, facilitating, and solving problems.

We provide examples of applying the peer intervention model to academic success in Chapter Eight, "Strategies for Academic Success." This is the only chapter that demonstrates an in-depth application of how peers may offer service toward a specific area of outcome. The chapter serves as an example of implementation, using as a topic academic success, which is a goal common to all students.

In "Using Campus Resources and Referral Techniques," Chapter Nine, we offer an overview of the process for helping students locate resources and making appropriate referrals to these resources. Among the discussed resources are physical support services and Internet and electronic resources.

xxiii

In Chapter Ten, "Ethics and Strategies for Good Practice," we introduce the need for standards of ethical behavior and discuss the issues of conduct that a peer educator might encounter.

As noted previously, we added Chapter Eleven, "Examples of Peer Education Programs in Higher Education," to present a range of examples of how peer educators function in a variety of services. This edition also provides a glossary as a resource aid.

As you begin the process of learning effective helping skills we encourage you to explore yourself and your potential for the future. It is the same exploration and encouragement that you will give others on a daily basis in your role of peer educator. We hope you find both training and serving others to be as exciting and personally relevant as we have in our own lives. You are in a position to make a difference in the life experience of others. We challenge you to make the most of the exciting life experience. Enjoy the ride!

ACKNOWLEDGMENTS

There are many who contributed to this revised work. We feel gratitude to them for their contributions of time and effort and, most important, for their willingness to share very forthright suggestions.

First, we greatly appreciate important inputs from the Jossey-Bass editor, Erin Null. She provided excellent suggestions with input from reviewers on how to make significant improvements in this edition. Her suggestions nudged and challenged us to open our minds to some new ways of presenting material. And this was done with the right amount of encouragement and support.

Next, we received a lot of informational inputs directly and indirectly from a number of professionals that were supervising and organizing peer educator programs. Direct inputs came from several professionals who offered interviews and described the details of their peer programs. We thank Mary Tolar, Carol Kennedy, Dianna Schalles, Sarah Tedford, Camilla Roberts, and John O'Connell for these inputs. Informally, we reviewed online descriptions from more programs than we can enumerate in a paragraph. This is another benefit of the Internet: providing "show and tell" access to the world.

Another valuable experience was visiting over a dozen classes where peer educators were being trained and receiving their ideas through open discussion. These students tried out many of the activities from the book and provided very candid feedback. Students not only helped students but they were also invaluable help to the authors. Special thanks to students Rebecca Steinert, Tammy Osborn, and Tammy Sonnentag for research and editorial inputs from students' perspectives.

I want to especially thank those who participated in the production of this book by offering suggestions, editing, research, and assistance with many of the details that made the final product possible. Eunhee Kim served as assistant in charge of research and made inputs with the chapter on student success. John O'Connell, a long time friend and colleague, served as a consultant on content for chapters on the college student and facilitative communication. Brenda Schoendaller managed to protect, organize, and make sure the detailed tasks were completed on time.

Extremely valuable contributions were made by two consultants serving as proof editors to read, correct, suggest, and improve drafts of this book. Shalin Hai Jew supported the completion of the first draft of the book. Both her expertise on technology and her writing skills were great assets. Katherine Harder, with only a couple of weeks notice, was able to help us polish the final draft. She was indeed a gift to find at the crunch time of preparation.

Last but certainly not least I want to recognize Ata Karim for contributing the initial writing of Chapter Three on "Enhancing Cultural Proficiency" and sharing his expertise in that area, and Rita Ross for adapting the concepts of culture and competence into practical applications for peer education training. She has also been a great source of personal support over the year of production.

We also want to recognize the authors who were the first to create an early version of *Students Helping Students* in 1979. Theodore K. Miller and Sue Saunders were pioneers in this effort, along with Steven Ender, coauthor of this book. We are grateful to these authors for releasing the copyright to us and letting their original text be updated and expanded. You will note sections that contain a reference to their work.

Fred B. Newton
Steven C. Ender

ABOUT THE AUTHORS

Fred B. Newton is director of counseling services and professor of counseling and educational psychology at Kansas State University. At the University of Missouri-Columbia he received an EPDA (Education Professions Development Act) fellowship while completing a doctorate in counseling psychology. He also has a master's degree in student personnel services from Ohio State University.

Dr. Newton's early career included teaching and coaching in the public schools, serving as director of a community recreation program, and directing the student activities program at a community college. He has held a faculty position in the Department of Counseling and Human Development at the University of Georgia and was coordinator of career counseling and associate professor of education at Duke University.

He has been active as an author and researcher, having contributed chapters to seventeen professional books and written over sixty articles for professional journals. Other professional contributions include over a hundred presentations to professional and other public audiences. He has been involved internationally with presentations in Europe and Asia and has publications that have been printed in Japan and Australia.

Over the past twenty years, Dr. Newton has served as a training consultant to students and staff in over fifty college settings, including colleges in the United Kingdom, Portugal, Romania, Taiwan, and Japan. He has helped establish workshops and training programs in areas of leadership, organizational development, and peer counseling. He has been involved with the implementation of six grant programs sponsored by foundations and federal government programs. Currently, he is director of Kansas State Comprehensive Assessment Tool, Inc., a nonprofit corporation that develops and distributes assessment instruments for measuring input and outcome variables on student success.

Dr. Newton has been recognized for excellence in his teaching and service contributions to professional associations. He received the Annuit Coeptis Award from the American College Personnel Association, the Walter Morrison Service contribution finalist by the Kansas State Foundation, and Emerging Entrepreneurs finalist by Commercialization Leadership Council of Kansas State Research Foundation.

Steven C. Ender became the ninth president of Grand Rapids Community College in May 2009. During his more than thirty years in higher education, Dr. Ender has held numerous teaching, counseling, and administrative positions and has published extensively in refereed journals as well as textbooks. His most recent professional position prior to the GRCC presidency was serving as president of Westmoreland Community College. A Richmond, Virginia, native, Dr. Ender holds a bachelor's degree in business management from Virginia Commonwealth University; master's and doctoral degrees in education from the University of Georgia; and has completed post-doctoral studies at The Snowmass Institute in Snowmass, Colorado, and Harvard University.

Among his honors and achievements, in 2002 Dr. Ender was named to the National Advisory Board for "Helping Teens Succeed," a college transition program. He received the Pennsylvania Association for Developmental Educators Award for Research and Publication in 1998, and the Award for Excellence from the Manchester Craftsmen's Guild of Pittsburgh in 1993. As a young man, he achieved Eagle Scout status.

Dr. Ender serves on the Economic and Workforce Development Commission of the American Association of Community Colleges, the Lifelong Learning Commission of the American Council on Education, and the board of the National Junior College Athletic Association as a presidential representative.

Dr. Ender resides in Grand Rapids with his wife, Karen Gislason Ender, and is the father of two adult children, Joanna DiCiurcio and Mason Ender.

CHAPTER 1

Peer Educators on the College Campus

LEARNING OBJECTIVES

After completing this chapter, you will be able to

1. Explain to others the role of college students serving as peer educators.
2. List several helping positions on college campuses that are staffed by peer educators.
3. Describe how your personal experience has demonstrated important principles of a helpful relationship.
4. Understand and be able to employ an active process model of learning that includes three elements—sensing, personalizing, and acting.
5. Explain the importance of role modeling within the helping role.
6. Define how the terms *peer educator, role model, mentor,* and *professional* may have similarities and differences.

The Case of Joe Freshman

Joe Freshman arrives on campus the summer before his enrollment and an ambassador gives him a tour of the facilities and a general overview of what it is like to be a student here. Joe also stops by the Financial Aid office to find out about his application for funding and talks with a financial advisor, who answers his questions. Later, he moves

---

1

into the residence hall where his resident assistant helps him get set up with residence life. Joe enrolls and takes a First Year Experience Orientation class, where he meets in a weekly seminar with a recitation leader. Part of the Orientation class assignment is to complete a career online assessment; a career specialist helps interpret his results. At mid-term, needing help with his college algebra, Joe makes an appointment with a tutor. Joe is determined to avoid the "freshmen 15," so he signs up for a personal trainer at the campus recreation center. If he needs health advice he has access to a SHAC (student health advisor), a SHAPE (sexual health awareness peer educator), or a SNAC (student nutrition peer educator). And, heaven forbid, if Joe has a problem and is accused of breaking the academic honesty code, resulting in an appearance before a student judiciary, he would be assigned a HIPE (Honor and Integrity Peer Educator) and may be told to complete an ABC (Assessment for Behavior Change) with a peer mentor.

Joe still needs to complete his first semester and he already has had contact with at least thirteen peer educators on campus. The potential for Joe is that he will meet at least twice as many fellow students serving in peer educator roles before he leaves campus. His first vocabulary word in college is *ubiquitous,* as in "peer educators are ubiquitous." Peers in trained support roles will be a very big part of his education!

This story about Joe might be hypothetical, but the examples of peer educators in this paragraph are authentic. The use of peer educators in the college environment has grown substantially over the past two decades. The involvement of undergraduates in peer assistance roles on college campuses has been identified in more than 75 percent of all higher education institutions (Brack, Millard, & Shah, 2008; Carns, Carns, & Wright, 1993). On today's college campuses, peer educators are involved in providing a wide range of supportive service activities. These services, cutting across a variety of peer educator roles, include providing information, explaining policies and procedures, orienting new students, making referrals, offering specific help strategies for problem-related counseling issues, implementing social and educational programs, enforcing rules, providing academic advising, facilitating community development, offering tutoring, helping with financial management, performing diversity training, and providing crisis intervention services.

Peer educators are valuable for an academic institution because they are experienced with the campus, they are economical to the budget, they can relate to the situations of fellow students, and they are effective. The student serving as a peer educator also benefits; the peer educator learns new skills, gains relevant practice experience, and contributes to the community. For some, it will last a year or two, and for others, it will initiate new career objectives and lifelong personal change. In either case, we believe you will find the peer educator role to be both challenging and rewarding. If you take up one of the many peer educator positions open on modern college campuses, you will have the opportunity to make positive and, in some cases, significant differences in the lives of other students. We believe you will find the personal rewards of serving as a peer educator substantial—and the responsibilities as well. In short, we believe this training program and your subsequent experience as a helping person will have a very powerful impact on your own life, allowing you to explore and extend yourself to make the most of your own best qualities.

3

Reflection Point 1.1: You, as a Peer Helper

Describe why you have chosen to pursue a peer educator position on your campus.

What personal characteristics do you possess that indicate that you are, or can be, a helping person?

A BRIEF HISTORY OF PEER EDUCATION

The use of undergraduates in helping roles on college and university campuses has a long and rich history. Students in residence halls have served as resident assistants, proctors, hall counselors, and advisers since the early 1900s (Powell, Pyler, Dickerson, & McClellan, 1969). Student tutors have been assisting their peers as a direct way to provide academic assistance since the colonial period of American history (Materniak, 1984). In the 1950s, a peer mentoring program, as a didactic education strategy, was implemented at the University of Nebraska. The success of this program led to the expansion of peer educating as a mechanism for improving retention and academic success (Sawyer, Pinciaro, & Bedwell, 1997; Terrion & Leonard, 2007).

During the past twenty years some significant changes have occurred in the use of peer educators. First, as we have already noted, there has been a proliferation in the use of peer educators into nearly every aspect of college academic and student service. Second, along with increase in the number of roles for peer educators comes broader use of multiple delivery methods. In addition to traditional one-on-one contact, there has been an increase in peer educators' involvement with organizational strategies, classroom and group programs, and Web sites and electronic communication. Finally, in the past decade more activist forms of peer movements have begun in response to issues of harassment, violence, and other trauma on campus. Such counter movements to

---

Exercise 1.1: Peer Educators on Your Campus

Identify the types of peer educator roles on your campus.

In these roles, what types of strategies are used for providing assistance: one-to-one contact, working with groups or organizations, online or electronic medium, or some combinations of all of these?

make the campus safer and more responsive as a community were due, at least in part, to an increase of shootings and acts of terror (Birchard, 2009). Peer educators are now playing a significant leadership role in campaigns to provide support groups, nonviolence, and better safety procedures for reducing trauma, connecting students to service, and developing more supportive campus communities.

Although peer educator involvement is possible in nearly every student service and academic department, our intent in this book is not to cover the job description and content information for all the ways peer educators may serve on a college campus. Instead, we focus on the basic skills for working effectively as a peer helper, no matter the specific capacity. This book is titled *Students Helping Students*, and in a broad sense that is exactly the purpose of this book: to provide preparation, skill training, helpful resources, and thoughtful discussion for students working as peer educators. We intend this book to be both a primer for preparation and a handbook of resources for those in the wide range of service roles and responsibilities mentioned in the paragraphs above.

The first step in this training process is to define key terms and concepts that will be used throughout the book.

DEFINITIONS

You have already seen that many terms seem synonymous with "peer educator." To name a few: peer counselor, ambassador, student coach, peer mentor, student assistant, class recitation facilitator, tutor, resident assistant, and orientation leader. Each of these descriptive names reflects the various nuances and characteristics of the roles and responsibilities taken on by the peer educator. *Peer educator* is a comprehensive and generally unifying term that encompasses the many other descriptive terms just given. Peer educators are students who have been selected, trained, and designated by a campus authority to offer educational services to their peers. These services are intentionally designed to assist peers toward attainment of educational goals. The following questions clarify further the concept of students helping students as peer educators.

What Is Meant by Students Helping Students?

Who is the student who helps and who is the student recipient of help? Are these upper class or more advanced students assisting younger and more novice students? Does this include graduate students? The defining characteristic of a helper is someone who is in some ways more knowing, more experienced, and more capable in a designated area of service than the people being helped. But class status, age, or years of experience is not as important as the *effectiveness* of the peer educator in providing service. For example, those who are motivated and capable of providing service might make more effective peer educators than those with higher status or more experience but less motivation to help. Most importantly, effectiveness can be enhanced through preparation and training. This book is designed to provide you with knowledge, skills, and personal awareness to prepare and enhance your effectiveness as a peer educator.

What Is Helping?

Along with *helping*, terms such as *facilitating, mentoring, advising, instructing, education, aiding, assisting, leading*, and *counseling* are used. These terms convey the specific function of a peer educator. But in truth, there are many shades of difference between the student helping with orientation, the student as a tutor, the student as mentor for achieving an outcome, or the student as an advisor. One basic characteristic of a peer educator is that of *provider*. A *provider* may offer a service of a specific nature; this can be information, support, or facilitating action such as decision making or task accomplishment in the best interest of another person. A helping relationship implies that there is *value added* as a result of the encounter. The peer educator is a *helper*.

How Is a Peer Educator Different from a Professional Helper?

A professional differs from a peer educator in level of training, preparation, experience, and by job designation. The professional must be qualified by meeting standards of competence and training established by the institution, the discipline, or other authority. Their titles such as counselor, professor, dean, adviser, or director denote both the status and level of responsibility. One important aspect of your training as a peer educator will be to learn where the level of your competence to assist others ends and where the knowledge and skills of the professional must take over

7

to provide the optimal learning experience for another student. We cover the importance of personal boundaries and knowing limits of peer service as well as the skills and knowledge necessary for making appropriate referrals and ethical behaviors in Chapters Nine and Ten.

Reflection Point 1.2: Peer Educator versus Professional Responsibilities

What are the primary differences between the type of assistance you are going to provide to other students and the assistance given to students in your sponsoring agency by your professional counterparts?

WHY ARE PEER EDUCATORS EFFECTIVE?

What the Research Says

There are several reasons peer educators produce positive results in assisting student success for a variety of outcomes. One explanation may be that the peer educator is slightly ahead in experience and awareness of what a student seeking help may be going through but not so removed as to seem unable to identify and understand his or her situation (Lockspeiser, O'Sullivan, Teherani, & Muller, 2008). Illustrating this idea, one student noted that relating with her peer educator was like "being able to relate to someone who has been through similar experience but still understands and won't judge me for needing input on what may seem unimportant." Indeed, sensitive topics such as dating relationships, health and sexuality, or personal finances may be discussed without the embarrassment of talking to a "more" adult figure (Good, Halpin, & Halpin, 2000; Sawyer et al., 1997). That students feel more compatible with a peer educator who has similar learning styles and who approaches the world from a similar generational perspective is exemplified in the Beloit College Mindset List, a yearly publishing of the events that have occurred and affected the lives of a contemporary cohort of students (see http://www.beloit.edu/mindset/). The world events, the newest technologies, popular entertainers, sports events, movies, music, well-known public figures, major political and social issues, wars, economic trends, fads and fashions, and even the popular lingo are ways that mark the times and frequently separate the generations. The underlying concept is that students seek advice from and are influenced by the expectations, attitudes, and behaviors of their peer group. Peer influence in many situations may be stronger than that of adults such as teachers, parents, and other experts (Mellanby, Rees, & Tripp, 2000).

Peer educators have been demonstrated to be effective helpers when provided systematic training in interpersonal communication and relationship skills (Carkhuff, 1969; Daniels & Ivey, 2007; Terrion & Leonard, 2007). Though effective human relations skills are useful in helping students with specific levels of need to explore and resolve questions of information, resource, support, and normal developmental transitions, they do not replace the more in-depth exploration of emotional, mental, or behavioral concerns that require expertise of a professional. A peer educator can be trained to meet some needs, but some needs require additional support.

What Experience Has Taught You About Helping

All of us have received emotional support, insight, or help resolving a problem situation from family, friends, teachers, counselors, or even strangers. Take time to acknowledge and understand what you already know about helping based upon life experience that has provided positive results.

Experiential learning results from the happenstance of moving through life. Instead of learning exclusively from the theory-based lessons of a book or class, you can also look at how

9

Exercise 1.2: Brief Moments That Make a Difference

Think over the past several days about the many little encounters you may have had—some with friends, some with family, but others maybe with people you hardly know: the clerk in a store, the person sitting behind you in a class, the individual who gave you directions when you were lost, or the instructor who made a special comment on your essay. Note the context of the encounter, what happened, and why it was meaningful to you. What was it about the quality of the interaction and the way the person responded to you that made it significant? Write down a short description of the encounter. No matter how short-lived in time the encounter actually was, make your description a brief story noting the action and the attitude, the situation, and the resulting impact upon you.

What was it about the encounter that made it meaningful, helpful, or created the positive impression? If you are learning with a group, individual members may share these reflections and explanations of the helpful encounter.

What can you take from this meaningful moment as a lesson for being helpful?

life experience has provided you with an important template for the *helping moment*. Perhaps you learned something about helping as a result of seeking out a person when a need was present. Or in many cases a meaningful event happened that seemed random, serendipitous, and unplanned, but it nonetheless provided you with extremely useful information, emotional support, and encouragement—it added to your well-being and made your day. The best way to tap this type of learning is to ask you to reflect on these moments directly and to share similar experiences with a group that you may be training with. Illustrations can also be shared by other peer educators. Exercise 1.2 can be done individually but it is more beneficial when the activity and discussion can be shared with a group.

Discussion

The following are examples from other classes of peer educators.

- A custodial worker in a residence hall offered a personal greeting and friendly smile each day to residents (who were feeling half-awake each morning) as they started off to class. This older lady, a first-generation immigrant, knew the names of nearly every resident in the hall and exuded an upbeat, positive attitude. Suddenly one day she was not there to offer her greeting, and many residents felt the strong sense of missing something very important. When it was found out that this woman had taken ill and was in the hospital, several residents rotated days to visit her in the hospital until she had recovered.

- Jayne took time out one afternoon for a ride on her bicycle and ventured down a riding path that led through an off-road park. Nearly eight miles out on the path, she ran over a rough stone and had a flat tire. Jayne had nothing to repair or pump up her tire and was left to push the bike home. About ten minutes later, another rider came by and offered to help. Even though this guy had a small repair kit, there was difficulty, and the tire repair took nearly 30 minutes to fix. She found out when the job was done that the "good Samaritan" helper was now going to be late for his job at a local convenience store. However, he refused to accept money for helping out and only issued a "Have a good day!" as he rode off in the other direction.

- Nearly every student in these classes had brief stories to tell about recent encounters: someone making a call concerned about not seeing her friend in class; an aunt who sent a "care package" to acknowledge a little-known but important anniversary; a boss who took time to explain the importance of doing a job correctly rather than handing out the prescribed disciplinary warning; a seven-year-old boy assisting an older man down a steep staircase at a national monument as closing darkness found the man hesitant about taking a misstep.

Lessons Learned

Take this exercise to the next step, and determine what the moral of the story might be in terms of what made the encounter meaningful. What is helping? What can you learn from any experiences that stand out from the simple act in an ordinary day or an extraordinary act that made a big difference in your life? Share and develop this list with people who are training with you in a group or, if working alone, write down your ideas and compare with the following examples gathered from one of our previous classes:

Helping is

- Less about the power or prestige of the person and more about sincerity and sensitivity
- Demonstrated by a sense of attention and interest even when not requested or spoken

- Action without a sense of personal gain
- A feeling of genuine, heartfelt, and sincere response to another
- Receptive and open acceptance of another without judgment
- Acting to do the "right" thing, a morality of action
- Made through small gestures with important meaning
- Inspiring without gloating
- Listening to the heart as much as the voice

Now make your own group list and discuss how being an effective helper is also an attitude, a disposition, an act of character, a gift of kindness, and a connection to humanity. There are many ways to provide significant gestures helpful to another person. Little things given freely can mean a lot!

THE IMPACT ON YOU AS A PEER EDUCATOR

You can expect that one of the most important outcomes of being a peer educator will be an enhancement of your own growth in both knowledge and personal attributes. Research suggests that college students who participate in peer education display significant improvements in leadership, gain interpersonal communication skills, increase peer-education relevant knowledge, develop higher levels of self-esteem, and create better personal health behaviors when measured on assessments before and after their peer education experience (Brack, Millard, & Shah, 2008; Good, Halpin, & Halpin, 2000; Yamauchi, 1986). As you help others solve problems, your ability to resolve complex issues increases. As you demonstrate empathy and compassion for others, your sense of emotional well-being is heightened. As you work to assist others, you will find your own sense of contribution and personal esteem will grow. Among a list of positive outcomes, program administrators—that is, those in charge of running peer educator programs—ranked the positive impact that the position had on peer educators as the most significant outcome of peer education programs (Ender & Winston, 1984).

If you are at the beginning of your training this is a good time for you to consider how this experience will affect you in significant ways such as those just mentioned. Even if you have had previous peer educator experience it is useful to reflect on how you are being affected. Having emphasized the benefits, though, we also think it important to discuss challenges; at times, you will question yourself and your ability. Most certainly this experience will provide you with opportunities for reflection. You will be likely to reflect on your decisions about relating to people, for example; you may also deliberate over choosing a career, and your experience as a peer educator may even cause you to look at your own values, ideals, and purpose.

The following reflection provides an example of the impact and change that may occur. It was written by a former student who served in several capacities as a peer educator, a student leader, and a study abroad ambassador.

Tammy came to college determined to be involved and make a difference. She became an officer in her residence hall, was elected to student senate, wrote articles for the newspaper, took a course in leadership, and spent spring break on service projects in the community. Tammy exemplifies what it means to be a peer educator. Determined to make college more than words on a page, she lived what she learned; she became involved and gave time and effort to provide service to others. But she also got back more than a few lines on a résumé. Her life took on new direction. College ended and she applied for a position in the program Teach for America. The next paragraph is an excerpt from an essay she wrote about how she has experienced change.

I have traveled to several countries, had to do the proverbial "stepping into someone else's shoes," and still was not prepared for what "Teaching for America" would mean. The mission, to move students two grade levels in their respective subject, is not all that Teach for America means, although it is a beautiful goal for a nation plagued by educational difficulties. In all actuality, it means ripping off your comfortable goggles. It means seeing for sure, with no protection, that life is not built into little boxes that are manageable. Instead you see that for sure, life is chaotic; that there are a myriad of ways to see that four-letter word. You see that learning about a new culture or a new language is nothing compared to learning how to be a kid again, and for sure nothing compared to being forced to truly face your own racist feelings that bubble forth from a place you never thought you had. The task of breaking down the walls of my own expectations against the realities of another life situation seemed nearly impossible. There was no magic dust to put my world into their minds and make it all right! It is frustration, anguish, and more.

It is when you sacrifice, when you are in pain, when you no longer want to do something that you are truly serving. And by no means is it as pretty as most would like us to believe; service is a battlefield. It is a violence upon the psyche, a violence upon the heart, a violence upon the mind that is so powerful; one does not walk away the same. If you think going into service is noble, it is. But, only after you have faced the fact that doing it removes nobility and you fully accept the title of servant can you truly serve.

Reflections on Being a Peer Educator

Nearly every peer educator, working in their specified role, will gain skills and knowledge from their experience. However, at a very personal level you will notice an impact upon your attitudes, values, perceptions, and self-understanding. This may not seem as dramatic as Tammy's experience described above, but it is more than likely that you will undergo some very clear and personal shift that continues into the future and affects the direction of your life. You will recognize the many changes that can occur from being conscious of everyday transactions that provide some level of impact.

INTRODUCTION TO THE TRAINING MODEL

There are three key components to training: knowledge, skills, and personal integration. In your preparation to become a peer educator you will need to work on all three areas. The chapters of this book address each of them.

Knowledge includes the major concepts that will be useful in your conceptualization and understanding of the helping function. The core knowledge base for helping others combines elements of psychology, sociology, cultural anthropology, and education. Specifically, this book provides some basic concepts of human development, interpersonal communication, cultural indoctrination, problem solving, group process, and leadership. However, even with a base of knowledge about any subject, you must have sufficient skills to communicate successfully and work productively with others. Some of these skills include the ability to listen, communicate accurately, show intercultural sensitivity, apply problem-solving strategies, lead groups, assess environments, and make referrals. Here you will be introduced to various strategies and methods to act successfully as a peer educator. Each chapter includes an introduction to the theory, but we emphasize how the theory applies to practice. Practice will include examples for use, "tips" to apply, and exercises to experience many of the suggestions.

Finally, the most important variable in the helping process is you! The most noteworthy ingredients of effectiveness are personal qualities, including self-awareness, accurate self-concept, confidence, commitment to others, motivation, and warmth. We emphasize that a crucial part of being a peer educator is being a role model. Throughout the book, you will be given opportunities to look at yourself and find ways to grow and improve as an example to others. These opportunities are presented in "reflection points."

The goal of a good role model is to emulate the qualities of self-awareness, personal growth, and the ability to self-manage behavior. It should be noted, however, that being a role model does not require perfection but an openness to being genuinely human and, while making errors, a willingness to understanding and developing yourself.

A Process and Reflection Model

The combination of knowledge, skills, and personal integration acquired in this training may best be accomplished through a process and reflection model of learning. Borton (1970) described this model by use of the terms "what," "so what," and "now what." The Borton approach gives one a systematic strategy to use when processing new material, and it asks the learner to define the relevance of this new knowledge from a personal perspective. The definitions of the three stages follow:

1. *What?* This process concerns the sensing out of differences between your original reaction, the actual effect it has upon you, and the intended effect. For example, you could ask yourself, "What is the difference between the intended impact of the material or information and my reaction to it?"
2. *So What?* This is the transforming stage, whereby the learner must translate the new material or knowledge into personally relevant patterns of meaning. You may ask yourself, "So what value does this information have for understanding my own life or my work with others?"
3. *Now What?* This is the action stage of the process model. Here the learner must decide how to act on the knowledge and apply the alternatives identified to other situations. You may ask yourself, "Now what am I going to do with this information?"

The model for training is depicted in Figure 1.1.

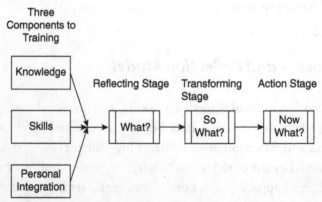

Figure 1.1. The Training Paradigm: A Process and Reflection Model
SOURCE: Adapted from Borton (1970).

Reflection Point 1.3: Your Thoughts and Reactions to Training

---

Given the themes of this chapter, the "what," "so what," and "now what" perspective might generate the following questions:

1. What did you think your training as a peer educator would entail? Did you enter with any anxiety or uncertainty? Do you find that there were major differences between your expectations of training and the information you have covered in this chapter?
2. So what do these differences mean to you (assuming there were any)? What implications do the expectations and reality of training have for you to enter fully and enthusiastically into this training experience?
3. Now what are you going to do to work through this if there is a difference between your expectations and the actual role of a peer educator that you are now defining?

In summary, the model of training we are suggesting is similar to the form of inquiry and learning that could take place on any topic. It applies to examining oneself in relationship to becoming a more effective helper or it could apply to a class on a science topic. For example, scientific experiments constitute a continuous cycle of inquiry that follows almost exactly the same progression—observing data, building interpretations, applying the interpretations, and checking the results. It is important that you view what is known from the world outside of yourself and then reflect upon these data for how they affect your own assumptions. It is important that you are open to challenge and experience the dissonance that then can lead to understanding, possible change, and continued growth. It is critically important to keep in mind that the material you will learn in this book will ask you to look at yourself and your own functioning as a human being. You will be a role model to those you are helping. Your level of functioning will have direct impact on those with whom you

19

work. It is very important that you know yourself and model the attributes of building on strengths and recognizing and working on weaknesses.

Training Assumptions

This training program is based on several assumptions (adapted from Ender, Saunders-McCaffrey, & Miller, 1979) important for you and your trainer to consider as you enter the program because they will lead you to more positive and long-lasting results when you share them and act on them. If you just go through the motions of taking a class with minimal expectations, you will miss the opportunity to be a true learner whose knowledge and skills will create change and indelible impacts. Alternatively, if you are aware of and share the assumptions driving the process, you will derive maximum benefit from it.

Learning Is an Active Process Learning, especially skill development, is not a passive enterprise. To fully benefit from this training experience, you must be an active participant. The principle that one must demonstrate commitment to personal growth and development if change is to occur applies just as much to peer educators as to the students who may be receiving assistance.

We encourage you to be an active learner in three distinct ways. First, through the use of the "what, so what, and now what" model, you are encouraged to employ a more reflective, thoughtful, and introspective learning style as you read the training chapters. The reflective model of learning is designed to assist you with this process. Second, embedded within many of the training chapters are exercises designed to assist you in thinking about new information and applying this information to yourself, your interactions with others, and the environment around you. These exercises will be assigned by your trainer. The third method of active learning occurs during the training sessions. Along with being thoughtful, you will take risks in your thinking, be challenged to hear and often accept thoughts different from your own, actively participate in role-plays and other simulations, and truly enjoy the acquisition of new skills through feedback and practice. The more you put yourself into this experience, the more learning will occur.

Peer Educators Are Self-Aware   You are entering a position that will require you to encourage others to make changes in some way. This may involve acquiring knowledge, shifting behavior, developing a different way of valuing an experience, engaging in more effective group activity, or finding ways of developing greater self-responsibility. If any of these changes are to occur with the students you are assisting, the students must show some awareness of their present behavior and make some commitment to change. The same is true with you. If you are not aware of your level of functioning in the area targeted for change with the student you are helping, it will be difficult for you to model the appropriate behavior—and difficult for you to advocate a change strategy with the student seeking assistance. We will challenge you throughout this book to become more aware of who you are as a person and a student. You are encouraged to incorporate change strategies into your own life when areas of improvement are warranted. Modeling the process for others provides credibility for what you are promoting. If you are unwilling to make a personal adjustment, it will be difficult for you to challenge others to take the risks necessary to promote change in their lives. As a helping person, you must be genuine and congruent with who you are as a person and what you advocate for others when promoting healthy, self-directed, and self-responsible behavior.

Training Takes Place in a Supportive Community   For change to occur, the support of others is usually critical. In this training experience, you are responsible for your own learning, but you are also responsible for supporting others in their learning experience. By this, we mean you should always try to encourage fellow students to take risks in their thinking, share their ideas, and practice new skills. In other words, you should support their attempts to master this new material. There is no place in training for talking down to others, assuming an authoritative attitude or demeanor, or making critical judgments about the worthiness of others' ideas and opinions. In fact, the opposite style has been found to be most successful in training: show support for others, provide encouragement to take risks, look for the positive rather than the negative qualities in others, and give feedback in constructive ways. When all members of the training community embrace these concepts, there is a greater opportunity for mutual benefit.

Training Requires Time, Practice, and Feedback   As you will be exposed to new content areas and be required to develop specific skills to help others, this training program should ideally occur over a series of weeks throughout a quarter or semester. You will need time to consider and reflect on new ideas, learn new ways of viewing the helping relationship, try out new ways of behaving as a peer educator, and master new skills. In some instances, to be truly effective, you will have to change your behavior or way of thinking. Long-term change does not occur overnight. It takes time to integrate new behaviors with thoughts. You cannot fully integrate new behaviors without practicing those behaviors.

The Trainer Is Your Role Model   As you advance through this training experience, look to your trainer as your role model. Just as you will be a role model to others, the person leading this experience is a model for you and will exemplify the helping skills you are here to learn. Everyone leads best by example. We trust that this old adage will manifest itself in your training experience.

Peer Educators as Role Models

Most people understand the folly of the parent who says, "Do as I say, not as do!" Learning is most likely to be accomplished when there is consistency between the instructional message and the behavior of the person providing that message. You will be most effective as a helping person if you provide a positive role model and thereby make it possible that you will become a significant person, a mentor, in the lives of other students.

Consider a role model who has made a difference in your life, and ask yourself the following question: Have I ever told this significant person about the important role he plays in my life? More often than not, significant others will not know that they are admired, observed, and even being emulated by you. People become role models because they are available for observation and have a special position of authority or are perceived as holding special qualities. Parents, older siblings, teachers, friends, leaders of organizations, or even those in the public limelight will often become role models. As a peer educator, you will be in a position to be a role model for other students on campus.

Your institution will entrust you with a position that carries important duties and serves in many ways as a representative of the college. Such a position engenders some immediate respect and admiration from others because you are expected to be responsible and accountable in helping other students. Thus, other students will look to your words and actions for guidance and leadership in regard to their own behavior. They may even try to emulate you in certain ways. Will the behaviors they emulate support positive qualities that show responsibility and respect, promote growth, and enhance their educational success?

For example, if you are a study skills instructor, do you practice successful classroom and study techniques in your own academic subjects? If you are a peer health educator, do you practice safe sex or abstinence? Practice responsible drinking? Balance your life with exercise and good nutrition? If you are a resident assistant, do you model respectful and cooperative community living? In summary, do you model through your values, attitudes, and behavior a lifestyle that is compatible with the goals of your peer educator role? This is an important point to ponder because you can count on the fact that students you work with will be observing your actions.

Reflection Point 1.4: Being a Role Model

Think about being a peer educator:

What behaviors describe a successful role model in the area served by your peer educator role?

So what are the differences between those behaviors and your own behavior?

Now what are some actions you can take to become a better role model for other students?

Tips for Being a Successful Peer Educator

1. Cultivate a genuine desire to be part of other people's lives, help them through the tough decisions, and see them become the best they can be. Be invested for a long enough time to make a difference.
2. Respect individuals and their abilities and their right to make their own choices in their lives. Avoid bringing the attitude to the relationship that your own ways are better or that participants need to be rescued. Convey a sense of respect and equal dignity in the relationship to win the trust of those with whom you work.

3. Listen and accept different points of view. Most people can find someone who will give advice or express opinions. It is much harder to find someone who will suspend judgment and really listen. Help simply by listening, asking thoughtful (but not leading) questions, and giving participants an opportunity to explore their own thoughts with a minimum of interference. When people feel accepted, they are more likely to ask for and respond to good ideas.

4. Appreciate others' struggles and feel empathy with them without feeling pity. Even without having had the same life experiences, successful peer educators can empathize with their partners' feelings and personal problems.

5. Look for solutions and opportunities as well as barriers. Balance a realistic respect for the real and serious problems that others face with optimism for finding equally realistic solutions. You have to be able to make sense of a jumble of issues and point out sensible alternatives.

6. Stay flexible and open. Recognize that relationships take time, and take the time to get to know your partners, learn new things that are important to your partners, and even be changed by the relationship.

We explore the qualities reflected in these tips in more detail throughout later chapters. Chapter Three will help you gain understanding of cultural differences and your responses to them. Chapter Four will help you enhance your listening and empathizing skills. And Chapter Five will help you broaden your problem-solving skills and strategies. The key point of being a peer educator is to understand that it takes a real personal commitment to enter into a relationship of this nature, and this commitment should be considered carefully as a condition of taking on responsibility as a peer educator. Some thoughtful reflection will enhance your role as a peer educator.

Reflection Point 1.5: Successful Peer Education

Think about peer educating:

What are some of the skills and competencies necessary for developing successful peer-educating relationships?

So what are your present strengths and weaknesses in these areas?

Now what are some specific targets of your training, as outlined in this text, that will be important for you to master to be a successful peer educator for another student?

SUMMARY

This chapter has provided you with an overview of students in peer educator roles on college and university campuses. In particular, the chapter focused on the historical expansion of undergraduates' serving in helping roles, the types of positions typically filled by peer educators, and the effectiveness that can be expected in these positions. In this chapter, you have learned what a peer educator is and what a peer educator can do. We have distinguished between the types of activities more appropriate for peer educators and those best offered by professional helpers.

The chapter has also outlined the three components of a learning process: knowledge, skills, and personal integration. It described the basic assumptions of peer educator training, as well as a method you can use to think about new information and reflect upon how this can be useful to your own situation and work as a peer educator. Because we strongly believe that people serving in helping positions are role models of effective living, we challenged you in this chapter to consider your present level of effectiveness as a student role model by identifying your strengths and developing action plans to focus on areas that may need improvement.

Regardless of the specific role you will assume on your campus, remember that you are joining tens of thousands of other students serving as peer educators across the country. The ubiquitous application and subsequent outcome research has demonstrated that the use of peer educators has the potential to make a major and positive difference in the successful development and achievement of college students. Enter into this training program with a commitment to be the very best you can be. Think seriously about role modeling and the mentoring relationship. Take risks to learn and be supportive of fellow trainees. Be positive rather than negative, supportive rather than judgmental, and active rather than passive. Training is a journey to new and exciting thoughts, ideas, opinions, and skills. Enjoy the trip!

CHAPTER ONE: SUMMARY QUESTIONS

1. In your own words, define the roles of students serving as peer educators on your campus.
2. What principles of healthy interactions are you able to identify based upon your experience in meaningful encounters?
3. Describe Borton's process model. What does he mean by sensing, personalizing, and acting?
4. Why are peer educators role models for other students on campus?

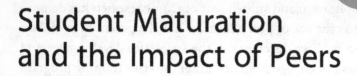

CHAPTER 2

Student Maturation and the Impact of Peers

LEARNING OBJECTIVES

After completing this chapter, you will be able to

1. Define key terms related to the maturation process including the following: growth, development, maturation, change, crisis, challenge, and dissonance.
2. Describe five principles that commonly operate in the human maturation process.
3. List some common crises that students face and offer some reasonable and safe ways to address them.
4. Explain the personal, social, and contextual factors that influence change and personal development in the college environment.
5. Identify several environmental conditions that have a positive impact on student development.
6. Use strategies that can help students make changes that will lead to positive growth and development.

The Case of Kaitlyn

Kaitlyn is a freshman still in her first month of college. It seems as though her life has changed 180 from just a few months ago in high school. In the huge lecture halls, it's so easy to ignore the professor by texting or to skip class altogether, things she never would have gotten away with in

---

high school. Her social life is different, too. She's having fun—it's been awesome to not worry about her parents' rules and to stay up until 3 A.M. talking to boys if she wants to—but she's a little lonely at the same time. She used to just go to the movies and hang out with friends she's known her whole life. But now, the new friends she's making go to parties where they all drink, something she didn't think she'd do much of in college. And her roommate is a completely different person than she is, so living together has been an adjustment. To add to everything else, she's getting kind of self-conscious about her appearance—she used to play a lot of sports, but now it's hard for Kaitlyn to find time or energy to work out. She's just got a lot of mixed feelings, and she wants to feel a little more secure.

It is natural and expected that people make significant changes as they grow and develop throughout life. In particular, students in the traditional college-aged group, those from about seventeen to twenty-five years of age, make many changes in how they think, how they feel, what they believe, what they value, and how they act in the world. College years are indeed a formative time when major decisions are made, and the actions that are taken in college set the stage for adult life. Exhaustive research has determined how students change and how the college environment may affect those changes. Pascarella and Terenzini (1991) summarized nearly thirty years of research on how students change in college and what happens in the academic environment that influences these changes. Although people seem to follow similar patterns of development from generation to generation, there will still be differences over time as society and the culture change. For example, the massive change in technology and society in the twenty-first century has led to a theory that transition into

29

Reflection Point 2.1: Change

Reflect on the ways that you have changed since you got to college:

What are examples of changes you have made? (Consider changes in
    your behavior, habits, attitudes, goals, or relationships with others.)
So what do you think influenced these changes for you?
Now what experiences can you identify that have influenced your
    changes in college?

adulthood now starts earlier and extends longer—in part because
of the greater number of options for students in living, work, and
social connections. In this chapter we address development and
change from a theoretical perspective, as well as from practical
observation of life.

Developmental issues can be understood by reflecting upon
your own experiences and the people you have known as a college
student. How have you and they changed? Students come to
college and try out new perspectives and different behaviors. For
example, you may know students who suddenly became party
animals, or who got religious and joined a church group, who
changed academic majors from science to business, or one day
turned in their backpacks and jeans for a suit and brief case.
Especially in the college years, the list of ways a person can change
goes on indefinitely. But what exactly is change? When are these
shifts in values and lifestyles normal? How and why do people
alter the way they are? When is change considered to be for the
better, and when is it considered to be for the worse?

YOUR OWN CHANGE AND GROWTH

Gaining an understanding of this process of personal growth and
change will be useful to you both as a growing student and as a
peer educator. As defined in Chapter One, your role as a peer

educator is to assist others in their adjustment, satisfaction, and persistence of their own educational goals. As an effective peer educator, you can be an excellent role model just by allowing others to see the way you approach your own choices, challenges, and opportunities. Research has consistently shown that peer educators are successful because of shared experiences that permit a connection to the student's situation and a feeling of ease in talking with a peer. Thinking about your own experiences and about the challenges faced by other college students will help you respond effectively the first time you talk with a student with whom you are working. The information in this chapter will not make you an expert, but it will give you enough understanding of human development to understand and assist students with strategies for dealing with normal periods of change.

DEFINITIONS

The meaning of the following few key terms will serve as a starting point for a better understanding of human maturation and the process of personal development and change: *change, development, readiness, growth, maturation, crisis, challenge,* and *dissonance.*

Change refers to alterations over time in student thinking, feeling, and behaving. Change can be based on a quality of choice or preference, including attitudes or actions, or it can be based upon a quantity shift such as additional knowledge, effort and skill or, in some cases, a lessening or reduction of behavior (Pascarella & Terenzini, 1991; Prochaska & Norcross, 2002; Rosen, 2000; Pascarella, 2006).

Development describes a series of changes that people typically experience over the course of a lifetime.

Readiness for change determines a person's stage of preparation for a transition or shift in his or her life. Readiness for change

31

is measured on a continuum that goes from not thinking about it to thinking about it to planning to taking action to maintaining changes (Prochaska & Norcross, 2002). The idea behind this model is that cognition, attitude, and behavior change do not happen in one step. Rather, people tend to progress through the different stages on their way to successful change.

Growth implies that the individual is moving forward toward maturity with greater complexity and differentiation.

Maturation implies that the individual is moving up to the next, higher level of development. You do this by learning from your past and adjusting to the demands of the present and future.

Crisis describes periods when a person must face an important decision and make a decision that could cause that person to move forward, backward, or remain the same. The presence of a crisis through an event, decision moment, or particular concern is referred to in this book by the word *challenge*.

A *challenge* may occur in one or more areas of life that could include family, school, work, or other situations. A challenge arises from new or changing circumstances combined with an individual's internal reactions (thoughts, feelings, attitudes, and reactions). Study abroad, which requires adapting to life in a different culture, would be a good example.

Dissonance is the discomfort and anxiety you feel when the *status quo* is disrupted. Often dissonance is experienced when your behaviors or actions do not match your beliefs or values. Experiencing dissonance frequently becomes the impetus to change in a way that will resolve the tension.

FIVE PRINCIPLES TO GUIDE YOUR WORK

Five principles of human development are worthy of consideration and should help in your work with others. Underlying these principles is the assumption that all students with whom you have contact will be in the process of confronting and needing to resolve a challenge as a normal part of their growth. Reviewing these principles will help you gain insight into how you can help others as they encounter various life challenges.

Principle 1: *Human growth and development occur as a result of pressure from three sources: outside or situational circumstance, biological changes, and the personal values and aspirations of the individual.*

The incentive for change originates in many ways. A new environment can create considerable anxiety for some people. That is why many peer educators will be involved with the orientation of new students or with freshman-year experience programs that help students adjust to campus life. Another example might include students' physical well-being and self-image. A peer educator working in a health or fitness center would help students improve their diet, exercise habits, and sense of body image. Another area for challenge and resolution concerns new and often divergent views on basic values such as relationships, religion, sex, and similar markers of lifestyle.

College environments and the readiness of students to experience new possibilities for themselves will lead to a period of life in which the potential for change is high. This period of potential change can be experienced as a very healthy point of discord when the student is open to entertaining new ideas, taking risks, trying out new behavior, and listening to alternative (sometimes conflicting) points of view. As a peer educator, you can play a supportive role in the weighing of options, the scrutiny of personal values, and the problem-solving process for choosing a new direction, even when the student is facing the challenge relatively cheerfully and without stress.

Of course, students may also experience the dissonance of change in some potentially unhealthy ways. For example, taking difficult courses and falling behind or not doing well on tests might challenge a new transfer student in the residence hall. Instead of facing the difficulty he might begin skipping classes, start drinking alcohol as a way to distract himself from his issues, and get into conflict with his roommate who is doing well academically. A peer educator, such as a resident assistant, might notice these behaviors and can play a significant role in confronting and responding to this student while there is an opportunity to make changes before consequences become as severe as flunking out. If the timing is right and the student is willing, the resident assistant may become part of the support network that can identify when a person is struggling with the challenges of the college situation and needs the intervention and assistance of a campus resource or authority.

Important to remember is that each student may grapple with a different set of issues and behave on a different level of readiness. Your job as a peer educator is to be aware of these variables and guide students toward successful maturation when possible.

> **Principle 2:** *We mature by making gradual changes over time and by facing and overcoming crises. Keep in mind, the term* crises *refers to the more significant challenges, ones that may relate to your identity, selecting a career path, forming relationships, finding meaning and purpose, choosing values and a moral code, recognizing diversity, and managing conflict.*

Normal development for most people is not a series of traumatic events but rather a continuous process of eliminating or resolving subtle and not-so-subtle challenges that create tension. Most of these challenges are quite predictable and normal. People's lives, for the most part, unfold in similar ways. Perhaps the major difference among individuals is the personal competence level in different areas of concern. For example, you and your friends on campus are all students, but some are better academically than others. A new college environment presents the challenge of finding out which classes you are best prepared to take, developing the autonomy to make it to class on your own, organizing your study times and approaches, and finding the resources such as libraries, computer centers, or tutoring services in a timely way. A new student may be good at taking notes but not as good at being assertive and finding assistance. Entering a new college environment presents a similar challenge to all students in that each individual must learn how to manage and adjust to the demands of classes. For some students, this is very natural and easy; for others, it may bring on a sense of crisis.

In your role as a peer educator, you will be working, for the most part, with individuals and groups of individuals who are experiencing this process of small changes that eventually will allow them to deal with the world around them more easily and to develop maturity. From time to time, you will run into individuals for whom the changes are at such a critical level that they find it difficult to adjust. For example, an international student is in a new country where everything—food, language, customs—is different may experience crisis in adapting to the new environment because he has not had to face such a challenge before or has not learned how to conquer the challenge earlier in life. Another example: if a person has never spent time away from home or has never been away without feeling homesick (even for a night or weekend), moving away from home and into a residence

35

hall may be a very traumatic experience. If, because of your assistance and the assistance of others, this person learns to adjust and feel comfortable in this setting, the student will have developed a strength that will follow her through adult life.

> **Principle 3:** *Maturation is a cumulative process, and therefore you have to master simple tasks before you can master the more complicated ones.*

Maturation as a cumulative process first shows itself in very young children, for example, when they are learning to talk. Initially a child coos and babbles, and later they start to mimic the way their mother and father speak. Then the child slowly begins to form a few words and finally starts to speak in sentences. A child who does not speak words clearly by age two will find it quite difficult to form whole sentences. This, in turn, will make it difficult for that child to express needs through simple communication, which will result in more dependency on the parent. Crises like this one can carry over into early adulthood. For example, a college student who is still very dependent upon a parent to make decisions and take responsibility, from waking up in the morning to washing clothes, could feel helpless when suddenly having to take over these responsibilities.

That maturation is a cumulative process is a principle that will have considerable influence in your work. Because you need to have certain abilities already developed in order to take on a new challenge, it is important to help students identify which abilities they need to work on in order to face a current situation. Finding the correct starting point is critical for later success. The key to locating a successful starting point is finding the place where an individual can stretch to new heights but not collapse under the strain of a challenge that seems unconquerable. Helping students develop the series of steps they must take to reach goal completion is a critical role for the peer educator. Learning how to help others evaluate their present skills in a needed area is the key to determining where to begin so that the individual can relieve the stress he or she is feeling. A good example would be helping a student understand the procedure for dealing with a grade dispute: a student should begin by making an appointment and asking the professor for feedback on how the grade was determined without coming across as confrontational, argumentative, or defensive.

> **Principle 4:** *Individuals develop at somewhat different rates, and each person has a unique way of adapting to personal challenges.*

The key to this principle is the concept of individuality. What works for you in regard to solving a particular problem may not work for someone else. Don't assume that someone else has attained the same capability, experience, and confidence in an area that you may have at the same point in your college career. Even though there are predictions of common challenges based upon general stages of life such as late adolescent or early adulthood, everybody takes life's journey with an individual set of skills, behaviors, and subsequent outcomes. This also means that a person may be highly developed in one developmental area but behind the peer group in another area. An example could be a student who has a strong background in science and is advancing rapidly and successfully through a pre-med curriculum. However, that same student is shy and lacks self-assurance in meeting new acquaintances and developing personal relationships. It is extremely important that as a peer educator you show respect and understanding for these individual differences.

37

Principle 5: *In each phase of maturation, an individual must acquire or master certain skills, knowledge, or behaviors that correspond with that phase.*

The knowledge, skills, and behaviors required at each phase are determined by the process of resolving earlier personal and intellectual challenges. Traditional-aged college students, ages seventeen to twenty-five, who successfully resolve the challenges they encounter at college are better able to address the challenges that will occur in later adulthood. Knowledge of the challenges that will face those you assist in your peer educator role will enhance your ability to provide effective assistance. It should be noted that although there are predictable tasks students of this age will encounter, which tasks will be confronted and when will vary considerably. Chickering and Reisser (1993) have outlined seven common areas of challenge for the maturing college student (Figure 2.1):

1. Developing a sense of personal competence in the physical, intellectual, and interpersonal realms.
2. Managing emotions effectively such as developing tolerance of others, handling loneliness, dealing with conflict, and handling strong feelings such as anger, depression, hurt, fear, desire, or anxiety.
3. Becoming more autonomous and learning to think and act on one's own; becoming less dependent on others while learning to act cooperatively with people in more interdependent ways.
4. Establishing an identity that defines one's self and presents this publicly in a unique but clear way. Identity includes a blend of other factors (emotions, purpose, relationships, physical appearance, and competency).

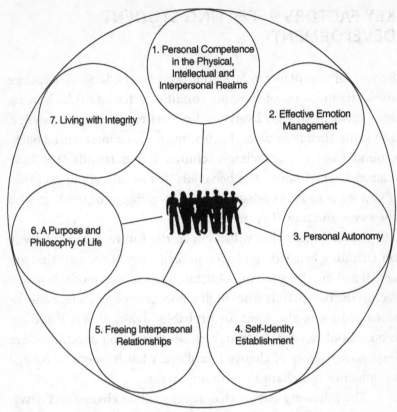

Figure 2.1. Chickering and Reisser's "Seven Vectors of Change"
SOURCE: Adapted from Chickering & Reisser (1993).

5. Interacting with others with tolerance and respect and developing the capacity for intimacy.
6. Developing a sense of purpose and philosophy of life that identifies clear goals and lays the groundwork for choosing one's future, including lifestyle and career.
7. Living with integrity so that one has an understanding of key values and beliefs that become blueprints for personal choice and provide a consistency between belief and behavior.

KEY FACTORS AFFECTING STUDENT DEVELOPMENT

Several factors play a role in the process of change for college students, and some of these are conditions that individuals bring with them to college. Every student has experience, knowledge, and skills already in place. Each student also comes with a background from family, schools, churches, and friends that have shaped a set of values and behaviors. It has often been said that if you want to know what someone is going to be, look at who they were and how they presently act.

Development that will occur in the future depends heavily on attitudes, behavior, and accomplishments of the past that are actualized in the present. Outstanding college football teams recruit the best players from high school programs; college admissions programs also look for probable high-achievers based on high school records. Although these preexisting conditions are important factors of change in college, what happens in college to influence this change is also important.

The following factors that affect student change and development are selected from research conducted by Astin (1993; 1999), Pascarella and Terenzini (1991), and Velasquez, Gaddy-Maurer, Crouch, and DiClemente (2001).

Involvement

Perhaps the strongest conclusion that can be made is that the more involved you are in school work and college activities, the better your knowledge will be and the more positive changes you will make (Astin, 1999). More specifically, how much the college experience will affect a student is determined for the most part by the student's level of engagement with college programs and activities (Gellin, 2003). The quality of involvement is important; in other words, to fully engage with action, energy, and commitment to the program or activity differs from merely saying you are a member or occasionally attending an event. Astin (1993, 1999) found that the more students are involved with campus life, the more they will be influenced by this engagement to learn and shape their lives. Therefore, factors such as living on campus, working on campus, joining campus organizations, participating in activities, and making friends with other college students will play a major role in the impact college has on the process of change for an individual.

Engagement is a two-way street; students must make an effort, and the people and programs of any given group or institution must present opportunities. Promoting engagement will be key in your position as a peer educator. A substantial amount of research indicates that peer instructions and peer interventions increase students' engagement in learning while also developing necessary changes (Astin, 1999; Gellin, 2003; Pascarella & Terenzini, 1991). The concept can be more simply stated this way: the more students are engaged in studies, the more they learn; the more students are engaged in college activities and events, the more they enjoy the college experience (Kuh, Hu, & Vestper, 2000; Kuh, 2003).

Cultural Expectations

A second factor that influences change and development is societal conditioning. For example, Gilligan (1982)—and other theorists viewing development from a female perspective—notes that women are more sensitive to their environment in terms of relationships, are affected more by relationship crises, and are more expressive of their feelings. Likewise, it is clear that people raised in various cultures will not have the same reactions to any given situation because of differences in the way each culture perceives the particular situation. The impact of cultural differences will be discussed in more detail in Chapter Three. However, this variable of societal conditioning is important to remember when promoting change and development among the diverse students you will work with as a peer educator.

Social Influence

One element crucial to individual change and development is the individual's social circle. During the college transition period, when people move from their family but have not yet entered the postcollege world, friends are the most significant source of influence (Feldman & Newcomb, 1970; Light, 2001). Friends provide a source of support, and by being a primary group to identify with also become the predominant source of influence during the college years. The social circle influences the student by establishing norms for how to act (from the clothes students wear to the places students hang out). By providing peer inclusion, recognition, and acceptance, the group of friends becomes the main way that the student feels validated. Congruence, or the ability to see overlap between sources of learning, is crucial to the more formal aspects of learning. Research has demonstrated that those students who make connections between what goes on inside the classroom and what they have learned from their friends outside the classroom have more satisfying college experiences (Zhao & Kuh, 2004; Pike & Kuh, 2005). Because of the importance of others the same age during these years, peer educators can be particularly influential as models and mentors to other students.

Impact of the Environment

Programs, events, and other opportunities offered by the university are also important for change and development. A college or university determines its educational direction by its philosophy and mission, and—more important—through the organizational activity that carries out that mission. Physical resources such as libraries, computer labs, and tutorial centers influence intellectual development; recreation centers, intramural sports, health centers, and parks can influence physical well-being; cultural events and student clubs available on a campus influence students' social and interpersonal development. However, beyond the physical structure and beyond the formal organizations, the most important factor is the interaction among the faculty, staff, and students. Peer educators can play a significant role in assisting students with making connections by acting as a link between students and the people, services, and other resources of the campus community. Remember, one of the most crucial factors in the educational and personal development of a student is the degree to which he or she is engaged with the resources, including people and activities available in the environment.

Compatibility Between Student and Institution

Lastly, the compatibility of the institution itself (size, philosophy, curriculum, and people) (Porter & Umbach, 2006) with the individual student will influence the potential for change (Tracey & Robbins, 2006; Wolniak & Pascarella, 2005). People who feel different or misplaced in their college situation may feel detached and indifferent and may potentially fade away or drop out without having much opportunity for growth. By contrast, people who believe they are in a compatible situation will tend to be a more comfortable, attached, and contributing member of the campus community. However, it should be noted that it is still important to have a degree of challenge and dissonance that can nudge a person toward expansion and growth. The right degree is important, though. For example, if your goal is to get an A on your test

Exercise 2.1: Balance Between Congruence and Dissonance

Review the five factors of student change just discussed.

Now choose one factor, such as influence of peers, impact of gender difference, or involvement with campus activity, and apply it to your own life. Do this by taking a blank sheet of paper and drawing a circle in the middle to represent you. In the circle use descriptive words or symbols to represent how you view yourself with regard to this factor (for example, the type of activity and involvement you have with campus life, or your identity from a cultural or gender perspective). Now around your circle, draw some additional circles representing other students (these can represent individuals or groups of students), and use descriptors or symbols to portray your perception of them regarding the same factor. Now compare yourself to the impressions you have of others in your college environment. Note the similarities and differences between yourself and others you know. How do these affect you?

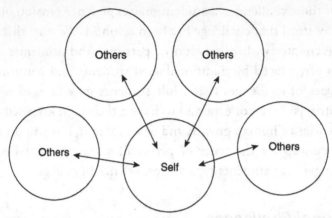

Figure 2.2. Circles to Evaluate Congruence and Incongruence with Peers

and you are used to getting Bs, you will be reasonably stretching your abilities because it should not be too difficult for you get that A. However, if you got a D on the last three tests and now you want to get an A, you may be asking too much of yourself and you will feel disappointed even if you get a B. The balance between what you are capable of and what you have to push yourself to do is critical in the change process. Your role as a peer educator is to encourage students to find their own niche in the college environment. The more compatible students feel with their situation, the greater their ability to transition through stages of change and development (Tracey & Robbins, 2006).

DEVELOPMENTAL CHALLENGES CONFRONTING COLLEGE STUDENTS

The next sections outline several real-life examples of typical developmental challenges confronted by college students in a number of key areas. These are situations, decisions, or tasks that need to be resolved and accomplished. Again, when confronted by

45

one of these challenges, a student may experience tension or dissonance until that challenge has been resolved. We start this part of the chapter with discussion of personal and academic challenges often faced by traditional-aged students and continue to the types of challenges that adult students may face. As a peer educator, you are not expected to have a thorough knowledge of all theories of human growth and development, but you do need some concept of the types of personal, social, and intellectual challenges that students typically experience in college.

Personal Challenges

When students enter college, they face challenges created by entering a new environment and taking on a new set of responsibilities. The situation will vary for each student and may depend considerably upon the nature and familiarity of the environment. However, all students will confront issues that will provoke reactions and challenges that need to be dealt with—and responded to—for a successful transition into college. These challenges may seem as simple as being responsible for waking up and going to class in the morning, but they can also become much more complex.

Take the hypothetical example of Lauren. Lauren is an only child who has lived most of her life in the same town surrounded by a regular group of friends and family. She has her own comfortable room at home and has a very set pattern of family rituals and responsibilities (like when the family eats dinner, who takes care of household chores, and what time her curfew is on the weekends). She arrives at college and moves to a Residence Hall room (about half the size of her room at home) that she shares with a roommate she has never met. The roommate seems nice enough, but soon it is obvious that the roommate has different tastes on how the room should be decorated and kept up. The roommate also has a boyfriend who spends a lot of time in the room without much consideration for Lauren's privacy. Lauren has morning classes and needs to get up by at least 7 A.M.; her roommate has later classes and likes to stay up very late.

It is clear that Lauren is up against a series of critical issues that create dissonance for her and demand major adjustments. Emotionally, she misses her old family and friends but is excited about her new friends and opportunities. She feels tension and conflict in dealing with another person in a small space but wants to find ways to get along and become friends with a person from a very different background. Her values are challenged on multiple levels as she makes decisions about the new people and activities in her life.

First year students have to make many kinds of adjustments. Here are some typical challenges:

Physically moving to a new place
Living with a roommate
Leaving parents, siblings, and friends
Living with people from other ethnic and minority groups
Taking the initiative to meet new and different people
Making personal decisions on a daily basis
Managing expenses and keeping a budget
Confronting noisy neighbors on the residence hall floor
Determining specific social groups to join
Socializing virtually in social networking spaces
Staying connected with friends through the Internet, phone, and
    other technology
Balancing a work and study schedule (more than half of college
    students work at least 12 hours per week)
Facing peer pressure to consume drugs, tobacco, or alcohol
Facing peer pressure to conform to new ways of behaving that
    may conflict with personal values and beliefs

47

Becoming more financially independent

Developing an identity apart from family and friends

Distancing from a "helicopter" parent who wants to know everything you are doing

Intellectual and Academic Challenges

Most college students will face a series of choices and need to make decisions about the nature and direction of their academic experience. Built into the typical college experience are critical moments that create dissonance—declaring a major, signing up for courses, receiving grades, finding financial aid, overcoming difficulties in learning a subject, and recognizing the need to get help. Students must resolve many of these situations in a college academic environment by dealing with faculty, resource personnel, organizational structures, and rules and procedures that in many ways embody the assumption that the student is now responsible as an adult to anticipate every need and carry through with a response. Here are some examples of these challenges:

Speaking up in class and asking questions

Visiting professors outside class (face-to-face, electronically, or by telephone)

Joining study groups

Managing heavy course demands and schedules

Completing difficult classes in areas in which the student may be weak academically

Figuring out multiple choice exams that ask for the "best answer" from a series of good answers

Understanding the registration, drop-add, course withdrawal, and other administrative procedures

Obtaining a tutor

Accepting the importance of the "general education" classes

Planning semester course schedules

Seeking assistance on campus when academic problems occur

Navigating the campus Web site to acquire helpful information

Balancing academic and social life

Physical Challenges

Students emerging through the late teens and entering early adulthood are often concerned about their physical appearance, physical competence, and manual skills. These areas are important for developing a self-identity in which you feel assured about your body image, are physically active and healthy, and have confidence in your physical attractiveness.

Take another hypothetical example. Ryan was involved in sports throughout high school, but when he reached college, he realized he could not compete at this next level. He kept up with some sports at an intramural level and through occasional workouts on his own time. After two years of college, Ryan realized that he was not as active as he once was and had gained about 20 pounds. He felt uneasy about not being as fit as he would like to be. Part of this was due to not having the same regular sports to play, but Ryan knew that he ate a lot of fast food because he didn't like to cook for himself in his apartment. He also was drinking when he went out and had also started smoking cigarettes on these occasions. Changing his lifestyle, dealing with new habits that were difficult to break, and staying disciplined on exercise and healthy activities were the issues now concerning Ryan.

Some physical challenges many students deal with include the following:

Coping with weight gain and loss

Learning to control diet and alcohol consumption

Competing athletically with other, more gifted students

Finding time to exercise

Accepting one's body type and working within one's own limits

Finding resources and accommodation to manage a disability

Forming positive health habits and learning how to break problem habits

Becoming self-reliant about managing stress, illness, or other health problems

Finding hobbies and physical activities that can be maintained over a lifetime

Interpersonal Challenges

Relationships are a major concern of college students and an area that causes many students to experience stress and anxiety. Making and maintaining connections has a profound impact on a student's life. As they mature through their college years, students will need different things from relationships. During the initial entry into college, a student may focus on finding a group to belong to and people to share activities with. Later, the more important priorities might be free expression of feelings and personal information as well as support. As interactions grow, relationship issues may become more complex and deeper—managing conflict or making meaningful commitments come to the forefront. Further examples of interpersonal challenges are

Becoming a part of a social circle

Developing and managing romantic relationships

Asserting oneself when personal rights are violated

Interacting with members of ethnically or otherwise different groups

Dealing with loss or separation from a significant relationship

Terminating relationships that are no longer positive

Tolerating the various forms of eccentric behavior demonstrated by boyfriends, girlfriends, friends, or peers

Sharing personal information with close friends and loved ones

Being cooperative in group projects and activities

Learning to show emotions in appropriate ways

Experiencing the personal benefits of helping others

Accepting the responsibility of a committed relationship

Managing conflicts

Being secure enough to say no to peer influences to engage in risky behaviors

Recognizing sexual orientation and, for gay, lesbian, bi-sexual, or transgender students, deciding whether to "come out"

Career and Lifestyle Challenges

The challenges of career and lifestyle become more prominent as students move into the last years of college. During this time, significant decisions come up that may have long-lasting consequences. Such decisions can become major challenges for college students and can be accompanied by significant dissonance. Here are some examples:

Choosing an academic major

Changing an academic major or minor

Deciding on appropriate internships, externships, study abroad, and practicum experiences

Deciding on a career path, military service, or graduate school

Deciding to "stop out" or drop out of school

Making significant decisions regarding issues of marriage and coming to terms with income needs and the lifestyle consequences of this decision

51

Unique Challenges for Adult Students

Today, there is a significant increase in the number of adults returning to college to begin or complete a degree, certificate program, or other type of continuing education. Adults returning to school (often referred to as "nontraditional students") also experience many of the personal and academic challenges identified for traditional-aged students. However, adult students may have several additional challenges in their life. For example, Gloria is a thirty-five-year-old single mother of two children, six and nine years of age. Getting a college degree in business is her long-term goal, but she will encounter many pressures and demands while getting this degree. Although taking care of her children is a major responsibility, she must also hold a job to pay the bills—and would like to "have a life" with time for enjoying friends and normal activities.

There are many adult students in college with equally challenging goals and responsibilities. Their challenges may include

Managing multiple personal responsibilities—home, family, and work

Adapting to the college learning environment and feeling confident with having basic study skills

Changing directions in work and career

Feeling comfortable in an environment that may be dominated by younger students

Finding and interacting with a supportive group of peers

Developing course schedules that are compatible with other responsibilities

Finding a place on campus to study, rest, and meet with friends

Commuting to class and finding adequate parking

Finding appropriate child care

Finding sources of financial support

Reflection Point 2.2: Facing Challenges

Consider your present life situation as a college student:

What significant challenge are you now experiencing in your personal maturation process?

So what human resources (peer educator–staffed programs) are available on your campus to help you overcome this challenge? Note: If you don't know of any peer educator services on your campus that could help, what professionally staffed college department could help?

Now what action could you take to make use of a formal peer educator service or an informal contact with peers?

Exercise 2.2: Life Challenges and the Peer Educator

Think about the area in which you are preparing to become a peer educator. From the preceding lists of personal, intellectual, physical, interpersonal, career, and adult challenges facing college students, identify the ones you might expect to most affect those seeking your assistance. Think of some additional examples of challenges or concerns common to students you may work with. If you are doing this exercise as part of a group training, compare your responses with others and combine them into a larger list.

CONDITIONS THAT PROMOTE STUDENT DEVELOPMENT

There are certain conditions that can be supplied within the educational environment that encourage and support an individual's movement through a transitional period. The following "tips" provide a summary of these factors and conditions that support the process of personal development. Each of these seven characteristics has implications for peer educators who plan programs and interventions to assist other students.

Tips for Implementing a Supportive Atmosphere

1. Take a genuine interest in the individual student's personal situation so that an atmosphere of support and care can be established.
2. Stimulate the student to become aware of options and opportunities outside of his or her normal life. Suggestion and nonthreatening forms of challenge can be give motivation for the student to move to a higher level.
3. Provide avenues (people, places, activities) for a student to explore the options and opportunities beyond the present situation.
4. When problems arise, demonstrate problem-solving strategies to move the student toward solutions. These may be ones you apply yourself or by referral to professionals in the field.
5. Help students assess where they are through reflection and feedback.
6. Be proactive by providing programs and activities that anticipate the needs of students based upon what is known concerning developmental levels.

Exercise 2.3: Environmental Influence

Consider the educational environment of your campus. Does this environment promote healthy student maturation? Support your answer by giving examples of campus characteristics, programs, and individuals that promote positive development. If your answer is no, what is the campus lacking? What could you and other peer educators do about any deficits you have noticed?

SUMMARY

This chapter has explored how students go through the process of change that accompanies normal growth and development. For traditional-aged students the college years provide the backdrop for a significant period of maturation into adulthood. For older students, college may represent some equally challenging transitions. The chapter summarized the concepts and principles of maturation and discussed the factors that can affect development. It also described the variables that promote healthy human growth, along with guidelines for how peer educators can have a positive impact when working with students who are dealing with issues involving change.

The way change occurs and people mature is important to consider as you successfully make your own transitions and as you prepare to understand this process in those you serve as a peer educator. Knowing the personal and academic challenges of students who need your assistance will provide you with a much stronger base of knowledge to help. In some cases the help you can provide is to refer students to another service, resource, or more prepared professional.

CHAPTER TWO: SUMMARY QUESTIONS

1. Review the list of developmental challenges in this chapter and determine the ones that are most likely to affect the students you will be helping.
2. Explain how the variables such as involvement in college activity, gender identification, peer group behavior, and faculty interaction will influence development and change.
3. Examine the five principles universal to human maturation. Choose one, and explain how that principle may affect your work in your peer educator role.
4. In your role as a peer educator, how can you help create an environment that stimulates positive growth and development?
5. Define the terms: *readiness, maturation, crisis,* and *identity.*

CHAPTER 3

Enhancing Cultural Proficiency

Ata Karim, Rita Ross

LEARNING OBJECTIVES

After completing this chapter, you will be able to

1. Demonstrate an awareness of and an appreciation for your own culture.
2. Define cultural proficiency.
3. Identify your own thoughts and behaviors on a matrix of response to culture.
4. Recognize and avoid forms of discrimination, stereotyping, and prejudice.
5. Define majority privilege and its impact on cultural proficiency.
6. Describe individual and institutional discrimination and how they impact cultures.

Ata Karim is the director of Multi-Cultural Services at Bellevue College. His prior experience was as senior associate director in the School of Leadership Studies at Kansas State University. He is a licensed psychologist and has worked extensively on issues of mental health and human behavior in culturally diverse populations and multicultural organizations.

Rita Ross has taught in both public schools and higher education for over thirty years. Her work emphasis has been to validate the learning effectiveness of students regardless of background or ability. She serves as a facilitator for exceptional experiences with gifted high school students.

7. Recognize obstacles to cultural proficiency.
8. Describe strategies that enable you to relate to individuals of many cultures, thereby fostering the mutual trust necessary for effective peer education.
9. Discuss your role as an advocate for those who might be oppressed by the majority culture.

●

Have you ever spent a day on campus without meeting someone strikingly different from yourself? Changing demographics put us into regular contact with diverse cultural influences, such as those of gender, ethnicity, race, religion, sexual identity, class, age, or ability. Colleges must create inclusive learning and living environments that enable all students to participate fully, regardless of cultural history. As a peer educator, you can be a major contributor to the promotion and demonstration of cultural inclusion. Regardless of your current levels of comfort and proficiency regarding intercultural interactions, your ability to relate to people from differing backgrounds can be strengthened, and you can become an agent of change in the communities to which you belong.

In this chapter we discusses the importance of creating environments that accept, reflect, and include many values, perspectives, and social practices. The following discussion of terms may help as you read:

The term *culture* refers to the infinitely complex, continually changing influences of background and preferences on the thoughts and behaviors of people and groups of people. These influences include sexual identity, socioeconomic status, and race but are not limited to these large-stroke groupings. Personal factors such as temperament, optimism, creativity, and unique experiences combine with the broader influences to provide each of us an individual framework for interacting with the world. Group cultures tend to be clearly defined and recognizable; the culture of the individual is infinite in variety.

To illustrate, within the African American culture you will find wealthy people and poor people and middle-class people. Some individuals within the African American culture are politically conservative; others are more liberal in their views. Some African Americans live in rural settings, while others are city-dwellers or suburbanites. Some are quite religious; others are agnostic or atheists. Some have large family support structures; others are loners. The combinations of personal factors within the African American culture are incalculable. Consequently, although *African American* describes a group culture, individuals within the group vary endlessly. An assumption that all African Americans are similar would be erroneous and naïve.

Culture, as used here, includes broad differences such as ethnicity, religion, or gender but also covers the unique outlook of the individual. Your culture largely determines your identity, as well as how you view the world and others. Understanding group culture and the culture of the individual is important to your work as a peer educator, and it is the major focus of this chapter.

Multicultural describes the interaction of distinctly separate cultures, such as when a community celebrates Hispanic, European, Arabic, and African traditions, or when straight people advocate for the civil rights of gay and lesbian citizens. In contexts such as these, the emphasis is on what makes the cultures distinct, rather than on the many ways the cultures intermingle with other identifying factors within individuals. For example, certain types of food, music, clothing, and family structure are unique to each ethnicity. We consider a collection of these influences to be multicultural. The cultures remain distinctly separate in identity.

Cultural proficiency refers to your ability to interact with people from different backgrounds. In order to develop cultural proficiency, you need to have an inquisitive mind and avoid pre-conceived ideas. It is very helpful to approach each interaction with some knowledge of different cultures, such as the notion that people from poverty often have strong social networks, or that Native Americans can be very hesitant to share their feelings in a direct manner. However, your most effective approach may be to allow each person to teach you about his or her unique combination of influences and their impact on outlook and behavior. Important to cultural proficiency is your ability to define and understand your own culture, which allows you to better comprehend perspectives that differ from yours. No one masters cultural proficiency. We all have things to learn about the life-views of others.

Prejudice means prejudgment. In other words, to be preju-diced is to make a decision before studying the facts. Judging a woman to be lazy because she is poor or judging a man to be incapable because he is deaf are examples of prejudice. We are all prejudiced. This is our nature as humans, and the tendency to sort people and identify those who are like and unlike us helps us make sense of the world. This tendency can impede attempts to connect with others, however, such as when establishing relation-ships as peer educators.

A *stereotype* is a view that generalizes or groups people into clichéd categories, based on indiscriminate judgment, oversimpli-fied assessment, or prejudicial attitude. "Muslims are terrorists" is a stereotype. So is "white men can't dance," or "black people are good athletes." You are using stereotype when you lump a group of people into one category rather than seeking to understand each person individually.

Bias refers to a perspective that is tilted in favor of or against a group of people. Prior beliefs can lead you to act in a biased manner unless you consciously work to overcome them. A math-ematics professor who believes that Asians are more capable than other students may involve Asian students in class discussions more often or have higher standards for them. In this case, Asian students comprise the in-group and all other students fall into the out-group. This bias is unfair to all students; the professor bases decisions on group status and fails to recognize the potential of individuals.

Whereas biases, stereotypes, and prejudices are thoughts, *discrimination* refers to the actions (sorting of people) that may result from unfair thinking. To discriminate means to differentiate, to separate according to differences. We do it all the time! When you choose a song to download or your favorite cookie or the closest parking slot, you are discriminating. You also discriminate when it comes to people, such as when you ask a store clerk for help or you sit by someone familiar when attending an event. You've chosen these people because of their differences, not at random. However, discrimination is a problem if you use it to treat people as if they are inferior. To build a building that is inaccessible to people in wheelchairs is discriminatory and reflects the perspective that the physically able are due more consideration because they are in the majority. Discrimination can also motivate institutions to enact unfair policies.

Empathy refers to the ability to feel what others feel. When you experience something from the other person's perspective, you are empathetic. For example, when you feel sorrow at another's misfortune, you are empathetic. When a friend tells you she got an A on a tough exam and you feel joyful, you are experiencing empathy. Your success as a peer educator will depend to a large degree on your ability to empathize. Others will trust you with their thoughts and feelings when they discover that you understand what it is like to be in their shoes. Empathy does not bear judgment. You are not determining right or wrong. You are simply sharing the other person's experience. Empathy is not sympathy.

Equity recognizes that people are not all the same but deserve a shot at the same outcome. When a college provides computers to those students who don't have their own, they are making the learning environment more equitable. Equity is about giving everyone a fair chance.

Some people say a fish would have a difficult time describing water. The fish has nothing to compare to water because water is all it has ever known. Before you can describe something as "wet," you have to understand "dry." You are like a fish in the water of your culture. If you have grown up and lived in the culture that is most common, that is, the majority culture, you are less able to describe your culture than someone who came from a contrasting background. If, however, you have been raised with a different religion, ethnicity, language, or other trait not common to most people where you live, you are a member of a minority culture, you deal with the differences every day, and you are very much aware of them.

The Story of Brandon and Tony

Brandon drummed his fingers on his laptop. He breathed deeply and recrossed his legs. He glanced at his phone for the third time in five minutes. Tony was late again. As Brandon mentally replayed the previous tutoring sessions with Tony, he became more and more impatient.

Brandon had become a volunteer tutor because he wanted to help other college students learn about a subject he loved. Math had always come easily for Brandon. He had sailed through the upper level classes at his suburban high school, and now he was earning a degree in mathematics and anticipating becoming a math professor in a few years. The opportunity to tutor other students gave him a chance to try his hand at teaching, and he had looked forward to working with Tony, his first client.

Tony had missed the first meeting altogether, with no phone call or notice. He just didn't show. The next week, he came a few minutes late, with no explanation, but the session went well. Although Tony seemed shy and was very quiet, he was obviously bright and seemed to understand when Brandon helped him work through problems. He muttered a "thank you" when he left. Last week, however, Tony arrived as Brandon was packing up to leave, almost thirty minutes after the meeting time. Again, there was no explanation or apology. Brandon helped him with a couple of exercises and then left, frustrated and disappointed that his efforts weren't appreciated.

Now Brandon was ready to give up. He decided to tell Tony he could no longer assist him and then find a student to help who would at least make it to the tutoring sessions. As he was putting on his jacket and stuffing his computer into his backpack, he heard a voice behind him, "Are you Brandon?"

He turned around to find a dark-eyed young woman looking at him. When he acknowledged that he was Brandon, she explained that she was Tony's cousin, Sofia, and she attended a parochial high school not far from the college campus. She and Tony lived near each other in a part of the city Brandon had never seen. He had heard, however, that there was a lot of poverty there, and lots of violence.

"Tony asked me to let you know he can't make it. I'm sorry I'm late; I couldn't find you." Sofia went on to tell Brandon that Tony was home with his younger siblings, who couldn't stay alone after school. Tony and Sofia both had their tuition paid with scholarship dollars, but there was not enough money for Tony to live on campus; he took the Metro home every day in time to care for the kids until their mother got home from work. In order to attend the tutoring sessions, Tony made the trip back to campus, which took 45 minutes, and used up the valuable Metro pass.

"Tony doesn't want me to tell you these things, but he really needs your help, mainly because our high school didn't have very good math classes. He's planning to quit school. Nobody in our family has gone to college before, and he doesn't think he can make it work. The trips back and forth are too expensive and he can't make it to your tutoring sessions in time to get the help he needs. Tony is so smart and we want him to make a better life for himself, but he won't listen to us. And he is too embarrassed to ask for help at school. He doesn't feel he belongs here."

Brandon was stunned. He asked Sofia for a contact number, since Tony didn't have a cell phone and had always made arrangements through the tutoring service or in person. It turned out Brandon and Tony both had a morning hour free on Wednesdays, when Tony was already on campus and wouldn't have to return for tutoring. Brandon also helped Tony secure a job as a cashier in the cafeteria so he could earn a little money to help with expenses. Perhaps most important, Brandon became a trusted friend to Tony. Their connection gave Tony confidence that he did belong in college. After both young men graduated, Tony was admitted to law school. Brandon altered his plans and became a math teacher in an inner city school much like the one Tony had attended.

Reflection Point 3.1: Cultural Misunderstandings

In the story, it is clear that Brandon and Tony each had good
intentions, but cultural differences led to misunderstandings
that almost ruined the tutoring sessions they both wanted. Think
about an event from your life (either experienced or observed)
in which multicultural misunderstandings caused a problem.

What was the missing knowledge that led to the problem?
How could the problem have been avoided or solved?

Exercise 3.1: Differences

Brandon came from a middle-class home; Tony lived a life of
poverty. Since they are students at the same college, the young men
may appear to have similar lives. At first glance it might appear
that their cultures are the same, but powerful influences can hide
beneath outside appearances. Make a chart with the side-by-side
headings

Brandon—Middle Class   **Tony—Poverty**

List differences in their backgrounds that might have an impact
on their respective worldviews. Some examples to consider might be
prior school experiences, living arrangements, external obligations,
availability of resources, confidence within the college culture, and
family support.

In what ways would treating Brandon and Tony exactly the same
way yield an unfair result? In what ways might a person from the

middle class be at a disadvantage if suddenly thrust into an environment of poverty?

PRINCIPLES FOR CULTURAL PROFICIENCY

The following five principles are important to the development of cultural proficiency. These guidelines may help you more effectively work with and relate to diverse students on campus both in your role as a peer educator and as a member of the community in general.

> **Principle 1:** *All of your assumptions are cultural, and may or may not align with the assumptions and understandings of others.*

People are cultural beings. As such, we tend to view and judge the world according to the cultural influences we've observed and experienced. Some of these influences are obvious to us; others are more difficult to detect. Both individual and institutional experiences contribute to these influences. We are likely to consider our own views as the right, the only, and the absolute ways of experiencing and processing the world around us. This natural assumption may lead us to make errors that prevent us from understanding unfamiliar ideas, behavior, and values.

Although our respective cultures make us who we are and enrich our lives, if we fail to shake free of biased influences when judging people, we forfeit the opportunity to know them in their cultures.

Principle 2: *When exploring the cultures of others, it is necessary to suspend judgment temporarily.*

Although it is not possible and would be quite anxiety provoking to suspend judgment indefinitely, it is possible to suspend the immediate judgment of an event or person temporarily, while gathering firsthand information to formulate a more accurate assessment. This is particularly important in situations where the immediate tendency is to base judgment on generalized information or stereotype.

Principle 3: *Both context and content are important.*

Many times, without regard for setting or circumstance, people judge the behavior of others. The same situation placed into a different context may require a different assessment. Take the experience of Brooke and Farzin an as example of the importance of context and content. Brooke met Farzin, a young man from Afghanistan, in her chemistry lab. At first, his halting English caused her to believe he was not very intelligent. He sometimes used the wrong words and sometimes stopped speaking altogether when terms failed to come to him. As they began to work with difficult chemistry problems, however, it became apparent that Farzin was quite gifted and able to simplify the most complex concepts so that Brooke could understand. Brooke began to imagine herself in Farzin's country, and she realized that Farzin was far more able to function within her culture than she would be in his. The context, not Farzin's intellect, was impeding his ability to communicate.

67

It is useful to pay attention to the context in which the behavior is occurring, as well as to observe the actual behavior. This yields a better understanding of the event or behavior in question than if the actions were judged in isolation.

Principle 4: *Becoming comfortable with discomfort is possible and necessary to the development of cultural proficiency.*

Anxiety is a normal response to an unfamiliar situation. When faced with intimidating cultural norms, accepting and conquering your anxiety will allow you to build effective intercultural relationships. Remaining engaged in an interaction despite some discomfort can lead to the reduction of discomfort over time. This is especially true in situations where the resulting interaction is positive.

Overcoming anxieties will also help you mature as a person. The resolution of discomfort promotes growth. Shrinking away from such situations and staying well within established comfort zones only maintain the status quo. Intercultural growth employs the same developmental principles that were discussed in Chapter Two. As discomfort is resolved, the benefits and enjoyment of intercultural interaction increase.

Principle 5: *Curiosity and deliberate inquisitiveness provide a richer, more accurate context for interaction.*

The more curious and inquisitive you are, the more you will be able to gather accurate information. This principle allows you to challenge existing belief systems as you critically examine new information. You will be able to make firsthand decisions about people and events that will be more accurate because they will be based on information you gathered for yourself.

STEREOTYPES

Cara's Story

One day in class, with no explanation, Cara and her fellow students were abruptly asked to "draw a doctor." Much discussion followed the activity. It turned out that nearly every drawing the class produced was of a white, male doctor, regardless of the gender or ethnicity of the artist. The exercise revealed a stereotype which may seem rather harmless on the surface. But as Cara and her classmates discussed the implications of the activity, they began to see subtle, yet powerful advantages experienced by those who fit the stereotype and mirrored disadvantages by those who do not.

The students were surprised to discover the hidden perception that doctors are white and male, a perception perhaps not uncommon in western countries. The expectation that a doctor will look like Patrick Dempsey is a reflection of a culture where white, male doctors are the norm. Unless exposed and addressed, this illogical perception could lead patients—even unwittingly—to choose only doctors who look like those in the drawings or cause leaders in the medical field to provide more opportunities to those who match the profile of a white, male doctor. People who do not reflect the stereotype may be discouraged from pursuing a medical career, simply because they don't see themselves in the role. This is not to say that the advantages should be reversed, but only that everyone should be able to pursue goals without the interference of stereotypes.

In this example, white males experience what is known as majority privilege. It is natural for the people who are in the majority to be unaware of their advantage. As a result, they often have a difficult time understanding the impact of the inequity. The members of the privileged majority did nothing to acquire the advantage, which to them may seem not to exist at all. They do not understand that reality is very different for those who do not share the benefits of the majority culture. It is very much like the fish trying to describe water.

Similar to the majority, minority populations suffer from their own stereotypes. Minority members can be blinded to individual differences within a culture they find to be puzzling or intimidating. The predominant culture is judged as a whole, making it difficult for a minority to relate comfortably with members of the majority.

Isabella's Story

An example: Isabella, a Latina peer educator from an ethnic neighborhood in the city, has been told stories about white people who treat Latinas as if they are inferior. These stories have alarmed her to the point that she has become afraid to interact with people from this group. The resulting stereotype has led her to suspect that any person from this population is prone to unfair beliefs and actions.

Isabella, a peer educator, has been assigned to teach a wellness class, which turns out to be largely populated by the students she finds intimidating. On the first day of class, Isabella's fears, based on stereotype, prevent her from interacting naturally with the students. She knows she must get beyond her stereotypes and recognize the students as individuals. This is a challenge, though; because her sensitivity to discrimination is heightened, she may, in a sense, be "looking" for it. In other words, she may be more likely to (mis)perceive students' intentions and in effect create the derisive behavior she fears.

If she can recognize that her apprehension is a response to stereotype, she can begin to override fears and initiate the development of positive relationships with her peers. Looking for commonly held values, practices, and beliefs, which are shared by many of the students, can begin this process. As Isabella begins to establish relationships with the students and shared interests are identified, she will find personal differences less threatening and will discover a new confidence when she interacts with the people she used to fear.

Exercise 3.2: Stereotypes

With your fellow peer educators, compile a list of traits, such as "blonde" or "nerd," that might elicit stereotypical thinking.

List instances when each of these stereotypes might impede communication or pose hindrances to group or individual goals.

Have you ever found yourself in an unfamiliar setting where your background or preferences were in the minority? How did you feel?

How did your actions reflect your feelings? Were you excessively quiet? Were you louder than usual?

What could you have done to quell any uneasiness and begin to relate in a natural fashion, free from the shadow of stereotype?

PREJUDICE

All multicultural communities must deal with the challenges posed by prejudice against culturally diverse individuals and groups. Prejudice can be defined as an attitude, usually with negative feelings that involve judgment about the members of a group. For instance, women may be judged as inferior to men when it comes to displaying and managing emotion. Stereotyping creates generalized labels that oversimplify difference, deny individuality, and limit possibilities. Prejudice acts in even more deliberate ways to diminish and even dehumanize other group membership.

Feelings of prejudice serve many functions: to maintain an advantage or control over another group, to scapegoat or create a source of blame for inadequacies or limitations that are present, to hold superiority of one group's set of values over another's, and to serve as a basis for justifying decisions as preferred knowledge (Brislin, 1993).

There are many types of prejudice that have often been used to identify group members as inferior and deficient. The following are common types of prejudice.

Sexism refers to prejudice based on gender differences. From the moment we are born, our cultures expose us to gender-related thoughts, feelings, and behaviors. Since men have historically been in positions of power, sexism is often associated with the denigration of women, which can lead to social, economic, or political inequality. Sexism is also apparent when men are viewed as less than manly for choosing roles typically belonging to females, such as caring for children.

Racism is prejudice toward members of ethnic groups who are different from the majority ethnic group in any society. The result of racism can be the marginalization of and missed opportunities for various peoples who are not in the in-group. Racism also occurs when minorities become prejudiced against majority members, such as when people from certain Asian countries believe all Americans are slothful and immoral.

Classism refers to feelings of prejudice toward members of a different, though not always "lower," socioeconomic class. Classism can also be thought of as a form of elitism.

Symbolic issues is a type of prejudice that occurs when one group views another group as interfering with or threatening important cultural values. Cultural symbols such as locus of responsibility, work ethic, value of time, and attitude toward authority can lead people from various groups into direct conflict (Brislin, 1993). For example, in Europe and the United States, recently immigrated people from societies where cultural values differ from the majority are seen as corrupting the institutions and society they are entering. This may occur because of differences in language, faith, and traditions (such as dress, living arrangements, celebrations or lack thereof).

73

Illegal immigrants to the United States, veiled Muslim women in France, and American pop-culture in South Asia are examples of imported cultures that cause distress to those governed by prejudice.

DENIAL AND RATIONALIZATION

Most people hesitate to admit prejudice toward another group. If you are afraid to identify and address your own prejudices, chances are you are denying them to yourself and to others. Denial is a common occurrence and almost impossible to avoid altogether, but it does not alleviate the harm of prejudice. Instead, the damage becomes greater as the prejudice is allowed to thrive behind the denial.

"Politically correct" language can hide underlying prejudices. We fool ourselves into thinking that words such as "African American" inoculate us from thoughts of prejudice, when they often only disguise the thoughts.

Rationalization is different from denial. When you acknowledge a prejudice but justify it without analyzing your true and perhaps unconscious motives, you are rationalizing your prejudice. For instance, if you believe that marriage and its accompanying privileges should be denied to homosexuals, and you cite as your reason a poll finding that 70 percent of the people in your state agree with you, you are rationalizing.

Another method of rationalization is to point to evidence that confirms your bias while disregarding conflicting evidence. We have a natural tendency to do this.

A third rationalization, used to the point of cliché, is to offer evidence of personal relationship with members of a group while maintaining a biased view about the group in general ("Some of my best friends are black, gay, Jewish").

Exercise 3.3: Personal Prejudices

Fill in the following incomplete sentences with the first thoughts that come to mind. Don't stop to work out politically correct answers. You are learning about your own thoughts and values and must be as honest as possible. You do not have to share these feelings and thoughts with others.

Women are ...

Men are ...

African Americans are ...

Whites are ...

Poor people are ...

Rich people are ...

People from my country are ...

Gays, lesbians, and bisexuals are ...

Now that you have explored how you think and feel about various groups of people, consider how you came to these thoughts and feelings. The task is to trace the learning sources and their influences on you. Take a category such as how you consider "poor people." Think of the messages that you received about poor people from parents, friends, religious institutions, media, government, and teachers.

Think of any other sources of information that are influential in your life. Identify them and the nature of the messages communicated by them. Did these sources verbally communicate assumptions about poor people, their values, work ethic, or ethnicity? Did they communicate their assumptions and beliefs more subtly, such as through their personal interactions with poor people? How have these messages impacted your interactions with students who in your eyes are "poor"?

DISCRIMINATION

As an expression of prejudice or stereotype, discrimination can, at the hands of an individual or an institution, harm a person or a group of people through words or deeds. Leaders who engage in stereotypical thinking may engage in discriminatory action against culturally diverse groups. Some argue that discrimination is the privilege of the powerful. In other words, only those who have the power to act on their prejudice are able to cause harm through discrimination.

As you recall from earlier discussion, we all discriminate, for many purposes. Discrimination causes problems when it is used to treat people unfairly. This harmful discrimination is caused by individuals and by institutions, such as clubs, communities, or governments.

Individual discrimination occurs when one person treats others differently, based on group identity rather than personal characteristics. It is likely that you consciously or unconsciously hold some harmful discriminatory beliefs, simply because that is the human tendency. As you identify and abandon these harmful beliefs, replacing them with an open curiosity about and appreciation for the many ways humans live their lives, you will become better able to build relationships with the diverse people you encounter. Examples of individual discrimination include making disparaging comments about certain populations, excluding certain groups from your friendship circle, or treating adults with disabilities as though they are children. Hate crimes are extreme expressions of individual discrimination.

Institutional discrimination can be observed when an imbalance of control emerges inside an organization, such as a government, school, business, or even a family. If one faction within the organization has a greater power than others, it is natural for discrimination to occur in favor of the majority faction.

One setting in which this can happen is in politics, where one race appears to be superior to others simply because the majority race is represented in greater number. (This is similar to the doctor-drawing experiment; someone who is asked to draw a politician might automatically draw a white person.) People become accustomed to this overrepresentation, leading to a perpetuation of the imbalance, and the culture tilts in favor of the majority race.

The same principle is found in corporations, schools, and even families, when factors such as socioeconomic, religious, or gender stereotypes prevail. If a school chooses textbooks and wall displays that reflect only one or two ethnicities, or if a family assigns only traditional gender roles to its members, regardless of interest or ability, it is practicing institutional discrimination.

Some types of discrimination found in institutions are obvious, such as when a state allows only people with driver's licenses or permanent addresses to vote, or when gay and lesbian soldiers must hide their sexual identities in order to keep their jobs. Other unfair discriminatory beliefs and practices, like some types of prejudice and stereotypes, are subtle, and can be very difficult to detect, such as when club presidents at a large, diverse university all happen to be white. Were there really no qualified candidates of a different race? We are so used to the "status quo" that we lose our objectivity and continue to accept practices without question. These hidden forms of discrimination gain power through their invisibility. Unless exposed and rectified, the discrimination continues unnoticed.

Individuals often unconsciously adopt the discrimination they observe in institutions. A habit of questioning the fairness of what you see will allow you to counter this influence and replace the institutional values you find to be unfair with your own ethic of judgment, consequently creating a more balanced, inclusive community.

Exercise 3.4: Discrimination

With your group, identify examples of unfair institutional discrimination, such as those discussed in the chapter. In what ways have these examples or could these examples lead to acts of individual discrimination?

Can you trace any of your personal prejudices to institutional discrimination you have observed or encountered?

What effects might institutional discrimination have on members of the culture of majority? How about members of minority cultures?

CULTURE

The previously offered meaning of the word *culture* outlines a complex term. As you recall, your culture reflects the influences of your personality as well as the groups to which you belong.

You may have heard terms such as *corporate culture* or *hip-hop culture* or *prison culture*. Intense environments create cultures because of the tremendous influence they have on the thoughts and actions of the people who experience them. Similarly, your own life experiences contribute to your personal culture.

Your culture is a combination of values, beliefs, and practices through which you view the world and through which you express yourself. Other people use these values, beliefs, and practices to identify you, and you identify yourself through your personal culture. You share many attributes with other members of your various groups (finances, family, friends, school, clubs, sports, job, music, religion, physical ability, gender, ethnicity, etc.), but your individual culture is unique to you.

If you understand and appreciate your own complexities, it is easier for you to relate to the many ways others interact with the world. Cultures cannot be ranked in order of value. Instead, they can be spread like a smorgasbord for us to enjoy. Like many good foods, some beliefs or practices may require time and more than one taste to appreciate. Some will never taste good to us, but we can respect that others find them enjoyable. And some cultures, like some foods, may be harmful!

No one is ever perfectly proficient at cultural understanding and appreciation. There is always room for growth. There is always a new value or practice to discover in others; there is always a hidden prejudice to discover in ourselves.

Exercise 3.5: What Is Your Culture?

Although your ethnicity or home country can strongly affect your beliefs, many other influences combine to form your culture. Actually, anything that contributes to your values, preferences, beliefs, or actions is a part of your culture.

Here is a list of factors that might play a role in the development of a person's culture. Do you recognize any as your own? What elements from your culture are missing?

Torah	Telenovella	Theocracy
The Rez	Braille	Fox TV
Foster care	Reggae	Progressivism
Community ovens	EbonyJet.com	Circumcision
Alcohol	Heaven	Gay-Straight Alliance
Farsi	Ramones	Salsa dancing
Howard University	Insulin	Eviction
NPR	Taxis	Tuition
First communion	Food stamps	Patriarchy
Bail	Immunization	Tattoos

Choose an item from your personal list of cultural influences that might be difficult for someone else to appreciate. How would you explain its impact on your life view in a way that encourages the other person's empathy?

When you study the items that are not a part of your culture, which ones might be difficult for you to understand in someone else's? Are there biases or prejudices that are impeding your ability to relate? What, specifically, can you do to overcome these preconceptions and build a trusting relationship with the other person?

COLOR BLIND

Stacy and Cho at the Freshmen Orientation Seminar

"I know she's going to say she's color blind."

Stacy sat with her roommate, Cho, in their Freshmen Orientation Seminar. The fellow students who surrounded them seemed to represent many countries and ethnicities. Stacy was predicting what the peer leader would do when she arrived.

"She's going to walk in here and see all these people from all these different places, and she's going to say it doesn't matter if we're black, white, blue, green, or purple. To her, we're all the same. I hate it when people say that. If they can't see my color, they can't see me. I'm black and you're Japanese, and we are not the same color! Jeeze!"

Cho, who was a little shy, was happy to have Stacy for a roommate. Stacy was outgoing and opinionated, and Cho, newly arrived from Japan, had learned more about American culture in the last two weeks than in all of her years in school combined. Just then, Cho saw Abby, the student seminar leader, in the doorway.

"She's here," warned Cho.

"Just watch. She's going to say it," Stacy predicted.

Short, red-headed Abby walked to the circle of chairs and took a seat. "Hi everyone. I'm Abby," she said. "I understand we have several countries represented in this class, and I find that very exciting. I want you to know ..."

"Here it comes. She's going to say it," whispered Stacy.

"... that we will all learn from each other this semester. I'm looking forward to discovering your interests and ideas

81

and I'm anxious to share thoughts about how to make this year a great experience for each of you.

"I'm going to pass around some cards, and I'd like you to write three things that are important to you on one side. On the other side, please list any fears or difficulties you've had since arriving on campus ..."

"She didn't say it!" said Stacy to Cho. "I can't believe it."

Cho handed Stacy a card.

"This might not be so bad," she said.

Reflection Point 3.2: Color Blind

Have you ever heard someone use the phrase "color blind" in the way it was used in the story? If so, what do you think the person who used it was trying to convey?

Why do you think Stacy was so offended by the term?

How might Abby's card exercise allow Stacy, Cho, and the other students to feel more included than a "color blind" comment?

OBSTACLES TO CULTURAL PROFICIENCY

Many feelings, beliefs, and actions can get in the way of individual and institutional cultural proficiency (Robins, Lindsey, Lindsey, & Terrell, 2006). Here are three that are commonly observed:

Lack of Knowledge

If you have never been exposed to certain cultures, such as specific ethnicities or sexual identities, it can be difficult to establish social connections with their members. You just don't know the subtleties of the culture, and you can inadvertently offend or place distance between you and the other person.

The first time you encounter someone from an unfamiliar background, such as poverty or a rural or urban setting, it might be helpful to establish common ground, perhaps by asking a harmless question such as, "What's on your iPod?" or "Do you miss home?" as a way to encourage her to teach you about herself. The trick is to ask questions that are not threatening but are engaging enough to promote conversation and new discoveries about one another. Although you want your questions to be natural and not seem like an interview, it is important to demonstrate respectful curiosity and to listen attentively when learning about the culture of another.

When you encounter someone whose dress or actions are noticeably different from your own, observe and interact with respect and curiosity. Make it your aim to discover the common views and experiences we all share, as well as factors specific to the culture.

Unaware of Majority Privilege

If you are a member of the majority culture, you are likely to experience benefits and advantages just because of your membership in the majority (in terms of race, gender, or economic

83

circumstances, for example). These advantages have not been earned through effort or achievement. In your aim to become more culturally proficient, it is important to be aware that these advantages exist. For example, the man at the bank may be friendlier and more receptive—intentionally or even unintentionally—to a woman in western dress than to a woman wearing a burqa.

Ask yourself if you benefit from the privileges of the majority. If you conclude that you do, be aware that your daily experiences may be quite different from those in the minority.

If you are a member of a minority culture, you are probably already aware of these advantages.

Believing Things Should Remain as They Are

Accessible travel and communication technology have allowed people from diverse backgrounds to mingle like never before. As a result, individuals and institutions find it necessary to respond to complex, dynamic populations. Policies and procedures designed for specific groups must be revisited and remolded to address the needs of people of many ages, races, religions, economies, abilities, and languages. It can be difficult to understand that these changes benefit all, especially for members of the majority culture. In order to accommodate a changing and diverse society, decision makers and those they represent must recognize the need to include all cultures when establishing policy.

THE CULTURAL RESPONSE MATRIX

Individuals and institutions respond to cultural differences in many ways. These responses include both thoughts and behaviors. Unless we actively share them, our thoughts remain hidden from others. Our behaviors, however, range from the secret to the

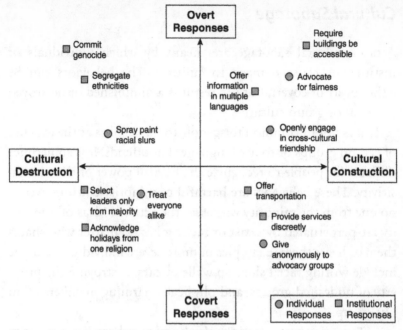

Figure 3.1. Matrix of Responses to Culture

obvious. The concept of plotting cultural proficiency on a continuum was proposed by Robins et al. (2006).

These overt and covert responses to various encounters with cultures can be constructive or destructive. Examples of responses are plotted in Figure 3.1. Both individual and institutional responses are represented on the matrix. For instance, committing genocide is both overt and destructive, so it appears in the upper left quadrant, whereas anonymous giving is covert and constructive, and is found in the lower right quadrant.

Ways of responding to cultures can be grouped according to the degrees of construction/destruction they cause. These responses can be devastating, affirming, or inspiring to cultures, depending on circumstance and context. The following paragraphs describe some of these groupings.

Cultural Sabotage

Acts of cultural sabotage are means by which individuals or institutions cause damage to cultures. The behaviors can be either overt or covert, but the result is a diminished or destroyed personal or group culture.

It is not uncommon for people to make jokes at the expense of certain groups or to use language that offends. It is sometimes difficult for people to recognize the hurtful power of their insensitivity. These behaviors are harmful to minority cultures even if no one from the minority witnesses the actions. Ideas of inferiority are perpetuated by sexist or racist jokes no matter who shares them or hears them. Examples of more severe individual sabotage include writing racial slurs on walls or cars, destroying the property of undesired groups, and physically harming members of an out-group.

These destructive actions also harm members of the majority culture because people are locked into the narrow thinking of stereotypes and therefore unable to enjoy the full spectrum of human expression.

Institutions are also known to overtly damage cultures, such as when only one language is allowed in a community, or when it is illegal for a transgendered person to use the public restroom designated for her gender identity. Some recognizable historical examples of overt institutional sabotage are the eradication of native populations in North America and the internment of Japanese citizens during World War II.

Institutions also act to destroy cultures covertly, such as when governmental calendars or policies promote one religion over others, or when public schools omit any mention of homosexuality in the sex education curriculum. The effects of covert sabotage are very powerful because they can be difficult to detect unless you are the victim.

Cultural Blindness

Like color blindness, cultural blindness is difficult to deter because it can disguise itself as helpful behavior. Cultural blindness occurs when you are aware of a cultural issue, but choose to pretend it doesn't exist or to ignore it. When you have a hidden prejudice or you are uncomfortable acknowledging an issue, denying it can make it seem to disappear. Instead, the prejudice thrives behind the denial, preventing authentic cultural interactions.

Everyone wants to be seen and to be recognized as an individual. Cultural blindness causes people of minority cultures to feel invisible or alienated, destroying the trust necessary for a productive helping relationship. Saying, "I treat all people the same" is an example of cultural blindness.

Cultural Ignorance

People can be unaware of the subtleties of other cultures. A history professor, discussing examples of cultural oppression, stated, "It's like when the Jews killed Jesus." A student said, "Excuse me, but it was the Romans who killed Jesus."

The teacher, obviously uncomfortable with being challenged, looked at the light-haired young man. "It's my understanding that the crucifixion happened at the hands of the Jews," he said.

"That story was spread to allow the Jews to be exterminated. It's false," replied the student. He was calm on the outside, but shaking inside.

"Why, are you a Jew?" asked the professor, who apparently thought the student was not.

"Yes, I am," replied the student, becoming flushed with the embarrassment of being singled out and called upon to defend his religious beliefs.

"Well, I didn't mean to offend you," said the professor, approaching and looming over the young man's desk.

87

"Let's just get back to talking about history," requested the student, hoping to divert attention elsewhere.

The student was humiliated at being in the spotlight and challenged for his faith. The teacher had no idea that the student was Jewish or that his insensitive comments would affect the student as they did. He was simply unaware of the nuances of the culture he was discussing.

Other examples of cultural ignorance include the westerner who doesn't know it is considered unclean to use one's left hand at the table in certain societies, or the African American who may not realize that lots of white kids don't have the strong support systems found in many black families.

As a peer educator and as a member of various communities, you will often be confronted with new ideas and practices. When you are faced with your own lack of cultural knowledge, it is important to be mindful of the feelings of others. This sensitivity will prevent hurt feelings and embarrassment, while allowing you to develop new understanding about the many ways people live their lives.

Cultural Awareness

You may know of some cultural influences that you have not experienced first hand. For example, a student from the inner city is probably aware of cowboy culture. He has perhaps seen movies with cowboys and read about cowboys in books and magazines. He knows horses and big hats are involved. He might even make fun of cowboys from time to time. But he really has no feelings about cowboys beyond his minimal understanding. He doesn't really understand the beliefs and behaviors to which cowboys ascribe. If he were to meet a cowboy, he might feel awkward. Perhaps he has no idea how to begin a conversation with the cowboy. He might find the cowboy intimidating.

Your own culture is one of many, and you will encounter the many ways people experience the world throughout your life. A respectful curiosity will allow you learn about thoughts and actions that might be unfamiliar and lead you to become more culturally proficient.

Cultural Tolerance

> What is tolerance? It is the consequence of humanity.
> We are all formed of frailty and error; let us pardon
> reciprocally each other's folly—that is the first law of
> nature.—Voltaire

Over the centuries and in various contexts, tolerance for others appears as a theme, valued and discussed by many. Acquiring a tolerance for various cultural perspectives is a step beyond demonstrating an awareness of them.

We are all vulnerable and we all make mistakes. Recognizing these imperfections allows us to accept others as they try to make sense of the world in their own ways. Remembering our similarities as humans helps us provide room for our differences. We begin to make places for everyone at the table; we include everyone, regardless of perspective.

When you declare that everyone has the right to pursue his or her own lifestyle, whether or not it matches your personal lifestyle, you are demonstrating tolerance. "Live and let live" is a statement of tolerance. Tolerance does not imply appreciation; in fact, it suggests a negative response to be overcome. You may not enjoy your roommate's music, but you put up with it. You tolerate it. Tolerance is a prerequisite to cultural fluency.

CULTURAL FLUENCY

Much the same way linguistic fluency allows insight and communication to occur through language, cultural fluency enables learning and collegiality between and within diverse cultures. Like language, cultural fluency can never be mastered; it is an ever-present, ever-improving tool allowing you to navigate the new situations you encounter. Cultural fluency is grounded in respectful curiosity and an appreciation for our differences that goes beyond tolerance. When you are culturally fluent, you don't know everything, but you do have some good questions and you know how to ask them in ways that promote understanding. You know how to listen with respect and how to respond in constructive ways to differences. You are actively looking for the hidden treasure in the cultures of others.

Cultural advocacy refers to actions that support or argue in favor of a culture. If you object to the telling of a racist joke, you are advocating for cultural inclusion and against harmful discrimination. Other examples of cultural advocacy are speaking to a campus governing board in favor of adding inclusive language to university policy, writing a letter to the college newspaper asking the writers to represent all cultures in their coverage of campus events, and petitioning for free child care during evening activities that are required for class. Decisions about whether to become involved in cultural advocacy, and in which contexts, are personal. The degree to which you are willing to advocate reflects your cultural fluency and your commitment to change.

Reflection Point 3.3: Cultural Proficiency

Revisit the story of Brandon and Tony. Referring to concepts learned in this chapter, describe Brandon's level of cultural proficiency at the beginning of the story. In what ways do you think he had grown by the story's end?

Tips for Facilitating Cultural Inclusion

1. *Awareness:* You must acquire awareness of yourself and of others. This includes accepting yourself as imperfect in order to accept that others are imperfect, also. We all bring biases, preferences, histories, and expectations to any interaction; recognizing that perfection is unattainable will allow you to focus on the strengths that you and others offer. When the emphasis is on the positive, people tend to develop their abilities and weaknesses diminish.

2. *Acceptance:* Since no two people are identical, no community is composed of identical members. When people come together in groups, large or small, their many perspectives and thoughts interact to enrich the experience for all. To diminish the diversity would be to diminish the complex qualities of the group. Healthy communities depend on the intricate interactions that occur when all authentic thoughts are endorsed. These interactions in turn depend on the unconditional acceptance of the individual.

3. *Determination:* Because you are a cultural being, you have specific notions about how to live that have been acquired throughout your lifetime. Your capacity to understand and relate to vastly differing lifestyles will not be fulfilled without determined effort. A commitment to this effort is necessary when establishing a welcoming climate for culturally diverse others. You must work through the challenges posed by intercultural interactions and resulting differences of opinion and perspective. Instead of clinging to one "right" way to live, you must employ more ecumenical principles, such as tolerance, respect, and faith in your capacity to work through differences. In addition, knowing that a false solution to a problem is no solution, you must also be determined to embrace a credo of honesty and fairness. Promise yourself that you will let integrity guide your thoughts and actions. Be sure people can trust what you say and what you do.

4. *Concentration:* When you are communicating, especially with someone from an unfamiliar vantage point, concentrate on what is being said in the moment, rather than worrying about

what to say next or anticipating a specific outcome. Focusing on the moment, rather than on yourself, allows you to be more fully attentive to the situation. When you fail to be thoughtfully attentive, your personal values and beliefs automatically interpret and judge rather than empathize with other people's words and behaviors. This lack of concentration makes the development of inclusive, accepting relationships unlikely. Instead, consciously listen for the intent of the other person as well as the literal meaning of his or her words. Speak in ways that are understandable in different contexts and try to understand others' frames of reference. This process facilitates the mutual insight required for effective, responsive relationships.

5. *Harmony:* The orientations of awareness, acceptance, determination, and concentration on the present lead to internal harmony, which is crucial for all human relationships. Your personal feelings of harmony will allow you to find and inspire harmony in others, and consequently promote effective, positive relationships and communities.

SUMMARY

This chapter presents and discusses ideas that are crucial to your work as a peer educator. Understanding the vast influence of culture and learning to navigate the various cultures you encounter will enable you to appreciate your own cultural influences and to build productive relationships.

Developing an awareness of various obstacles to cultural proficiency allows you to overcome them and move beyond their impediment. Prejudice, discrimination, and stereotypes are common, powerful thoughts and practices that must be exposed and managed in order to better establish relationships such as those of the peer educator. Sensitivity, respect, and authentic curiosity will be your allies as you interact with people from diverse backgrounds and beliefs.

Cultural proficiency is a developmental process that is never perfected. You continue to add, omit, and alter values and beliefs throughout your life.

CHAPTER THREE: SUMMARY QUESTIONS

1. How does your culture influence your worldview?
2. What does it mean to be culturally proficient?
3. In what way does institutional discrimination influence culture?
4. What are examples of "invisible" inequity? How do these inequuities occur?
5. In what ways can you overcome the influence of your own prejudice?
6. How does respectful curiosity promote cultural proficiency?

CHAPTER 4

Interpersonal Communication Skills

Creating the Helping Interaction

LEARNING OBJECTIVES

After completing this chapter, you will be able to

1. Describe the differences between ordinary, daily conversations and the special qualities of interpersonal communication that are necessary for a helping relationship.
2. Explain the differences between advice giving and interpersonal communications.
3. Communicate core conditions of helping, including empathy, respect, and warmth.
4. Demonstrate skills for physical and psychological attending.
5. Demonstrate listening and responding skills that encourage students to explore their own problems.
6. Demonstrate the ability to communicate "interchangeable responses" in a helping interaction.
7. Describe four types of situations you may encounter in the helping relationship that require you to refer the person to another individual who is trained and experienced in a specific area.

"... but, if you tame me, it will be as if the sun came to shine on my life. I shall know the sound of a step that will be different from all the others."

DE SAINT-EXUPÉRY, *The Little Prince*

Developing the communication skills necessary for becoming an effective helper rests on having multicultural competence (Daniels & Ivey, 2007; Ivey, Bradford-Ivey & Zalaquett, 2010). Chapter Three identified ways to understand and accept people from their unique cultural perspective. This chapter will show you how to build on cultural competency through enhancement of interpersonal communication that will facilitate positive outcomes in your work with students.

At this point you may be asking questions such as, Is it OK to give my opinion? Give advice? Tell my story? Be sympathetic? Act interested? Offer typical courtesies of conversation? The answer is not a simple no, maybe, or sometimes. In this chapter we do not intend to change your whole manner of communication; however, we will illustrate some of the limitations of everyday talk and demonstrate more successful ways to facilitate a helping response through specific methods of interpersonal communication. We start by looking at one of the most customary approaches to helping, which we call advice giving.

WHEN TO PROVIDE MORE THAN ADVICE

In your role as a peer educator, you will be called upon often by other students for assistance with figuring out problems in their changing personal and academic lives. In some instances, these concerns will be clear-cut; the student will need some specific information or action from you. For instance, a student in a residence hall may need some assistance in understanding a housing policy, such as a contract. This type of request requires you to respond with direct information. Or students seeking career guidance may need you to tell them where to find career assistance on your campus. This is also a request for action on your part. These types of requests are typically straightforward, requiring knowledge of specific resources. Your goal as a helper in these cases is to be direct and provide accurate answers.

However, sometimes students will seek you out as a sounding board and need your understanding and involvement. These situations typically require more in-depth communication because the students may describe personal dilemmas that are not clear-cut, easily identifiable, or quickly solvable. The students may be experiencing emotions such as confusion or anxiety in regard to the problem presented. They are clearly experiencing personal distress and are seeking your understanding and involvement to assist them in clarifying the problem and, quite possibly, identifying strategies for resolving it. Here is an example. A student approaches and tells you she is supposed to sign up for an advisor appointment for class registration next term. However, she adds, "I'm really embarrassed because I hate my classes, I'm doing poorly in my grades, and I don't have a clue what to say as my excuse."

This request for understanding and involvement requires responses that are very different from those for direct action or information. In these instances, you are being asked to enter into a relationship that requires greater proficiency of interpersonal skill. You are being asked to talk about issues that require the student to explore reasons for the emotions she is feeling. What is the "embarrassment" about? "Hating classes, doing poorly, and not having a clue"! These are all signals of something more going on in this student's life and will need more clarification and understanding before you will know the first step of assistance. In your helping role, your knowledge and application of interpersonal communication skills will help you work with the student to reach greater levels of personal understanding, ultimately leading to action or problem solving. In other words, your job is to help the student solve the problem, not to solve it for her.

DRAWING THE LINE BETWEEN ADVICE AND EXPLORATION

Many peer educators may find it hard at first to apply the strategies of more in-depth interpersonal communication to interactions with peers who need help. This is because we've all spent our lifetimes learning and practicing a different form of day-to-day helping—advice giving. For the most part, advice giving looks like the appropriate response when friends, family, and coworkers share their problems and concerns. In fact, this is what many people ask for and seem to expect, and in daily life, it often is appropriate. However, there are several problems associated with advice giving that make it a less effective tool for peer educators. It is important to understand when advice giving is the appropriate communication strategy and when a student needs more depth of personal exploration and understanding. Table 4.1 provides a comparison of the difference between advice giving and the skills of the helper that we refer to as interpersonal communications skills.

The following paragraphs describe the qualitative differences between advice giving and interpersonal communication.

Table 4.1. Comparing Advice Giving to Interpersonal Communication

Variable	Advice Giving	Interpersonal Communication
Interaction	Directed (talking to)	Collaborative (talking with)
Helper's role	Authority	Facilitator
Expertise	Reliable knowledge	Interpersonal relation skills
Time	Brief and direct	Extended for exploration
Function	Provides necessary information	Assists individual problem solving
Relationship	Limited (courteous)	In-depth (interpersonal skills)
Precautions	Advice does not always fit the perspective or need of another	Requires having accurate listening and attending skills
Limits	Must have specific knowledge	Must understand when need for professional assistance
Outcome	Not known	Outcome can be determined

ADVICE GIVING IS EASY

Giving advice is a relatively simple act. A person describes the problem, and you immediately give your best take on the situation. No problem exploration has occurred and, in fact, you will never know whether the initial problem that is presented is the real problem that needs to be addressed. For instance, a student complaining about a roommate borrowing her clothes without permission will not benefit from your advice if, in fact, the real problem is hesitancy to confront the roommate rather than what the roommate is doing. Perhaps this same student has difficulty dealing with most interpersonal relationships when conflict arises, and this "problem with the roommate" is really only a symptom of a greater issue. You might never address the real problem of conflict avoidance if you provide a one-minute sound bite of advice about the specific situation the student described. Instead, you need to learn how to draw out the underlying concerns—which the student may well not have recognized—and provide support while the student works out ways to deal with them. This approach may take some getting used to, but it is a very useful skill to master. For example, a student may tell you, "I can't stand my roommate any more, what should I do?" The quick advice retort may be "Yea, that's tough, why don't you just go apply for a room transfer. That will take care of it!" Quick advice does not allow an opportunity to better understand the possible underlying reasons for the student's statement. A better statement would, potentially, open the door for exploring more factors behind the initial comment. A more open response might reflect, "You sound pretty upset with your roommate; I wonder what your options might be to deal with this problem. What have you thought about doing?" This response does not solve the problem but it at least allows the student to pursue the issues behind the statement further.

The Helper Is the Expert

When people give advice, they are thinking and responding from a personal frame of reference: values, attitudes, past experiences, and present maturation level. Unfortunately, the recipient of the advice may be operating from a completely different set of personal values, attitudes, past experiences, and developmental level. What works for one person may not work for another person at all. The principle to follow is to recognize that the person seeking assistance is the most knowledgeable regarding himself or herself. The action to be followed must be consistent with who he or she is as a person, what he or she values and believes in, and the choice he or she is willing to live with.

Advice Giving Involves Less Time Commitment

A person who is in real need of your understanding and personal involvement requires a greater commitment from you in terms of time and attention. Problem exploration, self-understanding, and the identification of problem-solving strategies can rarely be dealt with in a few minutes of conversation. The skills recommended in this chapter require a willingness to spend some time with another student to allow for the best chance of successful problem resolution.

Advice Giving Demands Less Personal Energy

Advice giving does not involve much personal or emotional energy on the giver's part. You can quickly gather data, sort it through your personal frame of reference, and come up with a solution. Effective interpersonal communication, however, requires appropriate attending, listening, and responding skills within the other person's frame of reference. In other words, problem resolution occurs best when the person helped is at the center of the exploration process. You will learn that focusing your attention on another person and, as the saying goes, "walking a mile in their shoes" requires quite a bit of concentration. Effective helping is a high-energy and, at times, intense activity. You may experience some feelings of fatigue after a successful helping interview with another student, and you will probably feel somewhat tired mentally and perhaps emotionally.

Advice Giving Requires Knowledge but Fewer Interpersonal Skills

Advice givers bring their present maturation level, past life experiences, values, attitudes, and beliefs to the helping interaction. They filter their thinking through these personal dimensions and give advice. By contrast, effective interpersonal helpers have

100

developed several specific helping skills. These include understanding how people mature and develop; attending and listening effectively; demonstrating and communicating empathy, respect, warmth, and genuineness in the helping interaction; and implementing a problem-solving model. These are all specific skills that can be learned, practiced, and implemented.

Advice May Vary from Facts to Offering Opinion

Advice giving that offers a fact of information is based upon objective knowledge. However, if the advice giver offers a suggestion or recommendation about what a student should do then it is a subjective or opinionated action. Suggesting a course of action for another individual will usually be from the help provider's own frame of reference. This could show a lack of respect for the other person's ability to resolve the problem in a manner consistent with who he or she is as an individual. Also, if the solutions suggested do not work, the person who sought assistance has to take little or no personal responsibility for the lack of success. They can say, "I just did what I was told was best." Another way to think about it is that effective helping through interpersonal relationships promotes independence, not dependency. Effective helpers trust that others have the necessary human resources to discover and implement solutions to their problems, and they act as guides along the path of exploration, understanding, and problem resolution.

Reflection Point 4.1: Communication Styles

Think about communication styles:

What are the major differences between advice giving and effective interpersonal communication?

So what will be the major changes you will have to make in order to change from an advice giver to one who practices effective interpersonal communication?

CHARACTERISTICS OF A HELPING RELATIONSHIP

If effective helping is not giving advice, what is it? How will you know whether your interactions with others are helpful? What are the differences between ordinary, day-to-day conversations and those that can be described as helpful within the context of effective interpersonal communications? Ten characteristics can be used to distinguish between helping relationships and relationships that may not benefit those seeking help. The following characteristics and brief summaries have been adapted from Ender, Saunders-McCaffrey, and Miller (1979, pp. 51–53).

The Helping Relationship Is Meaningful

Both the helper and the person should benefit from the relationship. At times, it can be personal and intense. It is meaningful because it is relevant. It may both cause a little anxiety and also make some of your anxiety go away. It involves mutual commitment between the peer educator and the student seeking assistance.

The Helping Relationship Involves Feelings

In genuine helping relationships, both parties tend to disclose aspects of themselves that create some level of anxiety or dissonance. This self-disclosure may produce many feelings for both the peer educator and the person being helped. While talking with a person will emphasize thoughts more than feelings, the emotional aspects creating dissonance will also be revealed in both verbal and nonverbal ways.

The Helping Relationship Demonstrates Respect for Individual Self-Worth

The self-worth of an individual is respected in the helping relationship. Shame, preconceived notions, and deceit are not present in a relationship built on respect for a person's self-worth. Both individuals relate to one another as authentic and trustworthy human beings.

The Helping Relationship Takes Place by Mutual Consent

One cannot truly be helped if the helper is being coerced. The absence of pressure is a vital element in the helping relationship. Both parties should enter the relationship free of external pressure. This is a critical characteristic if genuine help is to be given and received.

The Helping Relationship Involves Communication and Interaction

In the helping relationship, both parties express and receive knowledge, information, and feelings. This information is exchanged both through words and nonverbal gestures. The more clear and articulate the communication between peer educator and student, the more meaningful the relationship.

The Helping Relationship Shows a Clear Structure

How structured or casual the relationship will be differs for each situation. However, there are two essential patterns—initiation or disclosure and reply. Responsibility for this structure is placed on both parties. In the beginning stages of the relationship, the peer educator will be required to initiate and at times explain the process of the helping relationship. As the relationship develops, however, the student will learn to take part more fully.

The Helping Relationship Is a Collaborative Effort

Both participants in the helping relationship work toward a mutually agreed-upon goal. Both seek out resources and contributions that will add to the partnership, moving toward the goal.

The Helping Relationship Is Designed to Produce Change

The significant element here is that the person seeking help will be somehow different after receiving the help. If the relationship was helpful, the peer educator and the student needing help will both describe the change that has happened as positive.

The Individual Seeks Understanding and Involvement

Although there may be many different reasons for seeking assistance, the student assumes that the peer educator can actually help him or her explore a concern and find potential resolution. It is crucial to the relationship that the student has confidence in the helper's abilities and believes the help is meaningful.

The Peer Educator Is Approachable and Secure as a Person

Effective peer educators develop a manner that makes other people want to seek them out for help. Their behavior is accepting of others and respectful of people in general. Peer educators need to free themselves from uncertainty, anxiety, or unreasonable fear, which may make them seem less approachable.

104

Think about the ten characteristics of a helping relationship:

What are the ones that seem most natural to you given your present style of helping?

So what characteristics may be difficult for you presently to model or try out?

Now what can you do to integrate some of these more difficult characteristics into your helping style?

INTERPERSONAL COMMUNICATIONS MODEL

Brief Background on Systematic Communication Skills

What are the attributes of effective helping skills? Training models for interpersonal communication skills have evolved over the past fifty years. Three assumptions have served as the basis for the development of these models:

1. Specific definable qualities are present during interpersonal interactions that create the conditions that facilitate positive personal exploration. Carl Rogers (1951) was one of the first to delineate and emphasize these qualities as necessary conditions for personal growth. They included genuineness, warmth, positive regard, and accurate empathy. These human relationship skills were further defined as helping skills over the following two decades (Carkhuff, 1969; Gazda, Asbury, Balzer, Childers, & Walters, 1977).

2. Interpersonal helping skills are definable, and these skills can be systematically taught and practiced through helper training programs. Training should be broken into very specific skill sets starting with basic attending and listening skills and

105

progressing to more advanced intervention and problem solving skills (Egan, 2009; Hill, 2009; Ivey, Bradford-Ivey, & Zalaquett, 2010).

3. Research on the application of interpersonal communication skills has shown that training leads to effective helping outcomes with both professionals and nonprofessionals in a wide range of disciplines. A summary of current research using microcounseling training indicated that training can be effective with a wide range of populations, including high school students, volunteers, teachers, and other skilled helpers (Daniels & Ivey, 2007). Similar models utilizing systematic interpersonal communication skills have been used to train peer educators with demonstrated outcome results (Newton, 1974).

Figure 4.1 shows the model that will be used for your training in the skills of interpersonal relationship for creating the

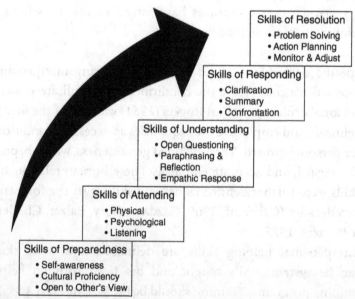

Figure 4.1. Incremental Steps for Helpful Interpersonal Communication

helping interaction. You will note that the first step, Skills of Preparedness, has been covered in detail in Chapter Three, Enhancing Cultural Proficiency. This area includes awareness of your cultural self, proficiency to understand differences with people of diverse backgrounds, and an accepting and open stance to other viewpoints. The last step in this model includes the Skills of Resolution, which is covered in Chapter Five, Problem Solving with Individuals.

Skills of Attending

To be effective in this helping role, peer educators must learn and demonstrate appropriate attending skills, active listening techniques, and interchangeable responses. Also, peer educators using this model must be able to remain nonjudgmental in regard to the problem they are hearing and must genuinely want to help the student who needs them. All these positive components of helping must occur within a relationship framework that can be categorized as having high levels of trust, respect, genuineness, and warmth.

Attending skills are at the heart of all other communication skills as they are the contact point between the person being helped and the helper. Daniels and Ivey (2007) define the components of attending as the 3 Vs + B (visual, verbal, vocal, and body language). Another way to describe attention is through the two dimensions—physical attending and psychological attending.

Physical Attending   Demonstrating appropriate physical attending skills involves focusing completely on the individual seeking help. Your body should be communicating nonverbally that you are really tuned in and interested in the person talking about and clarifying a problem. You will probably be sitting down or standing directly facing the other person, making good eye contact, and providing supportive expressions of warmth and caring. You will not be displaying behaviors that may be distracting to the person seeking help—no fidgeting, distracting body movements, multitasking, watching other people, or making judgmental facial expressions.

Psychological Attending Psychological attending is your ability to focus on the whole person. In other words, this kind of attending appreciates and understands the other person's feelings, thoughts, and intentions. Through psychological attending you could determine a factor such as consistency between what the student says and how the student acts. You will be absorbed in the communication and willing to address the small details of what the person says. You will be tuning in to such variables as the person's tone of voice, facial expressions, posture, animation, silences, pauses, and gestures. Everything is important. Psychological attending involves truly trying to enter into the other person's world, seeing and experiencing the world as he or she does. This will demand substantial concentration and energy.

Two other important psychological dimensions, respect and warmth, are also demonstrated through appropriate attending skills. Respect is the belief that most people have the capacity to be their own best problem solver. Respect can usually be demonstrated by good attending behavior such as refraining from doing anything for people that they could do for themselves and supporting people in their efforts. Warmth, on the other hand, is primarily communicated through nonverbal signals, which may include, when appropriate, a touch, a smile, or other facial expression.

Listening Focused listening is the ability to pick up through the verbal and nonverbal component what a person thinks, experiences, acts, and feels (Egan, 2009). One beginning test that indicates whether a helper is listening intently to the person disclosing the problem is the attempt to paraphrase the message just heard so that the student can feel secure that the person listening understands exactly what he or she is feeling. A paraphrase is being able to report back in a return statement the essential content of what has been spoken. Many peer educators have problems demonstrating this skill because distractions, both external and internal, can get in the way and result in missing aspects of the message.

External Distractions   Distractions in the immediate environment can minimize effective listening. For example, moving to a relatively quiet area can quickly alleviate noise distractions from the hallway. Just as distractive is your cell phone ringing or signaling a text message. If you don't manage these distractions you will have difficulty being able to concentrate at the level that shows you are fully available.

Internal Distractions   Simply stated, these are random thoughts that interfere with listening and we all have them; they might be yesterday's football game, your plans for the weekend, or something that you saw on the Internet. Internal distractions are more difficult to alleviate and require greater levels of personal energy and concentration to overcome. You have to actively stop these distracting thoughts as they come in to fully understand what the student is saying to you. This will take some effort and practice on your part, but it can be done.

Skills of Understanding

Interchangeable Responses   A paraphrase that repeats essentially the content of what a person has said, an interchangeable response, features the content but also includes both the feeling

109

Exercise 4.1: Comfort Zones

With a partner in your training group, sit facing each other. Experiment with the concept of physical distance and its relationship to comfort and warmth.

How do you feel when you sit one foot apart? Three feet apart? Ten feet apart?

Next, with your partner take a common discussion topic such as "what has your day been like today?" and hold a five minute conversation.

Pay attention to what has gone on during this conversation.

Identify physical mannerisms: gestures, smiles, nodding of the head or other nonverbal behaviors. What type of impressions did you receive from the verbal and nonverbal interaction?

Another way to practice paying attention to nonverbal behavior is to use the "mirroring" technique. One person creates nonverbal gestures, and the second person acts as a mirror, miming the same gesture back. Again, discuss your impressions and what you may have learned from acting as a mirror.

and motive that are being experienced. In the early stages of a helping relationship, your active use of interpersonal communication skills will demonstrate that you are listening intently and understanding the problem through a series of responses that are, in effect, interchangeable with the message you have just heard. That is, you will paraphrase what the student has just told you.

110

For example, a student who is having problems with an academic adviser may say, "I can't believe how much time I wasted this morning. Dr. Jones and I had an appointment to discuss my spring schedule, and I waited an hour, and he never showed up. This is the second time he has done this to me." An appropriate interchangeable response in this situation might be, "So you're pretty annoyed that your adviser didn't come to your appointment and you wasted a bunch of time waiting for him, and this wasn't even the first time that's happened, so it was even more annoying." This response is interchangeable. It shows that you get what the student is telling you and gives him the security to move on and figure out what else is going on in the situation. At the beginning, you might not know where the student will be going with everything. That is, the student's exploration of the problem may help him understand more about himself and get to a solution for the problem. It is the helper's job to help guide the process in a somewhat structured way. The interchangeable response will be a powerful helping tool as you aid a student in this process.

Empathy   Empathy is a critical and necessary dimension to interpersonal communication. To be empathic is to understand the other's world through his or her perspective and to know how he or she thinks and feels in regard to what is being said. Remember, this is how another person feels, not how you would feel if caught up in the same type of problem. Empathy is not sympathy. Sympathy may come off as pity or commiseration. Empathy, on the other hand, is showing an understanding of what the person is thinking, feeling, and experiencing. The better you are at attending and listening, the better your ability to empathize with the student you are assisting. There is a quality of knowing and understanding another person that allows you to experience something through his or her perspective, as if you were in the shoes of this other person; empathy is communicated

---

Exercise 4.2: Listening, Paraphrasing, and Interchangeable Responses

---

1. Find a partner with whom to practice your listening communication skills. First, have your partner say a short sentence (about ten to fifteen words).

   Now, repeat the sentence word for word. Just repeating another person's statement helps you to pay closer attention to what was said instead of interpreting the words into your experience. It is important to hear accurately the person you are listening to.

2. Once you can repeat a sentence verbatim, turn your attention to practicing paraphrases. Now ask your partner to tell you a story about him or herself. Paraphrase the story. Can you do this without leaving out any significant details?

3. Ask your partner to share a personal or academic problem. Afterwards, use a word to describe how you think your partner feels as a result of this problem. Ask your partner if you have correctly identified the most important feeling.

4. Ask your partner to share another personal or academic concern. This time paraphrase back the content you heard and the feeling, or feelings, you think your partner is experiencing. This is an interchangeable response.

by accurate verbal responses but it also is very much a "felt" experience. You will find that the ability to communicate empathically is a powerful helping tool. When you demonstrate this skill, the other person will realize that you are truly listening to the concerns being expressed and understanding the unique world of this person. In turn, you will help him or her develop a better personal understanding of the situation.

Skills of Responding

Summarizing The next step—after establishing rapport through attention, accurate listening, and exploring personal meaning—is to make sure you are orienting the interaction in the direction understood and agreed upon by both you and your partner. One way to verify this is to provide a summary of what has been discussed. The point of such a summary is to help focus what you are doing and confirm that you are going in an agreed upon direction. You might say something very direct, such as, "Let me summarize what we have talked about so far." This might be followed with a request for confirmation: "Is this the way you are experiencing our discussion or are there other points you want to add?" The summary also allows a person to seek clarification.

Clarification   There will be times when you will become uncertain or even confused by the conversation and will need to seek clarification. It is much better to ask for clarification than to act on uncertain speculations going on in your own mind—or to act as if you do understand even though you are lost. There are ways to seek clarification that will lessen what might seem like awkwardness or come across as accusing the other of being a poor communicator. The key to seeking clarification effectively is sincerity: you should be asking for help sincerely, not patronizingly; you should ask because you really want to understand and not because you are accusing the other person of lacking something. Another suggestion, when clarifying, is to ask questions that allow for more open-ended responses. Closed questions that can be answered "yes" or "no" or even multiple choice questions that limit possible answers will reduce rather than extend the possibilities for an accurate response. You may find the following phrases helpful in clarifying things: "I'm not sure if I understand what you mean by [whatever]," or "I'm not exactly sure what your situation is with [whatever area]." "Can you tell me more about that?" "Can you give me an example of [whatever it is]?" "Is there anything else that might be related to this that you haven't mentioned?" You

113

can adapt these basic ideas into questions that feel comfortable to you and sound natural to the student.

Confrontation At times you will experience discrepancies in what a person may be saying; something said at one point may be contradicted at another moment of the conversation. Such inconsistency may be a result of conflict between values and action or it might be a case of ambivalence. For example, many students have heard stories of ambivalence about a relationship. "I know he/she is not good for me because (fill in the blank why), but I still love him/her and just can't seem to give up and move on." Confronting or challenging discrepancies is important in order to have an honest and helpful encounter, but it must be done in a way that does not cause resistance or defensiveness.

Motivational interviewing is a strategy for helping individuals deal with ambivalence and sometimes resistance to change. The helper's role in motivational interviewing is to help raise awareness by pointing out a discrepancy; however, this should be done without judgment and should acknowledge the reluctance one has to give up or make changes; motivational interviewing and pointing out discrepancies should be done in a way that even embraces the other's right to choose a path that might be judged destructive (Miller & Rollnick, 2002). One way to describe this strategy uses the example of the martial art, aikido. Aikido does not resist, counter, or create defensiveness in another person but acts with respect to not harm and allow the other to be honored with the right to choose. Paradoxically, the lack of resistance permits choice and potential change to occur.

Interpretation Applying all of the aforementioned skills in responding you must, as accurately as possible, communicate your understanding of both the content and feelings you have heard. Rather than defending your initial understanding, you must then negotiate with the sender until there is agreement as to the sender's message. Using the statement above, for example, if the person responded, "No, I'm not really anxious about my parents coming to see me. I'm actually kind of relieved that they are coming this weekend because I'm going to be so busy after midterms." This new information clarifies what the helper needs to understand.

Demonstrating a Nonjudgmental Attitude

Within this type of helping relationship, you must refrain from interjecting your values, opinions, attitudes, and beliefs in regard to the issues being dealt with by the student you are assisting. It is important to take a neutral rather than personally biased stance. Whatever the problem, it must be resolved from within the student's unique world and values, not yours. A solution that works quite well for you may be completely inappropriate or undesirable for the student seeking your help.

In a helping interaction, keep in mind several factors to determine whether you can remain nonjudgmental. Three of these factors involve your own personal perspective and life situation—your values; your personal life, which includes concerns and issues you are working on currently; and other personal or academic problems you have decided not to actively resolve at this time in your life. The fourth deals with the complexity of the problem being presented.

Knowing Limits and Time for Referral

Your Personal Values From time to time, you may find it impossible to assume a nonjudgmental attitude because of your own personal values and beliefs. For example, consider the pro-life advocate who is assisting a young woman trying to resolve an unwanted pregnancy and is considering an abortion. It would be very difficult for a person who is pro-life to remain nonjudgmental in this situation. The appropriate course of action for a peer educator in this position is to refer the student to a more neutral person.

Your Personal Problems   It is very difficult to assist another person who is having a problem similar to one that you may be experiencing in your own life. For example, a peer educator who is currently struggling through a broken relationship will find it difficult to separate personal feelings and circumstances so as to truly enter, in a nonjudgmental manner, the world of a student seeking assistance with a relationship break-up. While sympathizing may be high when responding to this problem, true empathy will be difficult because a person has such strong personal identification with the problem. Referral to another helper who is not dealing with this same problem is recommended.

There will also be times when students tell you about problems that resemble personal and or academic challenges that you haven't resolved for yourself. It is very common for a person to have unresolved concerns and choose not to work on them, despite knowing that it would be better to do so. Maybe it doesn't cause a big enough problem to make you spend all the effort needed to fix it, but whatever the reason, you often know there is work to be done and are avoiding it. In this case, it won't be very realistic for you to be able to sit still and help others do that work for themselves. For example, a peer educator who has not yet chosen a major and is not really taking any steps to figure one out will, in all likelihood, not be very helpful to another undecided student. It would be too easy to enter into your own feelings on the issue to give the type of nonjudgmental helping that is described here. Again, these types of situations mandate a referral to another helping person.

116

Complexity of the Problem Some problems are just too complex for peer educators to help resolve because you do not have the training. Many of these involve personal and interpersonal issues that, given the age and life history of the student, should have been mastered long before reaching college. Examples of these significant personal concerns include students who are experiencing problems that cause them to be severely depressed or perhaps in some way dysfunctional. These students may be withdrawn, sad, and have little appetite; they may display antisocial behavior. There are possibly deeper psychological reasons for these types of behaviors with associated problems that must be solved. A peer educator is not the best person to work with these concerns, and a referral to a more qualified helper is required in these situations.

Any time other students indicate that they may be a threat to themselves (suicidal thoughts or plans) or others in the community (threatening others), you are involved in a helping relationship that goes beyond most peer educators' expertise. Also, if you feel nervous and upset when listening to another student's problem, you are in a problem area that is over your head from a helping perspective. Refer these students to your supervisor or another more experienced helper or professional service such as a mental health or counseling service.

Don't fear that you are pushing the student off onto somebody else, and don't feel like you haven't done anything. Your level of training and the fact that you are their peer makes you an ideal person to help students with certain problems, generally of a smaller nature and not as severe, such as helping a student find ways to meet new people or helping them figure out how to talk with a roommate about a conflict. And there are certain people who are trained to deal with more complicated or more severe issues, such as extreme depression and suicidal thoughts. By referring the students, you are making sure they have the kind of help

117

Reflection Point 4.3: The Helping Situation

Think of a time in the past when you have assisted a friend with a problem that was causing anxiety or distress:

What approach did you take when you helped this person? Specifically, did you just listen, give advice, or did you help discuss options?

So what approach would you now take if confronted with the same situation?

---

that fits the problem they are having. And this is the most helpful thing you can do in the situation.

The last stage of the Communication Skills Model calls for Skills of Resolution. You have gone through the first steps; the "now what?" involves very specific ways that problem identification can lead to goal setting and methods for solution. This will be covered in greater detail in Chapter Five.

Learning good interpersonal communication skills benefits from practice and feedback. It also entails understanding yourself and being willing to suspend your own opinions to allow the other person to explore themselves. Here is a series of suggestions that will be practical reminders of how you can improve your helping skills.

Tips for Sending Messages

Sending a message may seem instinctive—after all, you have been talking for as long as you can remember. Nonetheless, rather than just saying the first thing that comes to mind, consider the principles that will make your communications much more effective.

1. *Own your messages by saying "I" and "my."* Personal ownership includes clearly taking responsibility for the ideas and feelings that you express. Individuals disown their messages when they use terms such as "most people," "everybody," or "all of us."

Such terms, when you use them in your role as a peer educator, make it difficult for the person you are trying to assist to tell whether you really believe what you are saying or whether the statement represents the thoughts and feelings of others.

2. *Make your messages complete and specific.* Include clear statements of all necessary information the receiver needs to comprehend the message. Being complete and specific seems obvious, but often an individual you are helping will not understand your frame of reference, the assumptions you have made, the intentions for your communication, or the leaps in thinking you have taken. Although the person may hear the words, comprehension of the meaning of the message may be lost if you fail to be both specific and complete with your thoughts. Like all forms of effective helping communication, this takes practice.

3. *Make your verbal and nonverbal messages congruent.* When using interpersonal communication skills, both verbal and nonverbal messages will be communicated. In most cases, these messages should be congruent. For example, a person who is expressing genuine appreciation of someone's help will usually be smiling and expressing warmth in nonverbal ways. Communication problems can occur when a person's verbal and nonverbal messages are contradictory. For instance, think how you would react if a person were to say, "I thought you might want to know about this ..." but with a sneering face and a mocking tone of voice. The impression received is confused by two messages being sent simultaneously.

4. *Use redundancy.* Repeat your messages more than once, using more than one channel of communication to do so. This will help the receiver understand your messages.

5. *Ask for feedback.* To communicate effectively you must be aware of how the receiver is interpreting and processing your messages. The only way to be sure is to continually seek feedback concerning what meanings the receiver is attaching to your messages.

6. *Make the message appropriate to the receiver's frame of reference.* The same information may need different explanations depending

on whether you're talking to an expert in the field or a novice, to a child or an adult, to your boss or a coworker. You must be careful that you do not talk to a person on a level that is so complex as to be incomprehensible or on a level that is simplistic and insulting.

7. *Describe your feelings by name, action, or figures of speech.* Within this framework of helping, you will be working hard with helping someone else discover feelings about the situation you are exploring together. It is extremely important, therefore, that you are also descriptive in the explanation of your own feelings. You may describe your feelings by name ("That makes me feel so proud of you"), or actions ("This makes me want to brag to everybody I know!"). Use of these types of descriptions will help to communicate your feelings clearly and unambiguously. Also, by describing your feelings you, in turn, are modeling the way to aptly identify and express this important dimension of communication.

8. *Describe behavior without evaluating or interpreting.* When responding to the behavior of other people, make sure to describe their behavior rather than evaluating it. For example, "when you talk while I'm talking, it makes me lose my train of thought" rather than "you are being rude."

FINAL THOUGHTS

Remember the goal of interpersonal communication is not to solve the problems of others but to help them explore ways to better understand their own problems, develop and evaluate alternatives, set some personal courses of action, and then carry it out. Many people who have had help in the self-exploration and understanding phase can create alternatives and begin to take action on their own. What is most needed is a nonjudgmental, objective person to help them examine the discomfort they were experiencing. Once the source of this discomfort is brought into the light, many can go on to figuring out what to do about it.

On the other hand, for some people, understanding the problem is only the first phase of the helping relationship. They will need the peer educator to continue to provide assistance in identifying options, evaluating these options, and making a plan of action. Chapter Five presents many strategies you can implement when helping others figure out their options and make a good plan of action based on them.

SUMMARY

The types of interpersonal communication skills described in this chapter are quite different from those used in day-to-day conversations with others. In the context of a helping relationship, effective interpersonal communication skills are complex and require substantial practice to implement successfully. The basic skills can be viewed sequentially as starting with the stage of accepting and understanding cultural differences, as well as just being able to focus attention on the verbal and nonverbal expressions being presented to you. Within a helping relationship, you are primarily expressing your ability to listen effectively and with empathy. There are active ways to respond by clarifying, summarizing, and respectfully confronting discrepancies that will facilitate the student to explore concerns in more depth and gain deeper levels of self-understanding. In the next chapter you will explore several types of problem-solving strategies you may choose to initiate with a student after the problem has been fully explored, clarified, and understood.

CHAPTER FOUR: SUMMARY QUESTIONS

1. In your own words, describe the major differences between normal day-to-day interactions and the special qualities of a helping relationship.
2. When is advice giving an appropriate response in a helping relationship?
3. How is empathy different from sympathy?
4. What is an interchangeable response?
5. Describe situations in which it is best to refer an individual to another person in a more qualified or experienced helping role.

CHAPTER 5

Problem Solving with Individuals

LEARNING OBJECTIVES

After completing this chapter, you will be able to

1. Use effective communication skills while assisting students in problem solving.
2. Identify methods for exploring and analyzing problem situations.
3. Describe interview techniques and assessment tools designed to assist in the assessment process.
4. Explain the characteristics of successful goals.
5. Describe the relationship of behavioral objectives to goal setting and problem solving.
6. Formulate action plans that include ways to monitor progress and steps toward achieving goals.
7. Apply creative problem-solving strategies.

Chapter Four introduced interpersonal communication skills that equip you as a peer educator to connect, understand, and clarify personal needs when working with a student. These skills, when practiced effectively, can show positive results as an individual works through the self-exploration and understanding phases of problem solving. However, identifying a problem and actually solving that problem are different issues. This chapter focuses on the solution or action phase of problem solving. Problem solving often involves more than following a piece of advice or the simple directions on the package of a new product. Your role as a peer educator may include helping students get the end result they want in their lives. At the same time, the role of a mentor is not to take over and just tell the student what to do. Rather, you will ideally help students learn skills of problem solving so that in the future they are prepared for difficulties that come up and can deal with them on their own.

College students face many problems that can include deciding what courses to take, figuring out how to get along with a roommate, organizing time, dealing with strong emotions, finding a job, or managing a crisis. A first step when approaching a problem situation is to understand the underlying source of the difficulty. The "what" stage is determined by utilizing many forms of assessment.

ASSESSMENT AND DIAGNOSIS

Assessment is a process that assists in locating the source of a problem. Does the person have a gap, such as a lack of information or a skill deficiency? Is the person facing a barrier from within, such as a lack of confidence or personal confusion? Or is the barrier a conflict with others or with resources in the environment? The assessment process helps pinpoint the origin of the problem, which can then lead to determining a solution. Assessment will assist in charting the course and making a plan to be followed. When assessment is completed, the result should be an accurate diagnosis or determination of what is needed.

124

If practiced successfully, assessment is the starting point for goal accomplishment. Take for example students having difficulty deciding on a major. There are several potential sources of this problem that need to be assessed. Do they have a clear idea of their own interests, skills, or capabilities? Do they know about all the majors offered on campus? Do they know what careers they can get out of different majors? Do they know about job opportunities, requirements, and the job outlooks? If not, do they know the resources available for them to get this information? The structured interview is designed to ask these types of questions and begin the assessment process.

Structured Interview Techniques

The assessment-phase structured interview is the most common way to get information. Such an interview follows a deliberate format to gather information about someone's concerns, locate the sources of problems, and assess strengths and weaknesses. The structured interview operates from the basic principles of the interpersonal communication model discussed in the preceding chapter. To conduct a successful interview, you as a peer educator must follow a process in which active listening, respectful communication, and empathy become the cornerstones of the helping process. Here are examples of how the interview can be structured.

1. Ask open-ended questions that allow students you are helping to discuss their situation from their own perspective and in their own words. Take the example of a student who wants to improve physical fitness. Asking someone to describe what it would be like to be fit—permitting the student to elaborate on his or her own thoughts—is better than asking a yes-or-no question such as "Do you do aerobics?"

2. Follow leads of information from a student's responses to the open-ended questions by asking for clarification and expansion of specific points. "Tell me more about—" or "Help me to understand—" will seek further elaboration of what has been said.
3. Use paraphrasing and summaries of the student's responses to help pinpoint what the student sees as the source of the problem.
4. After gathering background information, make a tentative premise or hypothesis of what the student has described about the problem.

The following section describes how other forms of assessments can be obtained on a college campus.

Assessment Tools

Informal techniques for assessment may include checklists, surveys, or self-report questionnaires that are developed by your organization. They might also include surveys obtained from library resources or even reliable Internet sites. These tools may measure a wide range of student needs and interests in categories that include study habits, eating behaviors, wellness, career preferences, assertiveness, dating behaviors, stress reactions, and many more.

Formal assessment tools are also available through specialized professional offices on a campus. For example, career centers, advising centers, and counseling centers will frequently offer computerized programs or customized inventories that assess individual needs and interests. A student making choices about academic majors and career directions may need measures of personal interests, values, likes, and dislikes to gauge how well suited he or she is for a given academic major, career field, or occupation. Such measures can be provided by an array of online assessments that have been developed especially for student self-service or when working with freshman orientation, career exploration, and wellness promotion. In some cases, you as a peer educator may be working with an office where you will be trained and prepared to assist students with computerized interactive assessments and survey instruments. For example, at Kansas State University, online assessments have been developed for students to assess health behaviors (HBA, Health Behavior Assessment), learning (CLEI, College Learning Effectiveness Inventory), personal concerns (K-PIRS, Kansas State Problem Identification Rating Scales), and personal characteristics (PASS, Personal Attributes and Social Support). These instruments may be accessed at http://www.k-cat.org.

Self-Report Techniques

Many students can benefit from identifying their current behavior prior to determining a plan of action for change. For example, students who want to practice better time management would benefit from keeping track of how they currently spend their time. They could keep a daily log for a week or so to determine how they are using their time. An examination of this log, with the assistance of the peer educator, can help show where time is lost and wasted. Using this as a yardstick for comparison, a better schedule may be worked out. This same technique can be used when establishing better nutrition or exercise programs. It is always helpful to have a clear understanding of current behavior before trying to modify behavior.

Behavioral Observation

Another effective method that assists students with gathering information about themselves is behavioral observation and feedback. For instance, students learning effective job

127

interviewing techniques can video themselves during mock interviews. Viewing themselves then allows for self-discovery of strengths and weaknesses. This same technique is also helpful as students learn group leadership skills, the interpersonal communication skills model introduced in Chapter Four, or any other skill that requires an assortment of behavioral skill development.

Formulating a Diagnosis

One way to describe a problem is to determine three possible sources (see Figure 5.1, adapted from De Bono, 1971). One source of the problem may be a gap of some sort. A gap is a deficit, in this case a lack of information, an absence of knowledge, or a deficiency in skill. A second source involves the unknown of a novel situation. When venturing into uncharted areas, a person lacks past experience and is uncertain what is needed to prepare for the future. The novel situation demands that a person explore

1. The Gap = Deficit needing filled

2. The Hole = An unknown needing discovery

3. The obstacle = A barrier to be overcome

Figure 5.1. Three Sources of a Problem

128

new possibilities and be able to find creative solutions. Yet another source could be a barrier. A barrier prevents the accomplishment of a desired direction or goal. A barrier may be perceived personal limits, such as lack of confidence, indecision, or confusion. A barrier may also be outside the individual, caused by factors in the environment, such as a lack of resources or restrictions on behavior created by a social order such as a school, church, government, or family. Identifying the source and type of problem is a helpful prerequisite for determining a solution. Here are some other possible sources of problems:

Gaps: Lack of Knowledge About Self
Lack of information about options
Lack of skills

While considering different career paths, a student indicates uncertainty about the knowledge and skills needed to be an entomologist.

Unknowns: Inexperience in an Area
Tunnel vision with old solutions; need of new possibilities

"I really never had to take lecture notes in high school, so now I just write down everything exactly like the professor says it."

Barriers: Confusion or Conflict Within Self
Conflict with others
Limits within self, such as lack of confidence
Limits from environment, such as lack of support

"My parents always figured I would become a doctor like my sister, and I am afraid of disappointing them if I change my major."

STRATEGIES FOR PROBLEM SOLVING

An effective problem-solving approach starts with defining the problem from a positive perspective. In other words, if a person feels lonely a positive outcome would be to make friends; if completing class assignments on time is a problem the positive goal would be to improve time management. Positively defining a problem involves describing what and where the person would like to be when the problem is resolved. The positive outcome is the hoped-for goal.

Understanding why a person is unable to reach the desired goal requires the identification of what inhibits *and* what promotes the progress toward a goal. That is, fully understanding a problem involves considering the specific areas of concern, as well as the ways to achieve the desired resolution. After analyzing the factors surrounding a problem, you and the student can devise a plan of action that includes strategies for reaching the goal, along with methods for monitoring progress. Your listening and clear feedback provides a sounding board for students who are exploring problems. Clarification and understanding of a problem area will then lead to strategies for problem resolution. As a result, rather than *you* presenting a solution, you enable the students you are working with to discover their own solution. In other words, your goal as a peer educator should be to promote self-understanding and insights leading to student-initiated (rather than peer educator-initiated) problem resolution.

Resolving problems will require work and energy on your part and the part of the student you are working with. The next section discusses specific principles and methods for implementing goal setting, analysis of the situation, behavioral objectives, action plans, and outcome monitors.

Goal Setting

As the old saying goes, "If you don't know where you're going, you'll never know if you've arrived!" It is critically important that students attempting to resolve problems have a clear understanding of what they are trying to accomplish. The desired outcome, the goal that the problem statement should become, should be determined before completing the analysis and action stages. Goals with certain characteristics are more likely to be accomplished. These characteristics include personal relevance, positive outlook, clarity, and a reasonable level of attainability.

Successful Goals Are Relevant to the Person   Many individuals have established goals that are not really their own—that is, these goals are more important to someone else in the student's life than to the student pursuing them. For example, many students choose academic majors that may have resulted more from the encouragement and desires of parents, teachers, or friends than from their own initiative. Unfortunately, a major chosen in this way may have little in common with the student's values, interests, and abilities. It is not uncommon for a person to find it difficult to meet the challenges required to accomplish something when what they are doing lacks personal meaning and value. Exercise 5.1 challenges you to place yourself at the center of choosing significant life goals.

Goals Should Be Stated Positively   Positive thinking will improve the chances of successful attainment of a goal. Even when starting with a problem, a positive goal can be established because the flip side of a negative concern is the positive goal. For instance, if you did poorly on an exam and are concerned about getting a low grade in a class, it is best to describe your goal in positive terms. Rather than saying, "What do I need to do to avoid getting a D or

131

Exercise 5.1: The Board of Directors

Consider an important life decision that may be confronting you during the next several months. Many examples come to mind—changing a major, deciding where to live, transferring to another college, or purchasing a car. Whatever the issue, imagine that you will call together a board of directors in order to figure out where your preferences lie. This board of directors provides input into the decisions you make even though you will eventually cast the deciding vote. On this board, you may place several significant people whose input you value. For example, you might include your best friend, your parents, an adviser, someone you consider an expert, and an admired teacher. It is important, however, to prioritize your input over that of the board members by appointing yourself as the chairman of the board and giving yourself more voting power than the rest of the board.

On the first line (below), under the heading "Problem Description," describe the problem to be solved or decision to be made. On the next few lines, name the other members of your board, and place the options or inputs that you and the members of your board might suggest. Let's say that the decision to be made involves the purchase of a car. Input from board members suggests that you should consider factors such as gas mileage, dependability, needs for the future, and budget considerations. Remember, the board has been chosen to offer different perspectives, including expertise, new ideas, or even priority of what is valued. A hypothetical discussion of the options (possibly written down on paper, imagined in your mind, or even acted out by a group) determines which of the above factors are most important, and three choices are offered by your board (getting a loan and buying a newer model car; getting an older car with a reputation for good service; or assuming payments on a relative's car because this individual is looking for a new car). The final part of this activity is to weigh the options by putting a percentage value on the inputs from each perspective and deciding on the course of action. Remember, as chairman of the board you have the majority vote!

Problem Description:

Board Members:

Options:

Vote:

Exercise 5.2: Negatives to Positives

On the following spaces, list three problem situations you are facing, and then restate those situations as positive goals.

The Problem	The Positive Goal
Example:	Example:
Problem: I am feeling tired and unable to concentrate.	Goal: I want to improve my sleep to feel well rested and rejuvenated. (Rather than the negative: I want to avoid feeling tired and unable to concentrate.)
1.	1.
2.	2.
3.	3.

failing this class?" say, "What are the steps I can take to be successful and get a B in this class?" In other words, instead of thinking about what to avoid, focus on what to attain. Positive thinking usually generates energy and excitement, whereas negative thinking produces feelings of dread and boredom. In your role, help others by encouraging positive thinking and outcomes.

Goals Must Be Clear and Explicit   Goals are best formulated as clear, definable statements rather than a vague promise of a general outcome. A goal to be healthy or happy or successful may seem like a great outcome but the generalization does little to define what those concepts mean or how to achieve them in specific terms. Encourage others in the goal-setting process to write down their goals as specifically as possible. Writing can help clarify and crystallize the thought process. It also helps provide ownership for the student because, once written, the goal becomes concrete and real. To assist the student with writing a precise goal with specific outcomes, you can use the goal attainment measurement scale discussed later in the chapter.

Goals Must Be Attainable with a Stretch   For goals to feel worth pursuing, they must be realistic and attainable. At the same time, a goal has to push a person to extend his or her typical input of energy. For example, for a student who wants to be more physically active but does not like to run, a goal of entering and completing a marathon a couple of months after beginning a fitness program would be more than daunting and would stunt motivation. On the other hand, someone who does like to run and has finished long-distance races in the past probably could reach this goal after developing and completing a proper training program—and is therefore much more likely to find it worth trying. A well-stated goal may make a person reach beyond the present position, but it should not be out-of-sight.

Goals Should Be Measurable   It is useful to describe a goal with specific details from four levels—backsliding, current performance, easy improvement, and serious stretch. Goal Attainment Scaling is a systematic way to record your changes by measuring yourself against your own past performance (Marson, Wei, & Wasserman, 2009). For example, if a student's goal was to study

134

more in order to be more prepared for class, the four levels could look like this:

Level 1—Backsliding: A description of behavior if you were to fall back or do worse.

Example: I would study less than two hours per day.

Level 2—Current performance: An accurate description of the present behavior.

Example: I now study an average of two hours each day during the week and three hours on weekend days.

Level 3—Easy improvement: A description of behavior that is an improvement within easy reach.

Example: I would study an additional half hour a day and an extra hour on weekends.

Level 4—Serious stretch: A description of behavior that would stretch beyond your immediate reach.

Example: I would double my study time each day and include an extra three hours on weekends.

Setting goals allows a person to take control of life. Goals provide direction and meaning to each day. Goals promote an individual's sense of self-direction and accountability and also allow the individual to determine whether the things done every day are consistent with his or her goals.

Exercise 5.3: Goal Attainment Scaling

Identify one immediate goal you have at the present time. Choose a very specific area, such as increasing your exercise, meeting and making new friends, improving note-taking skills, or reducing time spent on the Internet. Remember, if working with a problem such as excessive time spent online gaming, change the negative into a positive goal: whereas "I want to stop spending so much time gaming" would be negative,

"I want to be more productive with my free time" would be a positive goal. After stating the goal, describe your present level, and then note a level below (backsliding) and two improved levels (easy reach and extended reach).

Performance Levels for Goal Attainment
Level 1 (backsliding):

Level 2 (current performance):

Level 3 (easy reach):

Level 4 (serious stretch):

Reflection Point 5.1: Developing Goal Statements

Think about goal statements:

1. What are the qualities of goal statements that make them more achievable? Restate these qualities in your own words.
2. Now imagine a situation in which you had a goal that did not meet these four qualities. What will happen if the goal is not relevant, positive, clear, and attainable? Can you give examples of such a goal and describe the result?
3. What strategies could you use when setting future goals to best ensure their accomplishment and your ultimate success?
4. Now state the goal as at least a tentative draft still allowing room for modification, so you can verify the diagnosis or determine the need to question the tentative ideas and explore the problem further.
5. Reframe the problem as a positive goal statement.

Identify where there is potential need for further informal or formal assessment tools.

136

Force-Field Analysis: Systematic Assessment of Strengths and Weaknesses

Kurt Lewin (1951) originally developed force-field analysis, and over the years, it has become a commonly used method to map a plan for goal achievement. This approach uses the idea that there are both driving and restraining forces that will either enhance or inhibit one's progress toward a goal. Drivers are actions that should produce positive results or help create positive outcomes. Restrainers are anything that seems to take away from intended outcomes. After you identify these forces, you can then make a plan of action. The student solving a problem identifies both types of forces and brainstorms activities that would help to eliminate the restraining forces and implement the driving forces. Then the student decides which of those activities will most realistically create a reasonable plan of action. Exercise 5.4 illustrates this process.

Exercise 5.4: Force-Field Analysis

This exercise starts from the point at which you have identified a problem and then restated that problem into a positive goal statement. The next step is to recognize the forces that will push toward improvement and attainment of the goal (driving forces) and those forces that will resist improvement (restraining forces) and maintain the situation as a problem. For example, if a goal was to improve overall physical fitness, driving forces might include regular exercise, good eating habits, and regular sleep. Factors that could prevent improved fitness could include eating too much junk food, frequently watching television while lying on the couch, or drinking too much alcohol.

Step 1: Write one of your goal statements from Exercise 2 in the box labeled "Goal Attainment" in Figure 5.2.

Step 2: On the sets of lines above and below the goal statement, describe at least four driving and four restraining forces that would affect attainment of your goal.

137

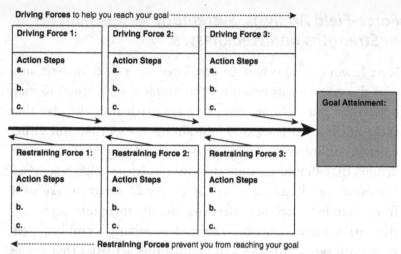

Figure 5.2. Driving and Restraining Forces

Step 3: For each restraining force, list possible action steps that you could plan and carry out to reduce the effect of that force or eliminate it completely. For example, if your goal is to study every morning before your biology class, and a restraining force is your tendency to sleep through the alarm, you might get a louder alarm, go to bed earlier, or have someone personally wake you up. Place these in the box underneath each of the restraining forces in Figure 5.2.

Step 4: Similarly, think of as many possibilities as you can for implementing each of the driving forces. Again, use the box underneath the driving forces to identify potential action steps for implementing the driving forces. If you were to use the driving force "to gain knowledge of good nutrition" in the example in Figure 5.3 below, you could list activities such as make an appointment with the Health Service nutritionist, visit a Web site providing nutrition tips, or buy a book on healthy meals for the college student.

Step 5: After completing a list of possible ways to enhance driving forces and reduce restraining forces, prioritize these potential problem-solving activities in order to target the most likely activities for success. For example, wanting to increase physical activity might be enhanced by having a workout buddy or by asking a friend to join you for three times a week workouts at the campus fitness center.

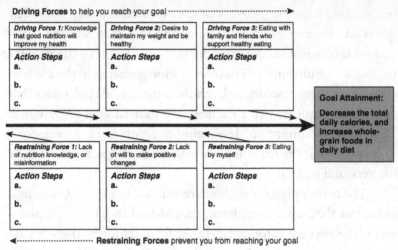

Figure 5.3. Driving and Restraining Forces Example

Figure 5.3 "Driving and Restraining Forces Example" shows how this may look for the goal of eating fewer calories overall and eating more whole-grain foods on a daily basis.

Now What? The Action Plan: Objectives and Activities

Once you and the student you are working with know (1) what you are trying to accomplish (goal) and (2) the student's strengths and weaknesses (determined through the analysis) in regard to readiness, you have a starting point for goal completion. It is now necessary to determine a specific plan of action. This is accomplished through the development of specific steps referred to as objectives that describe the student's intentions in an observable and measurable manner. In effect, a plan of action breaks down the larger goal into smaller and more manageable steps, or objectives; behavioral objectives spell out and make the plan recognizable in tangible ways. Objectives might include activities such as contacting a resource for information, researching a topic online,

139

or spending a specific amount of time on a class assignment. The key is an objective needs to be an action step that is observable—and such observable objectives are designed to move the student to goal accomplishment. The information gathered in the analysis stage of problem resolution determines the specific behaviors that need to be implemented to achieve the desired goal or outcome. This stage is similar to developing a contract or agreement—a blueprint that the student can use to chart progress and measure the eventual outcome.

The action plan for problem resolution is a list of behavioral objectives that, once completed, should lead to goal accomplishment. The peer educator assists in the formulation of these behavioral objectives and seeks to help the student determine that nothing has been left out. As the plan is being implemented, you as a peer educator may wish to create checkpoints—scheduled meetings to assess specific accomplishments that will provide a measure of how well the plan is going and how successfully the student is progressing toward goal completion. During these sessions, the plan may need to be changed if new information and the plan's progress suggest adjustments that will improve the chances for success.

It is obvious that action plans are never set in concrete, as, by definition, they are plans in action. Refinement is often necessary, and follow-up with students is essential to ensuring success. Completion of goals often leads to new areas of exploration and action plans. Life is always a work in progress!

Outcome Evaluations

The final stage of resolving a problem and achieving a goal is seeing and measuring progress. Peer educators can assist students in this process through the use of formative and summative evaluation techniques.

Formative Evaluation Formative evaluation is objectively charting progress on a plan of action. By meeting with the student periodically, you can find out whether he or she is staying on track. Has anything been left out? Is there a step the student is stuck on for some reason? Circumstances may cause you to have to modify the plan of action. To determine progress toward the ultimate goal, use data that indicate how well weekly objectives are being met or how well specified activities are being completed; then refer back to the goal attainment yardstick devised during planning to help determine progress toward the ultimate goal. New or expanded strategies should be formulated if necessary during progress checks.

Summative Evaluation Whereas formative evaluation is ongoing, summative evaluation occurs at the end of the action plan. Questions such as the following help create a summative evaluation: has the goal been achieved? Did it have the effect the student sought? For example, is the student satisfied with the outcome or has the accomplishment of this goal led to other questions or concerns? Again, in the area of academic majors, the student may have accomplished the goal of declaring a major. However, in the process of completing this goal, new questions regarding internships, minors, or other aspects of academic study may have arisen. The summative assessment process often leads to the development of new goals and behavioral objectives.

Problem Solving Leads to an Ability to Self-Regulate The best outcome of the problem-solving process is that the process itself helps one gain the confidence and skills for self-regulation. Self-regulation is the ability to modify your attitudes and behavior when your current ones are in some way detrimental to you or others. For example, Nick is a freshman who initially couldn't

141

manage his time and schoolwork along with a social life and personal activities, like working out. In order to achieve a better balance, he set a goal to coordinate his sleep, study time, and recreation to be more efficient and less wasteful. He developed a six-week plan using the problem-solving method of overcoming obstacles and the actions that would lead to success. As Nick progressed, he found that the tools of planning and action he was using to manage time could also be employed in other areas of his life. His success led to goals that included healthier eating and even a long-time dream of learning to play the guitar.

PROBLEM SOLVING OUTSIDE THE BOX

The problem-solving process we've focused on so far presents one system for assisting another person. The process of problem identification, goal setting, assessment of strengths and weaknesses, development of behavioral objectives, and constant refinement through assessment interviews can be helpful when addressing many types of student concerns. However, this process does not always work. People may find themselves in territory where they have little if any previous experience. They also may experience a nearly opposite yet equally trying situation in which they face a problem that seems very familiar, but the old and commonplace ways of acting in that situation are not producing results. In these cases, the use of common analysis may not be sufficient to resolve the problem. An option to explore the unknown or to break the tunnel vision of ordinary solutions is to use creative problem-solving methods.

Thinking outside the box is an important process for letting go and finding new possibilities. After all, there are many ways to achieve the same goal. Howard Gardner (2006) offers a framework that presumes people have the potential for using multiple forms of intelligence. Intelligence is really the ability and process to solve problems, and there are multiple avenues to achieve that end.

Creative problem solving requires being able to shift from the usual way of thinking. Five strategies are useful in making this shift: fluency, suspension of judgment, free association, mental stimulation, and artistic expression (Prince, 1971). *Fluency* relies on having a quantity of possible suggestions; one hundred ideas provide more possibilities than a limited few. *Free association* is a way to quickly generate a quantity of ideas by encouraging tangents or whims that come to mind and building quickly to new words, images, or possibilities. *Suspending judgment* sets aside the tendency to scrutinize each idea so that one does not thwart or inhibit possibilities. *Mental stimulation* requires strategies to think in ways that make the familiar seem strange, thus unlocking the mind to look at old patterns in new and different ways. *Artistic expression* requires you to use the tools of the artist as experienced by forms such as poem, song, picture, or metaphor.

Roger von Oech (1986) recommends four roles for implementing the creative problem-solving process. First you are an explorer when you search for new information and options. Second you become an artist when turning possibilities and resources into new ideas. Third you become a judge to evaluate

---

Reflection Point 5.2: Ambiance to Promote Creativity

What kind of setting would be most helpful to keeping an open and creative mind? Think of an environment that would free your mind and stimulate your thinking. Would it be indoors or outdoors? What backgrounds would stimulate your senses (music, lights, visual effects)? What tools, such as art pads and colorful pens, would be useful?

Now what activities, such as improvisation, charades, or make believe, could you use to generate an outside-the-box idea in your quest for solving a problem or finding a new opportunity?

the merits of an idea. And finally you become a warrior to boldly and courageously implement a new idea. The strategies presented in the next sections offer some simple ways to generate creative possibilities in problem solving.

Brainstorming

Brainstorming is a helpful way to explore and consider many new and even far-out possibilities. When you brainstorm, reserve judgment of each idea until later. Because brainstorming generates options without a "good" or "bad" evaluation of those options, it encourages free thinking, spontaneity, creativity, and the free association of ideas.

Perhaps you, as a peer educator, are working with a student who is having roommate issues. The student would like to live in harmony with the roommate but is bothered by the roommate's lack of consideration. This roommate is messy and leaves clothes, books, papers, food, and personal items scattered throughout the room. The student you are helping is unsure of what plan of action to implement, and you suggest brainstorming some alternatives for consideration. These could include ideas such as ignoring the situation, confronting the roommate about the unacceptable behavior, talking to the residence hall staff, picking up after the roommate, modeling more appropriate behavior, drawing a line on the floor and telling the roommate to never cross it, moving out, or spending a lot of time with a friend and storing critical belongings in the friend's room. Pushing the brainstorming even further may result in ideas such as hiring a "cat-in-the-hat" to talk with the roommate, designing a wall separator, or creating a loft to seal off two separate areas. Some—perhaps most—of these ideas may seem ridiculous, but the key to this process is generating as many options as possible for consideration. After the options are on the table, it is important to enter the artist phase.

144

Mind Mapping

Another creative problem-solving form is the mind map. Instead of the linear method as shown in the force-field analysis process (described earlier in this chapter), the mind map uses a spatial visual depiction in which the problem is placed visually in the middle of a blank page. Associations are then made from the initial starting point by attaching and building related images and ideas to the center point (Buzan, 2002). Tony Buzan, as an originator of the mind-mapping technique, now offers a software package to use with this approach.

Metaphors and Other Artistic Problem-Solving Designs

During the artist phase, the task is to incorporate the creative ideas into a picture that pulls various elements of a problem situation together. A common, everyday strategy for painting a verbal picture is to use metaphors to capture a unique situation that words, using literal definitions, cannot portray. Also, this can be accomplished in a group by use of expressive visual modes such as compiling a collage together with pictures from magazines or having a group devise a mural by adding their vision with pastels or crayons to a large white poster board. Metaphors and symbolic art expressions provide a parallel example that, although similar in ways, may also be viewed with openness to new possibilities, a flexibility to shift perspectives, and a tolerance for trying out a new or different reality (Newton & Wilson, 1991).

Metaphors can be analogies that compare one's situation to another circumstance. For example, a student may share frustration with mastering a course assignment by saying, "It is like playing solitaire when the deck has a missing card; no matter how many times I try, I can never win." Possibilities for a solution may first be viewed within the framework of the metaphor. In response, you might ask, "Are there ways for you to make new rules for the game? Are there games you could play that don't need that card?" The metaphor may provide some distance from the familiar pattern and yet also allow exploration of various options that are in some ways parallel.

Metaphors can be paradoxes, and paradoxes contrast opposing extremes in ways that help make new connections. Two roommates describe a conflict in which one likes the room hot while the other likes to sleep cool. Their problem might be addressed as experiencing what it would be like to "store ice cream in an oven" or "enjoy the benefits of a warm summer day while living at the North Pole." To experience the different perspectives through metaphor, one can "become" the metaphor and then look for solutions after experiencing the contrast and looking for mutual benefits.

A third way to use metaphor is to experience the problem as a story or fantasy. This is illustrated by the science fiction series *Star Trek*. On the starship there is a special chamber called the Holodeck. In this place a computer simulator can create a whole new environment and the person entering can escape into a fantasy to explore, rearrange, or try out new and unimaginable possibilities. Providing students the opportunity to create and arrange their ideal fantasy of what they had previously experienced as a difficult problem can aid and encourage them in finding new solutions.

Judging the Creation

The divergent or expanded thinking that occurs during creativity reaches a point at which possibilities need to be applied back to the problem situation. This is when the problem solver becomes

Exercise 5.5: Problems as Metaphors

Identify a problem situation in which you have felt stuck in regard to finding a satisfactory solution. Take a relaxed position in a comfortable chair, close your eyes, and imagine you are able to enter the Holodeck, where you can have a fantasy in which the ideal can come true. Once the ideas begin to form, sit up, and write your fantasy as a story with any dream elements that come to mind and suggest possibilities without the restrictions of present limits, real or perceived. An alternative exercise would be to think of possible metaphors for any dilemma you face and then to write a story about the metaphor and how you experience being a part of that metaphor.

a judge and makes decisions about which ideas and possibilities seem most worthy for future consideration. To do this, you must first establish the criteria for determining the worthiness of possible solutions. For instance, returning to the roommate conflict situation, these questions may produce helpful criteria: How bothersome is this behavior? How much time is left in the semester? Has the issue been discussed before? How comfortable is the student in confronting irritating behavior? Determine which criteria will best guide decision making. Typically, the seeds of good ideas are embedded in many of the options that were brainstormed during the creative phase. The important thing during the judging and analysis phase is to make a "force fit" that transforms the possibilities into a practical solution. At this point, you may again return to the concrete problem-solving model discussed earlier in the chapter and go through the steps of setting behavioral objectives and process-monitoring devices.

Implementing Bold Change

Courage is needed to think and problem-solve creatively. The person will often feel anxious about brainstorming creative solutions because they may seem unpredictable. For this reason, it is important to assume an attitude appropriate for an adventure that includes possibilities to make great new discoveries but also dead ends and setbacks. However, by holding the perspective that even mistakes and dead ends provide important learning, the person can continue to stay open to the new possibilities.

Another barrier for assuming a new behavior or attitude is the initial resistance that may be received from others in one's life—people may become uncomfortable when someone does not act in the predictable way. The person who is trying to change may encounter questions and objections about the new way of acting. Informing friends and family about the choice of a new course and asking for their support is one way to include others from the beginning. However, persistence and determination are qualities that aid all people as they enact change.

Finally, the attainment of any goal in which an investment of time and energy has been committed calls for a celebration of recognition. Ceremonies, rewards, and the sharing of recognition with important people in one's life should be built into any action plan. For example, one peer educator has shared a custom she has used in her family, the custom of using a celebration dinner plate. The plate is encircled with the words "You are special today." When an accomplishment or special event has occurred, the person is praised with a celebration dinner served on the special plate. Recognition and acknowledgment are often more important than a material gift.

SUMMARY

This chapter has introduced and given examples of several strategies that can be used when assisting others with problem situations. The strategies of goal setting, assessment, behavioral objectives, action planning, and creative problem solving have been explored. An understanding of these techniques and their application to specific situations will provide a method for helping students resolve problems.

CHAPTER FIVE: SUMMARY QUESTIONS

1. List four characteristics of a goal statement.
2. Define:
   a. Assessment
   b. Structured interview

c. Self-reporting techniques
d. Behavioral observation
e. Force-field analysis
f. Formative evaluation
g. Summative evaluation
h. Self-regulation
i. Creative problem solving
3. What is the primary characteristic of a behavioral objective?
4. How is formative evaluation used in the action phase of the problem-solving model?
5. How might a force-field analysis be used in conjunction with a brainstorming activity?

CHAPTER 6

Understanding Group Process

LEARNING OBJECTIVES

After completing this chapter, you will be able to

1. Identify the benefits and advantages of the group environment for helping students.
2. Name positive communication methods in group settings.
3. Explain how group norms are formed.
4. Describe the effects of individual role behavior on group interaction.
5. List levels of commitment by members of a group.
6. Understand how the group's task structure can affect decision making and successful accomplishment of goals.
7. Explain the ways that a peer educator can promote the involvement, commitment, cooperation, and action to achieve both personal and collective outcomes.

Groups are everywhere. You were born to a family and taught in class after class; you play on teams, interact with coworkers, live with roommates, and literally experience life as a series of group interactions. Although life experience seems to qualify everyone as an expert on how to interact and get along with groups of people, few people look carefully and systematically at this awareness. What makes a group work? Why do you enjoy interacting in certain situations but feel bored and uninterested in others? When is a group most productive or least productive? How does a group change and evolve over time?

Peer educators are frequently called upon to work with students in groups. Educational presentations, tutorial sessions, classroom seminars, service learning teamwork, leadership development experiences, and peer support activities take place in a group setting. The benefits of a group include the potential to learn from observing others, provide personal support and encouragement, try out ideas or actions while receiving feedback, and receive the incentive and motivation created by being part of a community.

This chapter will provide a focused way to observe your own experience in groups and determine which factors affect a group for better or worse. Concentrating on what is happening within a group and how the group functions is a matter of studying the processes or dynamics of groups. As a peer educator, you will find that the information and activity presented in this chapter increases your awareness of group processes and helps you make use of this awareness to increase your effectiveness when working with a group. Whether you are engaging a class in discussion, preparing a team to go out into the community to perform a service project, or helping an entering group of international students adapt to the new culture, awareness of what is happening with group members and learning intentional group facilitation skills enhances the opportunity for successful outcomes.

Reflection Point 6.1: Qualities of Effective Groups

Think of a group experience that has been positive for you. Perhaps you experienced the group as enjoyable, fun, productive, engaging, stimulating, or successful. Reflect back on your experience:

What distinguished the group as positive for you?

What qualities, characteristics, behaviors, or other such processes contributed to the success of the group?

What factors do you believe need to be present in any productive group?

In response to the above questions, the following comments were made by students in a training group:

- The goals of the group were very clear.
- People worked well together.
- There was a sense of belonging among members.
- Everyone took some responsibility to make the group work.
- People communicated directly and openly with each other.
- People listened to and respected each other.
- New ideas and creative suggestions invigorated the group.
- The team followed through with their commitments and plans.
- Roles and responsibilities were shared and interdependent.
- Differences were confronted and resolved.

Identifying the qualities of an effective group is the starting point for developing awareness and applying this knowledge to a better understanding and functioning of all kinds of groups.

ADVANTAGES OF GROUPS

Forming a group can often be the preferred method for assisting students. Groups offer a convenient way to provide information and education to several people at the same time. Groups serve as places where opinions may be shared, ideas collected, and problems solved. Groups concentrate the collective energy of several

153

people, allowing them to pool resources and complete a desired task. Peer educators are frequently asked to work with groups in areas such as orientation, advising, health information, and support services that focus on the special needs of students. You are most likely in a group right now, being trained along with other prospective peer educators who receive information, hold discussions, interact as a team, and provide support for each other in a group.

In college settings, people come together to make social contact for play, fellowship, work, and learning. Although the utility of using groups for a variety of educational, recreational, social, or vocational activities is well understood, the group setting can also facilitate personal growth, self-awareness, and change of individual behaviors. Peer educators play an important role in facilitating group environments that promote a positive atmosphere where personal growth and learning are most likely to occur.

Yalom and Leszcz (2005) describe factors that can operate within a group to support and facilitate personal growth. The following discussion synthesizes many of these factors.

When experiencing the self-disclosures of others, people can gain a sense of universalization, realizing that no one is alone in facing the problems and dilemmas in the world. On an emotional level, people may gain qualities of support from a group, such as a sense of belonging, respect, caring, and hope. Positive group experiences demonstrate to the individual the importance of relationship factors such as trust, warmth, understanding, belonging, and community.

Group interaction can also provide personal learning by way of other people through sharing information, imitating successful behavior, gaining direct feedback, or by direct suggestions. Interpersonal learning is an advantage that groups afford by being a laboratory for social interaction. Trying out new behaviors in a social context evokes reactions from others, providing an opportunity for learning in a way that is often parallel to the pattern of social transactions learned with family or friends in the past. Also, one's own perception of self may be validated—or confronted—by the sense of congruence or discrepancy revealed through interaction with others.

Chris's Story

An example of how a group affects an individual's self-perception may be illustrated by this story of Chris. Chris was a part of a service organization that had a group retreat to develop a sense of team and camaraderie. The retreat included a series of outdoor challenge activities in which the team members interacted to achieve certain outcomes. One activity challenged all of the team members to climb up and over a "Y" between two limbs in a sturdy tree about fourteen feet above the ground. The rules required team members to consider how to maximize the individual resources; for instance, they had to assist the strongest, most agile, and even most confident members to be in the right place at the right time to achieve the group outcome of getting all members up and over the limb safely. Once a member got over the limb, he or she could no longer help or support the remaining teammates.

Chris was very uneasy about this activity and lacked both the confidence and the physical attributes to believe he could achieve this outcome. After a couple of athletic students demonstrated how this could be done, two people, Sue and Ellen, noticed Chris's uneasiness and insisted that he go next in order for him to have physical support to meet the challenge. At first, Chris was very reluctant and indicated he would just sit the activity out;

155

however, with lots of encouragement, he started the task by receiving both physical and emotional support. The task was not easy for him and what was a thirty-minute activity soon went over time and started to consume what was scheduled as a break for refreshments. The pressure Chris felt increased, but the encouragement from the teammates went from subtle comments of assurance to insistence that "yes" he was going to achieve this goal. Forty-five minutes later, Chris went "over the top" to wild cheers of jubilation from the team and a celebration by the whole group.

At the time, this seemed like just a nice achievement during a fun day; however, two years later Chris walked in the office door of the group's advisor and articulated more strongly the significance of that moment. Chris said that up until that day, he had always felt different and less adequate than his peers. A genetic disposition had created muscular deficiency that although not all that noticeable to the eye, had been very noticeable to Chris, and he avoided sports and many physical activities to hide his weakness. "I always felt self-conscious and a little less significant than my counterparts because of this!" However, after that experience, Chris said he held another perspective that he really could be equal in the eyes of others, and people wanted him to succeed. Chris called this an experience that changed his whole attitude toward determination to engage fully with life.

A GROUP IS A SYSTEM

Of course, not all groups manage to provide the advantages described in the preceding section. Any group is a system, a complex set of interactive variables that may vary from healthy to unhealthy, growth enhancing to growth inhibiting. You can usually tell at once that something is wrong when you experience symptoms of a poorly functioning group—apathy, boredom, conflict, indifference, frustration, nonsupport, or inability to accomplish purpose. Because the group is a system, you can compare the function of the group to that of any organism you assess from both a holistic perspective and an analysis of the parts.

There are at least ten identifiable features that characterize a collection of people as a group (Cartwright & Zander, 1968).

Group members
- Engage in frequent interaction
- Define themselves as members
- Are defined by others as belonging
- Share norms of behavior on matters of common interest
- Participate in a system of interlocking roles
- Identify with one another
- Find the group rewarding
- Pursue interdependent goals
- Have a collective perception of their unity
- Tend to act in a common manner toward their environment

One way to understand the overall function of a group is to draw an analogy to the human organism and to check the functioning of this organism, the group, in the way a medical professional might conduct a checkup (Newton & Rieman, 1978). As an individual, you are an entity that at any given time may be healthy, growing, and improving, or you may be ill, shrinking, or deteriorating. If you are healthy, you might be taking steps to maintain your health and prevent problems from occurring—taking vitamins, getting exercise, talking to supportive friends, eating right, and having regular checkups—or you might be acting in ways that will eventually destroy it. It is quite productive to view groups

157

through a similar assessment of group health. The following section offers a way for you to conduct a check-up on any group in which you may participate.

Group Communication

Communication is the cornerstone of social interaction. Within any system, communication is a two-way process connecting one person with another to transmit ideas, experiences, feelings, or intentions. One aspect of the process is the ability to deliver (encode) a message. The second important part is to receive and understand (decode) the message. Personal factors that interfere with communicative accuracy are ambiguity and other failures in clarity, conflicting nonverbal signals, and interfering thought processes. Many factors within the environment may interfere with the communication process. Distractions of noise, both auditory and visual clutter, can interfere with reception of a message. In addition, in a group, multiple conversations and different status levels of the speakers affect the quality of listening—most people tend to listen more carefully to a leader, a friend, or someone they respect highly than to someone they perceive as lower in status than themselves or otherwise dislike or disrespect. Even distractions caused by meeting in a room in which the seating, temperature, or lighting is not comfortable may hamper the attentiveness of group members.

Success in communication may be measured in several ways. One way is to recognize the overlap in message between the communicator and the receiver. This overlap identifies the amount of shared meaning within the transmitted ideas, experiences, feelings, and intentions. The greater the percentage of message that is received, the higher the understanding of those facets of meaning (that is, ideas, feelings, experiences, and intentions). Another form of assessment examines the quality of the received

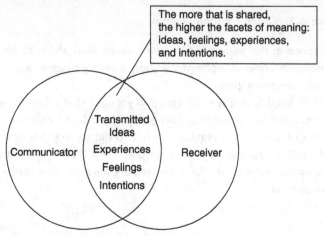

The more that is shared,
the higher the facets of meaning:
ideas, feelings, experiences,
and intentions.

Communicator   Transmitted
                Ideas
                Experiences   Receiver
                Feelings
                Intentions

Figure 6.1. Successful Communications

message, as it may range from very superficial and insignificant to very important and personally relevant. A third area of assessment includes the pattern of communication between and among group members, pointing out phenomena such as who speaks to whom, how often, and with what level of influence or credibility.

Little understanding between a communicator and a receiver leads to no sense or "nonsense." If there is some overlap, the shared meaning of ideas can result. Even more overlay, say, half or more, could result in shared meaning of thoughts, feelings, and intentions. A complete overlap between the communicator and the receiver would not be possible because there are always some unknown or mysterious or changing aspects of the respective individuals. Figure 6.1 illustrates this dynamic.

Group Atmosphere

Atmosphere refers to the tone of the group and may be observed in groups as a positive or negative energy. Atmosphere includes factors such as level of interest, motivation, and commitment of

159

Exercise 6.1: Group Communication

The purpose of this activity is for you to assess your ability to observe and distinguish how well communication is taking place in a group in which you are participating.

First, identify one specific group in your life that relies upon communication for its success. This group could be an informal collection of friends who regularly go out to dinner together or a more formal study group that gathers to prepare for a class project; it could even be an executive board for a student organization that meets to plan an agenda.

After you have identified this target group, read the six questions at the end of this exercise and, to the best of your ability, provide a response based upon your observation.

You may well find it difficult to frame complete answers to these questions based solely on memory. A useful alternative is to take an observer notebook with the six questions outlined to the next gathering of the group you have identified, and answer each question as you observe. Your answers will serve as a good pretest or demonstration of what you do observe and, also, those factors you have missed.

1. After observing a conversation, do the following: If two circles represented the sender and receiver of a communication, what would be the percentage of overlap (meaningful communication) between them?

2. What are the sources of communication loss in the group? Consider distractions in the environment as well as challenges or shortcomings with the sender and receiver.

3. How clear and specific are the expressions of the sender?

4. How well does the receiver attend to verbal and nonverbal cues?

5. What is the depth of communication taking place? Think of a scale running from 1 (very superficial—things someone would be willing to yell about on a street corner) to 5 (very significant—revealing very personal information).

6. If you were to draw a diagram, what would be the pattern of who speaks to whom, when, and how often?

This exercise has helped you identify the communication dynamics going on in this specific group. Now write a brief summary of your conclusion based upon these dynamics (*so what* does this all mean about how the group is communicating?). Based upon these conclusions make a further statement about what you think the group is doing well and what might be done to improve group communication in the future (this is the *now what* implication).

members. This will be reflected in the amount of investment in the group. Symptoms of high, positive energy include physical activity (talk, animation, and doing), good attendance at meetings or group activities, arriving on time, attentiveness to group tasks, expression of personal feelings, and conversations about group-relevant themes. Low or negative symptoms might be exemplified by attitudes that show indifference, energy directed away from the group, distractions or diversions to outside activity, suppression or concealment of emotions, denial of group importance, poor attendance at meetings and group activities, and tendencies for members to arrive late or leave early.

The most influential factor that affects group atmosphere is cohesion. Cohesion is a multidimensional construct that is composed of variables such as attractiveness, tolerance, unity,

Exercise 6.2: Group Atmosphere

Think about a group of friends, a study group, or a club or organization in which you regularly attend functions—perhaps the group you identified for Exercise 6.1. Answer the following questions to assess the type of group atmosphere that prevails and the level of cohesiveness present in your identified group. If you are being trained as a peer educator in a group situation, a second option could be to assess the group atmosphere that has developed to this point with other peer educators.

1. What signs of energy (activity, engagement) do you observe in the group?

2. Is the energy positive (supportive, encouraging, and full of lively discussion) or negative (argumentative, bored, and avoiding the issues)?

3. Do individuals identify and communicate a sense of belonging to the group or of distancing away from the group? Describe this behavior.

4. How do individual members express feeling (verbally or nonverbally) in the group? What do the expressions of feeling reveal?

acceptance, support, belonging, involvement, and even affection. The characteristic most indicative of cohesion is shared and mutual perception within the group representing the sense of togetherness and a feeling of belonging to the group (Fuhriman & Burlingame, 1990).

Normative Behavior

An important facet of group life is how well the group as a whole is able to identify and designate goals, perform routine functions such as decision making, and carry out its tasks. Several essential processes influence the group's task functioning. Initially, a group must establish strong, well-understood, yet flexible norms of behavior. Some norms are formally prescribed by agreed-upon standards, such as constitutions and by-laws, but usually informal yet tacitly understood expectations define group norms. Norms may include such behaviors as starting time, where people sit, when people speak up, the manner in which they speak, and even the style of clothing that they wear.

Because norms are often implicit, unwritten, or unspoken, people who enter any group are initially uncertain about the expectations for behavior and may feel the anxiety and discomfort that naturally result from dealing with an unknown. An important task for any new member of a group is to figure out the appropriate way to behave in that group and to gain practical understanding for how to function comfortably. For any new group, an initial function is to negotiate, oftentimes imperceptibly, the rules for how the group will interact. This sometimes involves controversy over preferences and could result in a vying between factions for a preferred way of acting within the group.

The initiation and acceptance of a norm into a group may be illustrated by the analogy of planting a seed. Initially, the seed of a new norm is to suggest an idea for a group behavior. This suggestion is made with caution and at times greeted with skepticism—"Why do we need this?" If the seed begins to sprout, the young idea may have to compete for space, recognition, and even the nutrients of support necessary to grow into a full-fledged norm. If the norm manages to overcome early resistance, it will grow to become a more frequent behavior of the group, one whose maintenance is reinforced and encouraged. There may even be pressure for those who do not observe the norm to conform and accept this behavior. Maturation of the norm is clear when the behavior occurs frequently and without question or dispute by group members. At this point, the norm seems to be a natural part of the group's routine manner of functioning.

Decision-Making Processes

An important facet of norm formation is the decision process. There are several ways that groups can make decisions. Decisions will vary by degree of authority and formality of procedure. A highly autocratic procedure would permit the individual with the greatest status (by position, seniority, popularity, or other determining factor) to dictate the decision. A highly democratic procedure might use formal methods such as voting or informal methods such as consensus making that seek input from all members. There are certain advantages and disadvantages of each method. A more autocratic method is typically faster and more clear-cut. It tends to work well for urgent or time-pressed situations though its quality is limited to that of the knowledge of the authority. A more democratic procedure generates a greater resource of knowledge, potentially heightens commitment of members to a decision, is perceived as more fair and inclusive, and allows the airing of differing opinions and issues about a decision.

Different decision methods may be used for resolving a variety of group issues. For example, a social group might vote on whether or not to hold a party, conduct a group discussion on the party theme, designate individuals, or call for volunteers to take charge of specific tasks, and then authoritatively be told by the budget administrator to set budget. The key to decision success is fitting the right process to the type of decision, the time allotted, and the level of importance for group input.

Conformity

The impact of group norms and group behavior may create pressure to conform and prevent deviations. Group norms develop out of the need for standard expectations and procedures; however, conformity occurs when the purpose is lost yet members remain obedient to a standard practice. As the metaphor admonishes, "it is important to not walk blindly over the edge of a cliff." A group needs a critical balance between maintaining predictability and innovation, between consistency and the infusion of new ideas, and between stability and vitality. If a group develops too strong a tendency toward conformity, it may overlook problems and act prematurely based upon the desire to have a common agreement. Too much conformity may also squelch creativity.

Membership and Roles

There are two levels of membership in a group—joining up and then committing and becoming involved. Joining occurs when a person is willing to try out a group, wants the status or favor of association, or sees joining the group as a corollary of a personal goal or commitment. An individual who initiates contact with a group goes through the necessary steps to join but may still withhold personal energies and avoid engaging completely in group activity. Eventually, if the group proves to be a good match,

165

Exercise 6.3: Group Norms

Your response to these questions will help increase your ability
to perceive norm-formation and decision-making processes. Think
back to one of the groups that you identified in the preceding
exercises.

1. If you were to help a new member become oriented to a group to
   which you belong, what four or five rules of behavior would you give
   to help the new person be "in the know"?

2. Identify two or three examples of innovative or unique behaviors
   that represent the possibility of new norms that are forming
   (planting or sprouting stage). These examples are characterized by
   being tentative, suggestive, and evoking reactions (for or against)
   from members.

3. Recall the last time you were with a group of friends and were
   trying to decide what to do for the evening. How did the group
   make this decision? Describe the methods used, noting especially
   the level of member participation and the degree of formality in
   making the decision.

the individual makes a commitment to participate and begins to invest time, energy, and resources toward the group purpose. A personal level of contribution will take on the distinctive form that suits the personality of the individual, influenced by the degree of personal engagement, and usually fits a niche within the group structure. For example, you may sit in a class every day, take notes, verbally interact only when questioned by the instructor, and fall asleep during lectures. Although you have joined the class so as to gain necessary credit in order to receive a degree, your participation is minimal and might be described as that of a passive student. In another situation, you may have voluntarily joined a sports club. You meet for practice on a daily basis, organize many of the practice schedules, socialize with teammates after games, and eagerly seek responsibility as a leader. You have joined this group and are engaged at a high level of activity reflected by a personal pattern or form described as a role.

Membership roles are a way to understand how individuals fit together in a group. Observing a sports team, the functional roles are clearly identifiable. For example, a baseball team has players in positions with very distinct characteristics (pitcher, catcher, or fielder). However, in addition to the defined positions and their responsibilities, the players have individual characteristics that describe what they personally bring to the game. Terry is the take-charge player who yells out plays to the rest of the team, while Sam says little but is a tireless worker in all team drills. Similarly, in any group, people will take on roles that fit their personality and allow them to fill a niche or function that is important to the group.

Some of these roles may seem to be supportive and necessary for the group's success, others may seem neutral or insignificant, while still others may block or interfere with the group's function. What follows is a list of generalized descriptions of member roles in a group. (Although these generalizations serve the useful purpose of defining types of member interactions, be cautious about applying them in practice—people's actual behavior always has an individual basis that may resemble the stereotype but is not defined or governed by it.)

Individual role-functioning in groups is often broken down into two areas: task functioning and maintenance functioning (Hershey & Blanchard, 1977). Some of the following characterizations are adapted from Posthuma's (1996) description of member roles. Examples of those fulfilling task roles include the initiator of ideas and information, the opinion seeker who clarifies and elicits ideas from others, the coordinator who links together inputs from different sources, the critic who evaluates the worth of a strategy or idea, the synthesizer who brings together divergent ideas into a coherent whole, and the energizer who stimulates the group to take action.

The maintenance functions will operate to support the way a group works together to accomplish tasks with less direct reference to the particular topic or theme that is the target of the group's work. Group maintenance roles include the harmonizer who attempts to reduce tensions and differences of opinion, the encourager who supports other members in the course of participation with the group, the observer who may serve as an objective reflector on what is happening in the group, the gatekeeper who facilitates involvement by members, and the doer who acts without need for recognition to get the job done.

Roles that can thwart or inhibit a group are adopted by people who often act out of their own needs or personality without regard for the group. Characteristics of these members could include the comedian who uses humor in ways that can distract the group from its task, the attention seeker who—through loud or dominating behavior—diverts attention from group activities, the blocker who seems to resist every idea or effort by being

Exercise 6.4: Membership Roles

Once again, think back to one of the groups you have identified in preceding exercises. If you are participating in a group training session, this exercise is particularly well suited for application to that group.

1. What three or four behaviors do you observe in the group that support the accomplishment of a specific group task? Describe the characteristics of people showing these behaviors and give a label that communicates their role.

2. Find evidence of distracting, disruptive, or other unproductive individual behaviors. Describe and label these as roles in the same way as for the preceding question.

Reflection Point 6.2: Observation of a Group You Are In

Consider your training group, or—if you're studying alone—another group you are participating in:

What role (or roles) do you carry out in this group?

In what ways does your role in the group support positive group interactions?

What are some additional role behaviors you could initiate that would contribute to the overall functioning of your training group?

negative or resistant, the victim who strives to get rescued or sympathy by self-deprecating statements, and the bully who attempts to coerce others to obey rather than work out what is best for the group.

STAGES OF DEVELOPMENT AND GROUP MATURATION

All groups go through different stages of maturation that influence the way they operate and will in many ways determine the group needs and behaviors that are foremost at any given time. Just as an individual develops from a dependent child state, moves through rebellious teen years, matures into responsible adulthood, and then declines toward death, a group will also progress from infancy to dissolution. Group development does tend to follow a sequence, with certain behaviors being more prevalent at certain times, but behaviors can overlap between stages, and the characteristics of any stage can be repeated at different times in a group. The important thing about understanding the developmental level of a group is to recognize that different factors or issues will require resolution and attention at different stages of maturation. Consider the analogy of individuals learning a new social interactive game. They must first understand the rules of the game and attain the basic skills of performance. Next the participants must figure out how to fit together, know what the individual roles will be, and find ways to coordinate with one another. When the initial practice sessions are complete, the participants in the game must work together and find ways to improve or correct mistakes so as to be ultimately productive. Finally, the participants may become proficient as a team. However, to maintain proficiency, the team must find ways to replenish, replace, or terminate the game.

170

Exercise 6.5: Stages of a Group

Since this section is asking you to reflect upon groups at different points in their development, anchor your responses for these questions by making general reflections on your overall experience as a group member.

1. What are common emotions experienced by individuals when they first enter a group? How are these feelings resolved?

2. What would be four or five characteristics of a group that has matured to the work stage? Give an example of a time a group has worked well and succeeded.

3. Identify three or four characteristics of a group that has stagnated and seems to have grown old. What are a few suggestions that you would make to have the group evaluate and possibly invigorate its stance?

FACTORS THAT PROMOTE POSITIVE GROUP FUNCTIONING

Remember at the beginning of this chapter we suggested that a group is a system that may function at different levels of well-being. Now that we have looked at the many variables that go into a description of a group it is important to go back and determine how well we can influence the group to maintain its strength or improve the overall functioning level. As a diagnostician, you need to identify the symptoms of both health and dysfunction—and then know and apply methods to promote and maintain healthy group functioning.

The following sections suggest ways for a group to resolve its problems, seek interventions to change unhealthy procedures, and help promote productive functioning. This information provides some tips and strategies that have the potential to improve a group. These suggestions are only a sample of the possibilities that may be applied in any given situation—they will give you a start, but the important thing is to stay alert and in touch with the group itself.

Communication

Earlier in the chapter it was noted that communication skills are the key element of social interaction. Communicating links and coordinates one part of the group, a person, to another individual or collective unit. If communication is not facilitating healthy group interaction, an intervention to improve these skills may be necessary.

Tips for Improving Communication Processes
1. Clarify messages.
2. Support group understanding of its direction and purpose.
3. Paraphrase what other members have said.
4. Encourage questions.
5. Share feelings and intentions with others in the group.
6. Personalize messages by saying "I" and "me" instead of "you" or "everybody" when offering opinions and reactions.

7. Be aware of personal congruence between verbal and nonverbal expressions.
8. Make sure that the group meeting space doesn't offer physical barriers and distractions that reduce the effectiveness of communication.

The Group Mood

Symptoms of high positive energy include physical activity, talk, animation, and activities directed toward the group such as good attendance, punctuality, attentiveness, expression of feelings, personally relevant discussion, and cohesive behavior. Low-energy symptoms might include indifference, activity directed away from the group, distractions and diversion to competing activity, suppression or concealment of emotions, poor attendance, tardiness, and premature departures. The following are actions you can take to influence group energy.

Tips for Promoting a Positive Group Atmosphere
1. Encourage clarification and direction of activity toward meaningful goals.
2. Confront symptoms of negative energy to promote honest discussion regarding reasons for occurrence. For example, if people arrive late, discuss the behavior and determine whether changes need to be made.
3. Encourage individuality and expression of personal opinion while linking those thoughts to the group's overall goals.
4. Recognize accomplishment of cooperative and supportive behaviors.
5. Model behavior that demonstrates willingness to try out new ideas, listen to other possibilities, and make adaptations to improve the way the group operates.

Group Task Behavior

An important facet of group life is how well the group works together to accomplish tasks. Having clear, functional norms, adequate decision-making processes, and conflict management and problem-solving strategies facilitates group performance.

Tips for Helping the Group Stay on Task

1. Make sure that norms are clear and understood, yet flexible and adaptable to changing needs.
2. When a conflict or crisis arises, suggest ways to openly express the difference without resistance or defensiveness.
3. For effective decision-making processes, consider context variables such as the type of decision, the time available, the expertise of leaders and members, and the amount of involvement necessary for a good choice.
4. Strive for win-win resolution of differences; avoid defining positions as wholly right or wrong. Win-win is the process of demonstrating that there are not two opposite sides or a dichotomous disagreement but valid points and information that can be gleaned from listening and joining the best from the various perspectives.
5. Be aware of healthy and unhealthy ways of disagreeing. Healthy disagreement produces clear distinctions of different opinions and ideas. Unhealthy disagreement produces reaction and defensiveness in ways that create emotional reactions rather than rational choice.
6. When making group decisions, support clear statement of problems, concise understanding of alternatives, criteria for prioritizing choices, and understanding of group resources.

Coordination of Activity

Coordination is concerned with how well the individual members maintain their uniqueness yet contribute to the total group in a way that moves the group toward its intended goals.

Tips for Improving the Group's Ability to Act in Agreement

1. Help group members express the desirable consequences of participating as an individual member of the group.
2. Have the group take time to assess the way individuals work together. Make sure the discussion avoids being judgmental and refrains from scapegoating or resorting to other individualized putdowns. Constructive criticism will focus on how to make improvements.
3. Support periods of creativity when new ideas and suggestions can be made, experimentation encouraged, and goals reassessed.
4. Encourage expression of both individual feelings and personal impressions of a collective accomplishment.

Exercise 6.6: Group Cohesion

Identify any group in which you are or have been a member. Imagine this group as a giant oak tree. (If this metaphor doesn't appeal to you, pick another—a building, a garden, an automobile, or a sand castle, or anything that reflects many diverse qualities.)

If this group were a tree, consider the roots, trunk, leaves, access to water, sun, soil, size, age, location, and other qualities. Pose questions such as the following about your metaphor: What parts of the tree demonstrate the strengths of the group? What parts of the tree may be deficient? How could the tree grow and improve?

Use the analogy to make suggestions on how this group could change, improve, or maintain its present state.

Maturation

The needs of a young child will vary greatly from those of a teenager, a young adult, a middle-aged person, or a retired person. It is useful to consider a group from a similar perspective by attending to needs at the five levels of group development.

Tips for the Group-Entering Stage
1. Find ways to become acquainted and get to know something about other group members through self-disclosing and demonstration of interest in others.
2. Have means for members to share expectations and interests in the group.
3. Ask members to express what they personally hope to gain by being in the group and how they would like to interact.

Tips for the Sorting Stage
1. Seek clarification of group purpose and direction.
2. Openly suggest means and methods for how the group will operate (establish common ground rules).
3. Encourage and appreciate various opinions and inputs from people.

Tips for the Cohesiveness Stage
1. Develop a badge of identity such as a name, a logo, or a set of common characteristics.
2. Recognize the norms that group members agree to follow.
3. Show acceptance of unique characteristics and contributions by individuals.

Tips for the Working Stage
1. Make use of problem-solving methods to help the group achieve its goals.
2. Gather ideas and disseminate duties to involve members in a system of complementary, interacting roles and responsibilities.
3. Consider ways to adapt and change when new situations occur.

Tips for the Renewal Stage
1. Hold retreats and have training sessions or reviews to look at ways to assess and potentially change the group.
2. Celebrate completion of goals and make decisions regarding how the group wants to carry on, or possibly dissolve.
3. Determine what it would be like to start over, reinvent the group in a new direction, or maintain the status quo.

SUMMARY

Much of your life is spent as a series of interactions with groups of people. These groups vary in levels of effectiveness (how well people work together to accomplish their purposes) and satisfaction of members (how much cohesiveness develops to motivate a commitment to be involved with group activity). Various dynamics operating within a group are identified as process factors. These include communication, norm formation, member interaction roles, motivation, group cohesion, decision-making

177

strategies, task accomplishment, and maturation level. This chapter has provided you with ways to heighten awareness of group process and make appropriate diagnosis as to how the group is functioning. Subsequently, members can use awareness to make choices, influence change, and generally move a group toward more productive outcomes.

A healthy group becomes a resource for providing information, sharing knowledge, accomplishing tasks, and enhancing personal learning that can be an advantage over individual contact methods. Group processes may enhance human work, with the whole being much more than the sum of the parts.

CHAPTER SIX: SUMMARY QUESTIONS

1. What are the advantages of assisting students in a group over working with them as individuals?
2. Identify what is meant by *process factors*. Define what *norms, communication patterns, group atmosphere, cohesiveness, roles, decision processes*, and *task accomplishment* mean.
3. Groups are characterized by going through stages of development. In your own words, describe two or three predominant characteristics of a group at each stage.
4. How can a greater awareness of group process enhance or improve the effectiveness and productivity of any group?

CHAPTER 7

Leading Groups Effectively

LEARNING OBJECTIVES

After completing this chapter, you will be able to

1. Identify strengths and weaknesses regarding personal qualities and competencies for leading group activity.
2. Distinguish different styles of leadership behavior and determine in what situations each style can be most effective.
3. Name and describe at least four theories prominent in the past fifty years for describing and explaining leadership behavior.
4. Identify five common practices of successful leaders.
5. Apply a leader planning process for working with a group that includes steps from initiation to evaluation.
6. Employ specific and effective leader strategies for working with groups in particular tasks or situations.

●

Researchers discuss the concept of leadership endlessly. However, few people who enter positions of authority receive any formal training or preparation to become a leader. As a peer educator, you will probably be asked to perform leadership tasks with groups of students. These tasks may include giving presentations, facilitating discussions, helping students work together to complete a project, or perhaps planning a social function. In addition,

179

when serving or assisting others, you may play a significant role in the development of positive group norms that facilitate self-exploration by permitting members to engage in meaningful and purposeful interaction.

At various times, you may be called upon in a group to inspire, motivate, mediate, moderate, support, demonstrate, structure, reflect, or evaluate. Depending on the present needs of the group, you may be very much in charge and at the center of the group activity, or you may find you will serve best by staying in the background and permitting group members to assume their own responsibility and authority. Some knowledge and principles of group leadership will help you look at your strengths and develop skills as a group leader. For instance, one principle of effective leadership is that rather than being top-down, leadership should be seen as being shared with the other members of the group. Also, in their book on "exploring leadership" for college students, Komives, Lucas, and McMahon (2007) emphasize the importance of understanding yourself, as well as understanding others, in order to become an effective leader. This chapter highlights the ways to be a reflective and receptive learner when developing the leadership skills to "make a difference" when you are meeting students in a group, organization, or classroom situation.

HISTORICAL PERSPECTIVE

What makes a good leader? This is a question that people have been asking for ages. This historical review summarizes how thinking about leadership has evolved over the past hundred years. One early explanation was the "great man" theory, which held that because of their superiority, certain elite individuals would naturally rise to the top as leaders. Another theory was the "Zeitgeist" ("the spirit of the age and its society"), which explained leadership as a result of situational determinants, such as time, place, and circumstance. That is, a leader emerges because of conditions present that matched the qualities of a person available to take control.

During the middle part of the twentieth century, more systematic studies investigated how leadership style would affect group performance. A classic study was the comparison of autocratic, democratic, and laissez-faire methods of Boy Scout leaders on the group life and individual behavior of children. White and Lippitt (1968) found that autocratic leaders created more dependence, aggressiveness, and discontent among group members; democratic leaders facilitated a more friendly, group-centered, creative, and moderately efficient membership; while laissez faire leadership resulted in detached members producing less work and work of poorer quality.

The next stage of research further clarified "effective leadership" as situation-dependent. Fiedler (1967) concluded from a variety of studies that group needs and context determined what type of leadership style was necessary. For example, task-oriented leaders performed best in less favorable situational structures: a group facing a time-pressed decision such as organizing to respond to an emergency functioned best with a task-oriented leader. Relationship-oriented leaders responded best in moderately structured situations. The conclusion followed that leaders must adapt their emphasis to the situation, or an appropriate leader must be matched to the right situational task.

Further research added new ideas to this leadership situation theme. Hershey and Blanchard (1977) added a dimension of group maturation, indicating that leadership style must change with the life cycle of a group. At earlier stages, a group will be more dependent on the leader's structure. As the group matures, members will assume more responsibility and need less input from the leader. The pattern of leader behavior may move along a continuum from dictating (telling) to persuading (selling) to facilitating (participating) to involving (delegating).

House and Mitchell (1974) emphasized the motivational factors of leader behavior, noting the key to leadership was to facilitate the "path" of persons to a "goal." Herzberg (1968) distinguished motivation as having many levels, pointing out that it is necessary to know the difference between direct, extrinsic motivators such as money and personal benefits and indirect, intrinsic motivators such as pride in accomplishment, personal satisfaction, learning, and growth. The significance of this group of studies was the emphasis on the leader's need to tap into the motivation of group members.

Another important contribution to the understanding of leadership came from case studies of significant national and international leaders from the past. James McGregor Burns (1978) concluded that true leadership is a dynamic and reciprocal exchange between leaders and followers. At first, the exchange might be as basic as the idea in the common phrase "You scratch my back and I'll scratch yours"—as in a politician's promise, "You vote for me; I'll support your issues." However, as people evolve, the exchange that happens in leadership also evolves. The exchange exceeds that of "helping" and becomes more about "empowerment." Burns says that the highest level is empowerment; a leader who inspires confidence in followers' abilities and then stimulates followers to act toward meeting their goals empowers others. Burns mentions Gandhi, Martin Luther King, and John F. Kennedy as examples of inspirational and empowering leaders.

The most recent discussions on leadership have highlighted the need for leadership to respond to changes created by the "new age" (Hesselbein, Goldsmith, & Beckhard, 1996). Leaders in the twenty-first century will be those who can assimilate the complexity, change, diversity, and new technology of their world and still take decisive and appropriate action. Furthermore, leaders need to accept the changing mindset whereby responsibility is shared across memberships and organizations rather than being held by one person who holds control and authority over the group. The effective leader models openness, invites feedback from others, admits and owns mistakes, receives assistance when needed, and is relaxed and open to new learning (Guttman, 2009).

In summary, the thinking and research on leadership has progressed from very general ideas to more specific detail of the role of the leader, but also the nature of the group and how leader style, group interaction, member engagement, and motivation will affect results. Peer educators will find that there is not one formula for being an effective leader, but having awareness and understanding of both the leader role and the group response will provide greater proficiency and adaptability to situations that occur.

Exercise 7.1: Qualities of an Effective Leader

Identify someone you know whom you regard as a good leader—someone whose style assists the group in functioning effectively and successfully:

What qualities, characteristics, or behaviors does this individual possess that contribute to the group's success? (Provide a list of three or four.)

What general ideas about leader behavior can be concluded from looking at attributes of specific people identified as successful leaders?

Go back over your list from the question above and identify qualities that you believe are strengths or attributes of your own.

What are some other qualities that you would like to possess but believe are undeveloped? Discuss how you could develop or improve in one or two of these undeveloped areas.

183

An Experiment on College Student Leadership

In his bestselling book titled *The Tipping Point: How Little Things Can Make a Big Difference*, Malcom Gladwell (2000) explained how a few significant people are able to initiate influence over many others in areas such as fads and other forms of social behavior. Soon after its publication, a group of peer educators decided to test Gladwell's thesis that *tippers* could have so much influence. This group of peer educators began with Gladwell's premise that those with tipper potential possessed certain characteristics, and then these students went about trying to identify who might be a successful tipper on their campus.

The criteria for who had tipper potential included that they were *well connected*, had *sensitive detectors* to student interests, and could communicate in a way that would *stick* in the memory of others. Over 500 students nominated peers who met these criteria. From the nominations, over 50 students were identified as *tippers*. These nominees were then sent a letter of congratulations and an invitation to participate in focus groups that would share ideas about improving student interest in wellness behavior. A majority of these students showed up for focus groups and brainstormed ideas for reaching students with important messages. The best outcome of this campus experiment was that many of these students became involved in carrying out several of the proposed ideas during the next year and became a part of the student wellness program. This experiment provided verification for identifying potential influence makers (Newton & Newton, 2001).

PRACTICES OF SUCCESSFUL LEADERS

Looking for common behavior in success stories as a way to identify practices of successful leaders, Kouzes and Posner (2002) surveyed and directly interviewed more than 500 leaders of organizations and businesses. They found five common practices: challenging the process, inspiring a shared vision, enabling others to act, modeling the way, and encouraging the heart. All these practices were common to successful leaders and were exemplified and implemented through specific leader behaviors. These practices are not magical or innate to an individual; they include attitudes, procedures, and skills that nearly anyone can learn and emulate.

Leaders Stimulate and Challenge

A successful leader acts not to protect the status quo but to stimulate and challenge a group or, as described by Kouzes and Posner (2002), to challenge the process. Such a leader explores new ways of doing things and is willing to take risks to assist the group; this leader sees a problem both as an opportunity and a challenge. Mistakes are accepted as a part of learning, and the process of change is experienced as an adventure. Skills of creativity and problem solving are important in this practice. A creative leader seeks many possibilities and is able to look at a familiar situation from a different perspective.

De Bono (1970) describes the difference between lateral (creative) thinking and *status quo* (vertical) thinking. Vertical thinking is analogous to digging a hole. Once you have started, you continue to dig the hole bigger and deeper. Because of the investment of time and commitment of energy, it is very difficult to give up this space even when it is not working to meet one's purpose. To think laterally is to choose a place that is

185

experimental and uncertain. De Bono's idea of getting stuck in the "hole of familiar patterns" is often referred to as "tunnel vision," or an inability to see new alternatives. For example, many groups follow a set of rules and procedures because "that's the way it has always been done," even when the rationale for the customary way of acting is no longer known. A successful leader knows when to question routine and get the group to act with relevance to the present set of circumstances and group purpose.

It is not necessary for a leader to come up with every new idea or to provide the ingenuity for every shift in direction. Rather, the leader can be a facilitator of creative process, using strategies such as asking provocative questions (such as "What has been your most memorable event today?" or "What would make this meeting most enjoyable?"); setting up experiments (such as every person contributing one object that is in his or her present possession as a way to ascertain a common group theme); and involving people in retreats (everyone could make a sandcastle that represents an ideal concept such as building bridges between different groups of students); brainstorming sessions (such as one focused on how many functions can be identified for a roll of dental floss); or even art exercises that elicit more creative, right-brain ideas.

A leader promotes challenge and change by rewarding those who make suggestions and seek new possibilities. Because a shift to new or different ways of doing things will initially heighten anxiety, a leader must demonstrate that the stress of change can be managed and is an acceptable part of the stimulation for something new to happen. Finally, an important function of the leader is to help a group determine which of the new options and possibilities are truly good and useful ideas to follow. A healthy person and a well-functioning group both have the imagination to create, the courage to change, the resilience to recover from a mistake, and the excitement to continue into uncharted areas.

Leaders Activate Focus and Goal Direction

Promoting and directing a group to clearly identify its mission and purpose is an important responsibility of a leader. Kouzes and Posner (2002) referred to this as inspiring a shared vision. For example, when a teacher begins a class discussion period, the first question could be, "When you leave this class period, what would you like to have accomplished?" It is not sufficient for a leader to impose a goal on the rest of the group members. Successful leaders engage followers in a manner that elicits the personal commitment and energy of each member toward some shared ends. The goals of all members need not necessarily be the same, but there must be a mutual acceptance that all can benefit from the interaction and cooperation of the group activity.

The task of inspiring a vision implies that a leader must have the tools of a visionary. A visionary uses lessons from the past (knowing the pluses and the minuses, the strengths and the weaknesses), identifies the needs and purposes of a group at the present, and can see future possibilities. To inspire a shared vision, then, a visionary leader must be able to bring ideas together in a way that two things are preserved: both the unique aspirations of individuals and the mutual considerations of the group.

How may a group leader inspire a vision that has the greatest opportunity for success? Look at the six factors below that could be considered a checklist for determining an idea's potential for becoming a shared group commitment.

Leaders Support Member Involvement

The third practice of successful leaders is to enable others to act. An old Taoist proverb attributed to the philosopher Lao Tzu says it this way: "That leader is best whom people barely know of, not

---

Checklist for Determining Group Commitment to an Idea

☐ *Value or principle*—The idea is important to a core belief of the group membership.

☐ *Credibility*—The idea is grounded in evidence of its worth. There is a rational, justifiable basis for pursuing the idea.

☐ *Inclusiveness*: The idea is shared so that all members can be a part of the vision.

☐ *Clarity*—The idea is communicated with enough illustration to be vivid in the minds of the group members. Clarity provides a common certainty for the context, including purpose, action, and outcome.

☐ *Positive Perspective*—The idea is stated in an affirmative way that communicates the hopes and anticipations of members.

☐ *Passion*—The idea taps the emotions and the hearts of group members, providing a driving force for accomplishing the vision. Passion can be the zest and enthusiasm that keeps members engaged and prevents apathy and indifference.

so good who people obey and acclaim, and worst whom they despise. Of a good leader who talks little when the work is done and the aims fulfilled, the group will say, 'We did this ourselves.'" The emphasis in the most effective groups is to attain a team or "we" atmosphere in which the commitment and energy of all group members is activated. The activity most central to engaging others is to facilitate cooperative and collaborative behavior.

Harrison Owens (1997) describes a process called "Open Space Technology" whereby no preconceived structure or agenda is imposed and the leadership empowers the group to self-direct. Open space requires full engagement of the group membership, and it has been found to produce greater investment of members and provide more diverse inputs and creative solutions that speak directly to the needs of a rapidly changing society. Margaret Wheatley (2006) says that the world of today *has* changed and instead of the chaos and frustration that might occur when organizations try to hold onto an old way comes the opportunity for a reorganization that finds productive creative possibilities starting with the smallest face-to-face groups that all of us interact with in our daily lives.

Leaders Model Effective Behavior

The fourth practice of effective leaders is to set an example for others. Kouzes and Posner (2002) describe it as modeling the way. An exemplary leader emphasizes the importance of action over words. It is the opposite of the parental admonition, "Do as I say, not as I do." Included here are six areas in which leaders can model the way for a group.

- A leader demonstrates behavior that is consistent with a set of values or principles. The leader can clearly identify the principles that a group stands for and then act in ways that will establish, promote, and maintain those values.
- A leader communicates in a manner that is clear, understandable, and up-front. This can be accomplished by stating the purpose and motivation for any group activity or agenda. The leader avoids covert, hypocritical, and ambiguous messages.
- A leader demonstrates a caring and respectful attitude toward others when in face-to-face contact and also shows a sense of consideration and dignity for others outside the immediate environment.

189

- A leader shows engagement and works intently toward completing the tasks of the group. A true leader energizes a group by modeling the commitment and effort needed to make things happen, inspiring the group to establish strong norms for hard work and achievement. However, to be productive, a leader must also pay attention to counterproductive factors such as job stress, burnout or fatigue, or emotional tension, and work to reduce or prevent them.
- A leader acts to maintain behavior that reflects fair play and integrity and establishes standards for ethical conduct.
- A leader models effectiveness, the single most important action a leader can demonstrate.

Leaders Recognize and Reward

An organization will thrive best when there is recognition both for doing the little things that make a difference and for reaching goals and succeeding in major accomplishments. Sincere acts of unselfish kindness, observations and gestures reflecting interest, and acknowledgment of individual uniqueness are all ways a leader is responsive and encouraging to members. Reinforcement of even small steps toward group goals provides participants with incentive and a sense of progress. Recognition may vary from routine acknowledgments such as "That was a good idea" to regular updates or reports on what individuals have accomplished. Personal messages commemorating birthdays, refreshments at meetings, or acknowledgments of specific individual contributions toward special events are also valued incentives to members. On a larger scale, at significant points of the group's life, it is important to have celebrations to note accomplishments such as award ceremonies and "We did it!" parties.

Exercise 7.2: The Group Time Line

The following activity can be completed individually or with a training group. If completed in the group setting your training leader or teacher will direct you on how a group will undertake this task.

On a large sheet of paper draw a line that divides the paper in half horizontally along the midpoint. Next divide the line into three parts and label these parts past, present, and future. Identify a group that you have been actively involved in while a college student. If you are working with a training group you may wish to use this group as the example, although another group can serve the purpose. From the vantage point of the group's history, its present activity, and its possible future direction, identify significant milestones in the life of this group. Locate and label these points chronologically on the time line.

What can you summarize about the purpose, methods, and successes of this group?

What does the history and present status of the group's functioning have to do with the future possibilities of this group?

What steps or measures could a leader take to make it easier for this group to assess and determine future directions?

PRACTICAL TIPS AND STRATEGIES

As a peer educator you may encounter a variety of situations that will interfere with what you want to accomplish in a group or class. Students may come late and leave early, a cell phone may ring, someone's sarcastic comment may create a reaction, few responses may be given to a group question, your request for volunteers may meet a deadly silence, and you—as the leader—may begin to wonder whether you could do something to make things better. Leading a group is not easy, but there are definitely ways to deal with many of the difficulties encountered in groups and, more important, make the experience one of the most exciting and productive ways to work with students. In this section we describe many practical strategies that a leader can use to enhance the functioning of a group. Although the section will read like a cookbook and is indeed meant to provide examples for many specific situations that you may encounter, it will not be an exhaustive list of all the strategies that may be needed in a group. As noted for earlier sets of suggestions, these tips are designed as a starting point, not a final answer to every problem.

Building a Cohesive Team

Nearly any group will benefit when members develop a sense of identity and commitment to the group with which they are involved. A sense of team identity may be less important for a group that is coming together briefly to receive or share information. However, even during brief contacts, having a sense of the value, purpose, and common benefit from the experience can increase participants' attention and engagement with the task. For a group that will have continued involvement and personal investment over time, the development of a cohesive team atmosphere is essential.

Team building has both personal and group dimensions. It begins when individuals are able to share information and get to know others in the group on a personal basis. The personal alliances that develop become a basis for positive communication, a working relationship, and a determination of how individual needs, interests, and capabilities will fit into an overall group purpose. The group dimensions are then generated by the process of identifying common denominators that lead to the group goals; the group dimensions are further developed through the interaction of group members as they work toward realizing the goals. When members have a strong identity and a sense of belonging with a group, they will have a greater investment in and commitment to group activities. Examples of how to do this follow.

Tips for Team Building

1. Provide an icebreaking activity soon after the formation of any group so members will gain personal contact with others. Icebreakers can be as simple as getting the name and shaking the hand of persons sitting next to each other in a lecture. Or for a group that will interact more closely, an icebreaker could be more involved and personal; for example, members might share values or purpose ("three principles that guide my life") or personal information ("my proudest moment in the past month").

2. Hold an initial session in which group participants express individual expectations and goals, determine common and complementary interests with other members, and formulate group goals.

3. Demonstrate the significance of cooperative and collaborative effort within the group by providing a simulation, game, or group task. Then have the group members discuss how they were able to interact together. An interactive game using art supplies to build a "product" is an example of a typical group

---

task. More elaborate team-building processes may have a group do skits or role-plays that depict the special qualities of their members and the outcome of their collective identity.

4. After the initial stages of team building, take time for periodic assessment of team interactions. Include a review of how the group communicates, identify team accomplishments, and gather suggestions for the future. Use these times to celebrate collective successes and look for ways to reinvigorate the group and make improvements for the future.

Making Decisions and Accomplishing Tasks

Typically, a group organized to achieve an outcome must make several decisions before taking direct action toward that outcome. The decision process is often the most critical moment in the achievement of a group goal. The way a decision is made can determine the quality of input given to the decision, the degree of members' commitment to carrying out the decision, and the definition for knowing when a task or goal is complete. A leader must attend to three important considerations in leading the decision process. The first is to determine ways to define and clarify the question or problem to be acted upon. The second is to determine the manner in which participants will provide input and come to resolution. The third is to determine how any decision will be carried through.

Facilitating a group's implementation of a plan and accomplishment of designated goals is a critical aspect of leadership. It may include strategies for assessing what tasks need doing and who can do them, evaluating how well each task was done, and organizing a celebration of successes at the end. Through this process a leader may seem more like a manager and problem solver. However, while implementing systematic organizational strategies, the leader will also need to be aware of and adapt to special needs that may arise; for example, a successful leader will notice and help resolve individual differences that may result in conflict.

Tips for Decision Making and Task Accomplishment

1. Clarify the decisions that the group or organization needs to address, stating issues, problem areas, organizational objectives, and the context for needing a decision at a given time.
2. Define the methods for reaching a decision. A formal organization may use a clearly defined written set of procedures, such as Robert's Rules of Order. However, most organizations will use less formal decision-making processes that allow for a wide range of involvement and participation from members.
3. Generally, significant decisions that will affect all of a group's members and require a strong commitment from participants should follow procedures with high levels of member input. Providing means for open discussion and some form of democratic resolution will make for better decisions and may be a necessity for successful group support and accomplishment.
4. Decisions that are less significant, relate to carrying through detail, or pertain to subgoals already established by group input can be delegated to individuals, committees, or other units given the authority to efficiently and expeditiously make an ad hoc decision.
5. Be prepared to make decisions for the group when face-to-face group decisions cannot be made or emergency time restraints eliminate the possibility for group input, but consider group interests carefully in such decisions.
6. Delegate tasks to group members in a manner that considers the fit of an individual's capabilities and interests with the job at hand. When possible, use voluntary input and self-determination of members to guide the process. The more members feel they have a clear and definitive role in contributing to a task, the greater the group involvement.

195

7. Provide job descriptions, task definitions, time parameters, and other structure in very clear terms when making delegations. Follow up decision-making and task-delegation sessions with written summaries that clarify and reinforce what has been determined so that all group members are clearly aware of expectations.
8. Use checkpoints and follow-up sessions to note progress and accomplishments of any group decision.

Impact of Physical Environment

The physical environment can critically influence a group's nature of activity and level of performance. It is important for a leader to anticipate, when possible, the optimum conditions of meeting space by planning and arranging space needs. Consideration should be made for physical comfort (including such factors as temperature, lighting, seating), freedom from distractions (noise, competing activity), and seating arrangements appropriate for the tasks of the group.

Tips for Using Space
1. Check out any space that will be used for a group in advance to make arrangements or resolve problems. It is important to know whether there is adequate seating arranged in a manner that facilitates the type of interaction desired. See Figures 7.1–7.4 on seating arrangements.
2. Make sure that whatever writing surfaces, visual aids, and other supplies the group may need are present or available.
3. Be sure the environment is conducive to the task, including lighting, temperature, and the elimination of distractions.
4. Follow up to make sure that any special arrangements or refreshments are ready on time. One of the most inefficient ways to start a meeting or hold any group activity is to waste time and

energy by unlocking doors, finding chairs, or locating a resource that could have been taken care of by careful preparation.

When considering seating arrangements, remember that they need to be tailored for the kind of interaction you have in mind. Various options have both strengths and weaknesses.

Theater Seating   Row seating is best used for providing information via lecture or similar presentations. A theater format provides the speaker with good visual contact with the audience. It also allows the audience to have direct visual and sound access to demonstration methods and media aids. However, this arrangement is not good for stimulating discussion or active two-way involvement with participants.

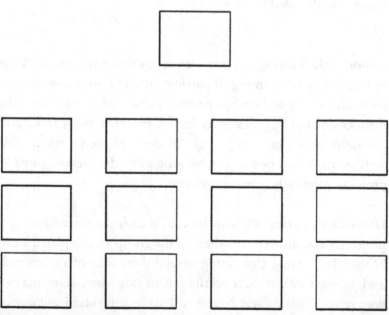

Figure 7.1. Theater Seating

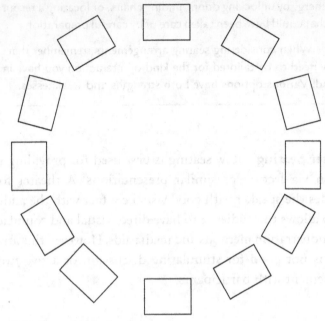

Figure 7.2. Roundtable Seating

Roundtable Seating A conference room setup permits face-to-face interaction among all participants. This promotes discussions and dialogue between people. Table surface can serve the function of holding materials, notes, or other work tasks and communicates a businesslike atmosphere. However, roundtable seating would not permit easy viewing of media presentations or promote physically active movement.

Horseshoe Seating When the goal is to focus discussion on a project or a problem rather than on the group and its plans, it can be useful to arrange the seating around three sides of a table, with a whiteboard or flip chart on the fourth side where someone can keep track of points and decisions. This retains the advantages of

Figure 7.3. Horseshoe Seating

the roundtable setup while diverting members' attention from each other.

Living-Room–Style Seating   Tables can be a barrier when more informality, interpersonal contact, and participant movement is desired. When you want to establish such conditions, set up a casual arrangement with comfortable seating that removes tables and other barriers from the meeting space.

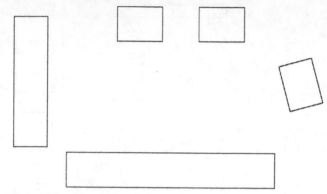

Figure 7.4. Living-Room Seating

GROUP EXPERIENCES FOR INTERPERSONAL GROWTH

As a peer educator, you may facilitate support groups or structured experiences that focus on personal growth or interpersonal behavior of members. Such peer support groups include those focused on wellness (exercise and diet), recovery (campus Al-Anon, Alcoholics Anonymous, and eating disorders), self-improvement (overcoming shyness, leadership training), and identity (international students, women in engineering, and gay and lesbian students). Whenever the purpose of a group experience includes self-disclosure and self-improvement, it is very important to establish the conditions of safety and support for promoting personal exploration of what most people consider to be private and vulnerable information. After establishing necessary conditions for personal revelation, it is important to create a helpful atmosphere where open exploration, enhanced personal understanding, and potential growth can occur. In short, a leader has responsibilities for establishing an ambience in which personal information can be safely shared and a process through which self-exploration and discovery can take place.

The most important caveat for all peer educators is to recognize that you are not a professional counselor. It is essential to establish the purpose and limits of any peer group that is focused on personal exploration and growth. Orientation to ground rules of the group may help establish these limits.

Necessary Conditions for Self-Disclosure

First, the development of trust is essential for people to share information about themselves in a group situation. Trust is a condition earned through demonstration that the group environment will be safe, accepting, caring, respectful, and honest. Although it is often helpful initially to describe these conditions to group members and suggest that they be operating principles, the trusting environment becomes a reality when the leader and members consistently display the promised behaviors. Group members will initially be cautious and reserved, testing the norms and integrity of the group to ensure that it is a safe place. This is a normal process, so a leader must allow time for testing and confirmation of group norms so that trust can be assured.

A second important condition is the provision of openness. We often communicate in a way that may disguise or hide underlying feelings, motivations, and intentions; such a communication style protects against the vulnerability and discomfort, even the rejection and belittlement, that we fear may result from expressing our real thoughts or feelings. Personal learning at a deeper level, however, necessitates that people be open, frank, and candid in their communication with others. This does not mean that a person must reveal every private thought and feeling in a group, but it does mean that what is chosen for disclosure must be sincere, honest, and clearly communicated.

A third condition for self-disclosure is effective listening between group members. When people disclose information about themselves, it needs to be heard. More important, it needs to be understood from the individual speaker's own frame of reference. We discussed the development of effective communication and listening skills in Chapter Four. A leader of a support group may need to promote effective listening and communication skills through instructional activity, good modeling, or interventions that take place based on the evolving dynamic of a group.

Helpful Interacting

A group environment may provide the opportunity for participants to benefit and learn about themselves in ways they could not manage on their own. The following are factors that describe the advantages of personal learning occurring in a group. First, individuals obtain many ideas through the demonstration and example of others' behavior. Another's actions provide a role model, serving both to suggest possibilities and to show strategies that can be applied to one's own life. Similarly, when a person tries out a behavior in a group, the group is apt to provide feedback and reactions—letting the experimenter know how the behaviors came across and offering suggestions on how improvements could be made. The very act of trying out an idea or behavior in a group can bring the validation and support of others, which leads to more confident initiation outside the group.

A group also supports the building of self-acceptance and improved self-esteem. Yalom and Leszcz (2005) describe one of the ways a group does this as "universalization." Universalization is a process that reveals people's similarities and expresses the reality that many people share many of the same problems and insecurities, as well as many of the same hopes and dreams. To know that one is not alone in dealing with the difficulties of life provides both a sense of relief and a prospect of hope. A group also serves as an emotional outlet to release pent-up feelings, experience the support of acceptance after revealing the inner self, and receive the internal reward that comes with contributing and giving to others.

Tips for Leading Support Groups
1. Describe clearly to all group members both the purpose and the limitations of the group experience.
2. Provide a discussion of potential ground rules for the establishment of trust, support, and open communication in the group. Allow group members an opportunity to give input and discuss how these guidelines may be implemented.
3. Ask group members to share initial expectations and personal goals for what they would like to accomplish through the group experience.
4. Initiate process interventions within the group to create an open atmosphere where members can share impressions of the communication, trust, and other dimensions of group interaction.
5. Use a problem-solving approach in a manner that emphasizes the positive, such as "What did you like about this group session?" and "What are ways that we, as group members, could improve our listening skills?"
6. Provide a summary of each session that reflects on what has been accomplished and emphasizes the meaning or understanding of the session. Allow group members to summarize what they learned.
7. Make sure that closure occurs before the completion of any group experience intended for personal growth. Closure should include dealing with unfinished business, which means allowing group members to ask questions or deal with group issues that they feel are incomplete. Closure should also reflect upon the meaning of the experience, what has been learned, and how that knowledge can be used beyond the group. Finally, there should be a time to say good-bye and acknowledge the importance of others.

SPECIAL PROBLEMS CONFRONTING PEER EDUCATORS LEADING GROUPS

Underparticipation by Members

When people are uninvolved with group activity, they tend to miss meetings, arrive late, or leave early. However, even without attendance problems, other behaviors can show minimal participation and engagement. People who don't feel engaged with a group are apt to be reluctant to speak up or verbally interact, even when opportunities are solicited. They may also allow themselves to be distracted easily from group focus by doing things such as looking out a window, texting or frequently checking their phone, or holding unrelated conversations with a friend. Boredom or indifference may be observed through blank looks, avoidance of emotion, and a general lack of energy or engagement shown by physical lethargy and refusal of eye contact.

Although the symptoms of disengagement are clearly observable, the causes may be less certain. First, the behaviors could signal a lack of clarity and purpose for the group, a feature that may be common during the forming stage of a group but should diminish quickly once the group becomes established. A second cause of apathetic and disengaged behavior is a lack of commitment to a group. Some people will attend or join a situation because it is a requirement or an expectation and not because they are personally invested. The attitudes of those who are required to take a class they do not like, who join a group with little interest but think it will look "good on the résumé," or are just there because "everybody else is doing it" are instantly recognizable. A third factor includes individual personalities—some people may feel too shy, uneasy, or inexperienced to speak up, show involvement, or make assertive input to group activity even though they actually do care about what the group is doing. Fourth, lack of

Tips for Increasing Involvement

1. To facilitate more equal involvement from all types of personalities, shy as well as gregarious, provide simple methods that solicit total participation. For example, have everybody write down an idea, and then have each member share the idea by writing it on a visual board or flip chart. Break the group into smaller groups to initiate more active participation, perhaps starting with two people and building to smaller face-to-face groups, especially when the group is larger than twelve people.

2. Keep the group focused so that all members know the task, the limits of time, and the need for staying on track to accomplish specific ends. Establish clear and specific norms for when a meeting will start. Adhering to those norms communicates an expectation that they will be followed consistently. Finishing a meeting on time with the task accomplished can be an equally rewarding outcome for good group performance.

3. Challenge a group to make an investment in the activity of the group, so that everyone recognizes that his or her involvement is a high priority and a worthy commitment for the group. When this is done openly, it will challenge the uncommitted to make a decision, and, if still unwilling to make an investment, they may leave voluntarily.

4. Observe group behaviors that show a lack of involvement. Communicate your observations to the group in an open way, without indictment or hostility, inviting members to discuss what is going on with the group and what can be done about it. For example, make an observant inquiry such as, "The group seems tired and detached today. Is something going on that we should talk about?" This method of open discussion invites group members to make inputs and possible suggestions as to how the group can be improved.

involvement may reflect problems within the group dynamics. Some people may be afraid of criticism, making a mistake, being embarrassed, or losing status through their actions. This could be due to group norms that create defensiveness, such as hostile comments or threats, ridicule, disrespectful statements, demonstration of prejudice toward subgroup members, or a sense that no one cares or is interested in the individual. To correct these symptoms, a leader must be able to diagnose the cause and have ways to respond to the appropriate issue.

Conflict Among Members

The good news about conflict in a group is that it indicates that people are engaged and are willing to provide opinions. It also means that differences of opinion can be aired and that ideas can be openly evaluated for their pros and cons and strengths and weaknesses. Unfortunately, the presence of difference and conflict typically leads to feelings of tension, but again this can be positive, as tension at a certain level will engage and energize a group.

Tips for Dealing with Conflict

1. Set ground rules for looking at all sides of any issue and for openly discussing differences. Suggesting that the group make a list of both the pros and the cons of any disputed issue can accomplish this goal.

2. Separate the issues from personal attachment. Avoid tactics that polarize and personalize groups into win-lose situations. Be clear that hostile tactics are not tolerated—there is no room for defaming statements about individuals ("Your ideas are always bad"), throwing blame at individuals ("If we fail it will be your fault"), or using blackmail ("If this decision is made, don't expect me to be involved").

3. When a decision has been made and a direction determined, be clear to group members that it was important to have had everybody's input and that it is equally important in the future to continue to have everybody's support. Make sure that everyone gains the understanding that even people who oppose the majority's ideas are considered as providing valuable input now and in the future.

The bad news about conflict and differences is that when it creates cliques within a group, members may feel polarized and sometimes alienated. This is especially true when differences are viewed in a win-lose context. It is important to value difference without creating individual defensiveness and to promote scrutiny and critique of ideas and group decisions without attaching the worth or viability of the person to the outcome. The key to dealing with conflict and difference is finding an acceptable balance of critique and resolution in which differences actually promote better group outcomes without alienating group members.

Problem Personalities

There will frequently be people with personalities that have a negative impact on a group, either by blocking effective group practice or creating interpersonal difficulties. It would be a difficult if not impossible task to identify in this chapter a comprehensive description of the potential types of difficult personalities that one might encounter in a group. However, we can cite a few examples and provide some tips for encountering difficult individuals and responding in general to these situations.

Monopolizers Groups will often have members who tend to dominate verbally and bring undue attention to them. Initially this type of behavior might be a relief to others, as it takes responsibility and effort off themselves for group participation. However, it soon becomes apparent that domination by a few will deter a more balanced group participation and limit positive input from those who do not wish to compete with an aggressive personality. Deference will lead to many members' showing less interest and becoming annoyed with the domination. A common problem with a domineering type is that leaders and other group members accept the behavior initially and then find it difficult to deal

207

with the monopolizer when the behavior is recognized later as a problem. Confronting a person at that point feels inconsistent, as though the initial acceptance set up a sort of contract as to what behavior would be accepted in the future—and the typical monopolizer will be quick to take advantage of any reservations the group or its leader may show.

Manipulators   Some people will seek many ways to have a sense of control and protection for themselves. One set of strategies this type of person may adopt includes forms of seduction, in which they draw support from others by feigning interest, showing fragility, or attracting attention in an alluring way. Manipulative people often communicate a dependency on others and a need for rescue or support, which makes them particularly difficult to confront.

Distracters   This type of individual may sidetrack a group with behaviors that lead a group off task. They may clown around and use humor to get off the subject or may just be loud and disruptive by talking to a neighbor while the group is conducting business. Again, these people can be difficult to deal with because they have a good defense response when they retort that "they were just trying to have a little fun."

Aggressors   An angry or attacking person will create considerable disturbance in any group. Confronting such a person presents the opportunity for a fight or debate. But to acquiesce and avoid the conflict creates acceptance of an environment that a hostile bully will dominate. A group will often disintegrate if hostile behavior is allowed to continue.

Harmonizers   Some people will try so hard to please, help others, or create a peaceful, no-conflict atmosphere that their

208

Tips for Dealing with Problem Personalities

1. Take initiative by taking time at the beginning of a group for members to discuss positive ways in which they can interact and be productive.

2. Confront unacceptable behaviors while still demonstrating acceptance of the person. Make it clear that you can be annoyed, displeased, or angered at a behavior without diminishing the person's character. For example, "I appreciate how much energy you show in the group, Terry, but I also observe that your behavior doesn't allow others who are more quiet to provide input" is likely to get much better results than "Sit down and shut up!"

3. When confronting a person, be factual and explicit about what you observe and how such a behavior affects the group. For example, use a statement such as, "I notice that the side conversations taking place are distracting attention from our group activity." Do not use judgmental labeling such as "That was dumb," "You're acting stupid," or "Quit being a baby."

4. Be direct and honest. Do not use satirical remarks or innuendo to get your point across. "Megan, your talking on the cell phone while we are meeting is distracting me" is more tactful than "Megan, do you have to make that date on group time?"

5. Ask group members to respond to specific observations as a way to process their reactions to a person's effect on the group as a whole. Examples might include such statements as "What are those of you who were silent today thinking and feeling?" or "I sense that many people seemed to back off when Kim got angry at Jon; can we discuss those reactions now and how they may be affecting our interactions?"

6. If certain member behaviors are very destructive, and the group is not an appropriate place for discussion of individual behaviors, meet with the individual on a one-to-one basis outside the group setting. Be prepared to suggest alternative behaviors or other options for the

individual. However, you still may have to define boundaries of behavior for being a part of the group, which may include a necessary step to suggest severance from the group or organization.

7. If a person's behavior seems to reflect personal issues or trauma in his or her life, be willing to refer that individual for professional help. Do this in a helpful way that shows concern and interest.

Exercise 7.3: Self-Evaluation of Your Leadership Practices

Kouzes and Posner (2002) identified five practices of successful leaders. Briefly state what these practices are. Then reflect on your own behavior in working with groups:

Look at your strongest and weakest leadership practice and suggest how you would lead with your strength and enhance your area that could be improved. Why did you select these particular qualities?

What do you suggest could be a way to improve your weakness or make better use of your strength?

behavior actually does more harm than good. For example, they may act to gloss over any conflict quickly so as to avoid tensions in a group, thereby short-circuiting issues of difference that may need to be discussed. They also may be quick to provide support, and their typical response attempts to help by overloading the person with suggestions ("Have you tried this . . . or this? And this is what I did last year") or provides potentially false reassurance ("Don't feel bad; I'm sure everything will turn out all right").

SUMMARY

There is a wealth of information about how leaders can be most effective in working with groups. In spite of the early theories that a person is born to be a leader or that a leader emerges automatically as the result of special circumstances, there are very clearly identified principles, attitudes, skills, and strategies that can be developed by any individual. Effective leaders do not call attention to self but instead are able to provide very important subtle qualities that provide impetus for group members to engage, create, and assume responsibility for a group to achieve goals. Subtle qualities include stimulating, inspiring, encouraging, and modeling a right way. When a leader acts in these ways group members will truly engage and own results as their own and will be able say "we did it ourselves."

CHAPTER SEVEN: SUMMARY QUESTIONS

1. At one time, studies of leadership looked at individual traits, problem situations, and group tasks as the variables that determined who could become a leader. More recent emphasis

has been placed on leader attitudes, skills, and the ability to engage others in ways that model and motivate participation as a team. Take a position on whether you believe a "leader is born" or a "leader is made." Explain how your position impacts your view of yourself as a leader or your view of those you'll be helping.

2. Burns says that the highest level of leadership is empowerment; a leader who inspires confidence in followers' abilities and then stimulates followers to act toward meeting their goals empowers others.

3. Assume that in your role as a peer educator you have been given the assignment to meet with a small group of students in a freshman residence hall who have been identified from their first set of midterm tests as being at risk for failing their classes. The hall director has sent a letter to these students instructing them to meet with you at a designated meeting time in the next week. Make a list of five or more things you will do to prepare for initiating this contact with these students. Why did you choose these five things?

4. What are four necessary conditions for establishing trusting and helpful group interactions when leading support groups for personal growth experiences?

5. Define the following words:
   a. Situational leadership
   b. "Tippers"
   c. Universalization
   d. Empowering leadership
   e. Conflict resolution

CHAPTER 8

Strategies for Academic Success

LEARNING OBJECTIVES

After completing this chapter, you will be able to

1. Recognize that learning is influenced for better or for worse by personal factors unique to each student's attitude, confidence level, time management, learning style, and study habits.
2. Understand the importance of internal motivation and self-awareness to learning.
3. Know the differences between active and passive approaches to learning.
4. Conduct an assessment interview to help students determine how effectively they use study strategies.
5. Assist students in developing a plan and using resources to improve learning effectiveness.
6. Define the following terms: self-regulation, personality style, prioritizing, balanced lifestyle, and self-efficacy.

●

Regardless of your peer educator position, one element will be common to all helping roles on any campus: you are working with college students, and they are engaged in a learning environment. Most students strive to achieve some level of success. College *success* could mean many different outcomes for any individual; however, commonly held definitions include acceptable grade averages, retention toward a degree, opportunity for career enhancement, attainment of productive life skills, and personal satisfaction. What do we know about how well students succeed in college?

STUDENT ACADEMIC SUCCESS: WHAT DO WE KNOW?

Data on college students and their success, measured by a variety of outcome standards, are less than encouraging. To understand the "bad news" of the difficulties and barriers that prevent students from achieving higher education goals is to also identify some of the solutions for promoting success. This overview is provided as a backdrop to identify what can be done to help students succeed.

Students Are Frequently Underprepared

According to the National Center for Education Statistics (U.S. Department of Education, 2003), an average of 28 percent of entering college freshmen in fall 2000 required at least one remedial course (reading, writing, or mathematics), and the proportion was much higher at public two-year colleges (42 percent). About three-fourths of all institutions and 93 percent of two-year institutions offered at least one remedial course for enrolled freshmen. This is a clear indication that these entering freshmen need remedial academic work to compete in many college classes. Their need for remediation has been linked to the intensity of

214

their high school preparation (Sax, Astin, Korn, & Mahoney, 2000). Implications point to the need for better preparation before entering college or a willingness to provide early intervention with incoming students to bring them "up to speed."

Students Are Vulnerable to Dropping Out Early in Their College Career

At four-year colleges, the majority of college students who drop out do so within their first two years (National Center for Education Statistics, 2007; Porter, 1990), and about 20–25 percent of freshmen leave college during their first year in college (ACT, Inc., 2002). Especially for first-time freshmen, the transition from high school to college can be demanding and stressful, and their vulnerability to academic, social, and emotional adjustment difficulties can lead to leaving college before their second year (Tinto, 1999; Upcraft, Gardner, & Associates, 1989).

Many Students Do Not Attain a Degree

We also know that across the higher education landscape, the statistics regarding student success as measured by semester-to-semester retention rates and graduation rates of two- and four- year degree programs are disappointing at best. At two-year institutions, graduation rates are approximately 30 percent within three years; at four-year colleges and universities, only six out of ten students actually earn their four-year degree (National Center for Higher Education Management Systems, 2009). It is becoming more and more of a priority with higher educational institutions to increase the retention rate. Because peer educators work to increase other students' probability for success in college, you can be a major influence in this priority outcome.

215

The fact that you are reading this book and doing this reflection indicates that you are still a student in college. However, think back and describe any point at which you had thoughts of leaving college and doing something else. If you never considered leaving college, think of a friend who did. What was happening that could have led you or your friend to leave? Why did you stay? Were there academic, personal, or situational reasons that influenced you?

Looking to the future, what do you believe are your chances of staying in college to reach the goal initially charted for your academic career? Might there at any point be reasons that you would choose a different direction? What would those be?

What Determines Whether Students Will Succeed?

It is important to both the institution and the student to understand what happens during the educational experience that creates a successful outcome or, as in some cases, a disappointment and a potential detour on what set out to be an educational path. College success is important to students because it demonstrates that they are meeting the expectation to achieve desired learning goals, thereby improving their chances of meeting long-term personal and career goals. Is there a crystal ball that can predict success? No, but considerable research has gone into trying to answer this question, and predictive formulas have been offered. Figure 8.1 groups these predictors into three categories of impact factors. Next we talk about which of these variables are key intervention targets when working directly with college students.

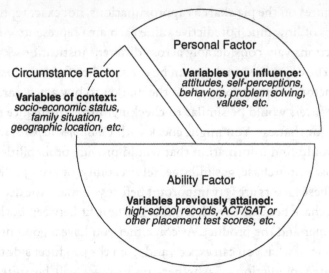

Figure 8.1. Factors Affecting Academic Performance

THREE CATEGORIES OF FACTORS INFLUENCING STUDENT SUCCESS

A good place to start in understanding Figure 8.1 is to consider the prospective college student as a consumer, a person prepared to "buy" into a product, education, to improve his or her life. The prospective student will probably need to submit some information to the potential college of choice. This information could include transcripts of past academic work, scores on achievement tests such as the ACT or SAT, and maybe recommendations or representative work samples. Most of these are "preconditions" we have labeled *ability factors*. They are used to predict acceptance to selective institutions, placement in appropriate class levels, or compatibility with an institution. As the pie chart indicates, these variables comprise about 50 percent of the prediction of the student's likelihood for academic success. Note, we are using

217

the figures on the pie chart as approximations, not exact representations of how much predictive value each area represents. Actual predictions vary considerably across different institutions.

The consumer analogy can be expanded to further illustrate this factor. Suppose you were in the market to buy a new car. The *ability factors* would be similar to checking out performance standards for that car. You might check with *Consumer Reports*, where you would find information that would provide probabilities for the cost of purchase, gas mileage, serviceability, or even preferred use. These factors are very important before you make the decision to purchase because they determine the best fit between both the consumer and the product. As consumer you have a good understanding of what you can expect, and from the producer side there is a good prediction of whether the product will be suited to your desired outcome. A key point about this category is that it represents a stable set of variables that will not be easy to alter once the decision is made. You cannot make a limousine out of a Volkswagen. Matching a student's ability, interest, and experience to the right institution is best done through initial decisions; otherwise dissatisfaction and altered course of direction, such as transferring or dropping out, would be an expected outcome.

The second category is labeled *circumstance factors*. These factors are based on your situation as determined by where you have come from and the conditions that you must live within. They include your socio-economic status, ethnicity, geographic location, family background, or even having to work a job and take care of a family while getting an education. These variables will definitely influence one's investment of time, energies, and motivation toward the college experience.

Again, we can illustrate how circumstance factors work to predict a student's "fit" with a college by going back to the consumer analogy of finding a successful mode of transportation. Situations like having to commute an hour each day in traffic, living in a frigid climate, and needing to take four kids to soccer practice all could influence the choices about the right car for the right circumstances. This is the same for education. Situations do affect the choices you make and how well you are able to balance education with the rest of your life. The pie chart indicates that this category represents about 10 percent of the influence on outcome probability. A student may decide to change some life circumstances that may alter and have an impact on academic success. For example, one might decide to cut back on work hours in order to have more time for study. Or a student might search for the right institution that is most adaptable to a specific situation. For example, to accommodate having a full-time job, one might seek more flexible options online or through a community college. However, the reality is that circumstances may not be easy to change and involve choices that are already a given part of a person's life, thereby making this area less likely for interventions by the peer educator.

The final category that influences college success is labeled *personal factors*. This third category includes a number of personal variables that are typically within the power of a person to influence, direct, or enhance in some way. Returning one more time to the transportation analogy, you personally can make a big difference in a car's overall performance by monitoring how fast you drive, performing regular maintenance service, learning better driving skills, and knowing what expert mechanic can help you solve a problem. This category is almost entirely within your control! Educationally, personal factors may include attitudes (motivation, work ethics), self-perceptions (confidence, self-efficacy), behaviors (work organization, study habits), problem solving (critical thinking and decision making), and values (personal preferences, beliefs).

Evidence indicates that many personal factors, described as psycho-social variables, have significant influence on college

219

outcomes (Robbins, Lauver, Le, Davis, Langley, & Carlstrom, 2004). Looking at very specific personal factors has confirmed further evidence of a link between these attributes and academic outcomes such as grade point average and retention. The following list illustrates several types of personal factors shown by research to affect student success:

- Engagement (Astin, 1993; Kuh, Cruce, Shoup, Kinzie, & Gonyea, 2008; Pascarella & Terezini, 1991)
- Social and institutional support (Kuh, 1996)
- Intrinsic motivation (Bong, 2004)
- Self-efficacy (Chemers, Hu, & Garcia, 2001; Friedlander, Reid, Shupak, & Cribbie, 2007)
- Individual preference and compatibility (DiTiberio & Hammer, 1993; Dunning, 2003)
- Stress management (Davidson & Beck, 2006; Pritchard & Wilson, 2003), and well-being (Newton, Kim, & Newton, 2006)
- Organization and study approach (VanZile-Tamsen, 2001)
- Self-regulation (Lahmers & Zulauf, 2000; Nonis & Hudson, 2006)

Next we define how the above terms represent personal aspects of students' lives that can make a difference in the success of their college experience.

PERSONAL VARIABLES THAT MAKE A DIFFERENCE

Learning Is Engagement

Learning is work! It is not a passive activity to be pursued with a lackluster attitude. As with all work, energy is necessary and must be focused on the task at hand. Just as with physical work, at the end of a long study activity, most of us will feel tired and depleted mentally. Our brains are tired. This is compensated for, however, by the satisfaction of a job well done. Considerable research has shown that engagement—investment of one's attention and activity—toward educational goals is imperative for successful outcome.

Engagement includes more than study and activities assigned in the classroom. Research has shown that students involved in extra-class and informal activities including social activities, concerts, sporting events, and organizations increase their motivation and commitment to their overall educational experience. The student who becomes involved with college life on many levels has made an investment of time and energy that pays offs in dividends of satisfaction and higher academic performance.

Engagement Provides Connections to Support

Effective students are able to identify and make connections with resources in their environment. These resources include peers, instructors, and service personnel who can provide support, information, and personal development resources. On the peer level students will connect to a social network, an identity group that will provide much of the social interaction and time commitment including the living environment, social friendship group, and sometimes those taking classes in a major or special cohort group. Social contacts can offer emotional support, social outlet, and examples of how to manage college life, including time commitment and study habits. However, social influence may also pose problems by creating distractions from personal goals, bad habits such as excessive partying, or nonessential time wasters. The overall environment of college life may range from formal curriculum and bricks and mortar to extra-class activities and social events that can serve as a seamless part of the educational mission; in the other extreme, the environmental context may include

221

opposing forces counteracting the overall effectiveness of the educational mission. The peer educator is most helpful when able to assist the student partner to be able to view the impact of the whole social and environmental impact upon their educational experience. It is also important to understand the resources that would be available for the student and understand how to take advantage of these in a timely and proactive manner. Good students make use of campus resources.

Internal Versus External Motivation

Most of us work more productively and earnestly when we are internally motivated. This seems to be especially true for college students. The more relevancies the student experiences between the hard work of study and the life goal being pursued, the more likely he or she will stay focused on the hard work required to master knowledge and skills. Determining a major that fits with future life goals is a tremendous motivator for many students. They can see the connection between courses and the sustaining work and lifestyle they hope to have upon graduation. College makes sense when there is a strong connection between academic success and success in life.

For many college students, however, motivation seems to exist external to the learner. These external motivators may be, for instance, parental expectations, the need for lower-cost medical insurance, satisfying a significant other, or simply delaying the decision of "what next in my life after high school." When it is time to buckle down and apply the hard work of study, these external motivators provide little incentive to complete the learning task. Unfortunately, many students motivated by external factors never experience the satisfaction of successful study and academic accomplishment leading to life goals, work, and a profession. Because they are motivated by external factors, they approach academic work passively; therefore, they fail to generate sufficient energy and related academic work strategies to assure success in the learning outcomes associated with the study experience they implemented.

Internal Motivation Facilitates Active Learning

The contrast between external and internal motivation can be seen in the respective types of learning that take place: passive and active. Consider the task of reading an assigned chapter. Most dive right in, with great expectations of finishing the assignment successfully. But what is success? They start strong, but they often finish weak. When tiredness begins to set in, they often ask themselves, how many more pages must I read to finish this assignment? They flip through the chapter to find the end. They note the page number they are on and the last page number of the chapter. They mark the end with a bookmark and mentally count the number of pages to completion. The reading goal becomes reaching the bookmark rather than understanding the text. Do you recognize yourself through this description? If not, congratulations! You are more likely an active reader. On the other hand, if you see yourself in this description, you may be more of a passive reader, and you have some work to do. An active reader would have glanced through the chapter, noted heading and subheadings, looked at summary questions or statements, and perhaps generated questions they seek to answer as they read the chapter.

There are many strategies that distinguish the active versus passive learner. Table 8.1 describes the differences between an active and passive learner for specific learning tasks. These strategies include establishing a work environment for study, setting goals, balancing time and activity, reading actively, finding one's voice in the academic conversation, using to-do lists, and developing and using study groups.

223

Table 8.1. Differences Between Active and Passive Learning

Learning Activity	Active Learner	Passive Learner
Reading	Reads to answer questions Reads to make connections between ideas from various sources	Reads to finish the assignment
Study	Uses learning drills	Glances through notes, without any plan
Learning environment	Establishes a work setting	Random settings (reads in bed, on the couch in front of TV

Reflection Point 8.2: What Does Going to College Mean?

Are your reasons more internally or externally determined? Answering this question sets the stage for subsequent work.

Think of yourself from the point of which you entered college as a freshmen student. What reasons best describe your intentions for being in college? Why did you choose to go to college? What did you want to get from the experience? Try to come up with at least four or five reasons. Be open and candid with yourself to make clear reasons that include personal and social, as well as academic and career.

Looking at your list, label which of these would be categorized as external motivators and which ones more internal motivators.

Now, looking at yourself from the present moment, have your reasons for being in college changed? In what ways have they changed?

Learning Demands a Confident Attitude

A necessary condition for successful learning is the belief in one's ability and knowledge about how to learn. This sense of confidence applied to learning is called self-efficacy. Self-efficacy is gained through past experiences, observations of other people's successful behavior, reassurance and verbal encouragement from others, and the recognition that past successes can be applied and adjusted to new situations (Bandura, 1997).

Most students enter college with optimism that they will do "OK." However, that optimism may be quickly challenged when encountering problems such as finding that expectations can be higher in college courses and that freedom or discipline to act is now the student's responsibility. This leads to the conclusion that when coupled with organized, meaningful actions, self-efficacy is necessary for successful outcomes. Conversely, students showing discouragement and signs of being defeated are not likely to follow through with purposeful action. The lack of confidence may create an inability to act and the probable self-fulfilling outcome of failure. Such self-defeatism can be seen in the example of Eric.

Eric's Story

Eric failed the first mid-term exam in his geology class. Having stayed up all night memorizing the name of igneous and sedimentary rocks, he thought he was prepared. The questions were difficult and his failing score meant that passing the course would take a lot of work. Discouraged, his interest in the class lagged, he found excuses to miss the voluntary lab experiences, and finally he stopped going to class altogether. Eric had other options such as finding a tutor, making an appointment with the instructor, or changing his study habits to plan ahead better, but it just seemed easier to "give up."

Think of a time when you encountered a challenge that was somewhat novel but you felt confident and determined to tackle that challenge and believed you would be successful. What gave you the confidence to feel that way? Were there strategies that you used previously that could be applied to the new situation?

Now think of an opposite situation in which you encountered a new task and felt that you had no idea of what to do and how to do it. How did you think and act in this situation? Was there a tendency to give up, or did you go ahead and try to see whether you could figure out what to do no matter the outcome? What did you learn from this type of challenge?

Know Yourself: How to Use Personal Strengths

Individual differences require challenges to be met through approaches best fitted to your style, your interests, and your best manner of interacting with the world around you. It is important to know and understand how you operate best in the world. A good place to start is identifying your personal style or what we sometimes refer to as your personality. One dimension of personality includes the way you prefer to interact with people. For example, do you consider yourself more of an introvert or an extrovert? Introverts tend to reflect and observe before acting, and extroverts tend to act and then reflect. Or another personality difference could be whether you prefer lots of structure and direction, or whether you prefer greater room for exploration and creativity without structured restriction. The Myers-Briggs Type Indicator and other similar personality inventories provide considerable information for understanding the impact of personality on tasks such as how you organize your room, choose a career, or get along with a friend (Myers & Myers, 1995).

Individual personality differences also apply to student learning experiences. When students individually work, learn, communicate, or complete team projects, they have individual preferences that often require less effort, come more naturally, or better fit the circumstance (DiTiberio & Hammer, 1993; Hirsh, Hirsh, & Hirsh, 2003). For example, extroverts are high in verbal and interpersonal skills, whereas introverts value reading and individual time and need quiet for concentration.

Similarly, people have different learning styles or preferences for taking in information; depending on the learning style, seeing, listening, reading or writing, or acting may be preferred. The simple test of your preference is to recognize a preferred method for receiving and recording information and instruction in order to understand and use a concept. If you were visiting a friend who lived in another city, how would you prefer directions be given? Would you like a visual map carefully outlining all landmarks or would you rather be told in conversation? Or would you prefer to "walk" through the experience as though you were acting it out? Having preferences for receiving information applies to learning. Which way do you learn best—by the use of text, diagrams, images, spoken directions, or action-oriented demonstrations such as lab work? Using your preferred learning modality enhances retention and recognition.

Learning Improves by Managing Stress and Maintaining a Sense of Well-Being

The management of one's personal overall well-being affects performance in intellectual, emotional, social, and physical domains. The traditional college-aged student, eighteen to twenty-five, can enjoy life with vitality, resilience, and usually without the constraints and demands that may inhibit possibilities as one moves into more set life patterns further into adulthood. College is time

227

that students can explore new behaviors such as staying up all night, eating pizza at 3 in the morning, drinking alcohol to excess, and taking on more than a few daring chances because it is fun. As the saying goes, "these are the best of times," yet stress due to a variety of pressures is cited as the most common symptom affecting students' physical and mental health (American College Health Association, 2009). The freedom for college students to experiment and make choices about their lifestyle is an important developmental step. A recent study of college freshmen indicated that students with positive health behaviors had higher grade point averages and overall greater life satisfaction (Newton & Kim, 2009; Newton, Kim, & Newton, 2006). Positive health behaviors included in the study were healthy eating, vigorous or moderate physical activity, personal management (including relaxation, sleep, time, creativity), and reduced alcohol consumption. A well-balanced life that includes sufficient sleep, good nutrition, exercise, social outlets, and time for recreation are part of a successful lifestyle.

Learning Is Using Time and Organization Effectively

Let's consider the situation of a hypothetical student named Suzie. Suzie enjoys college life—she has many friends including three roommates in an apartment suite, she belongs to a sorority, she is on a student activities committee, has a part-time job working as a lab assistant, does aerobics three days a week, and is taking a full load of required classes in order to qualify for a special internship next term. Suzie would say she is happy to be in college, but she would also say she is feeling stressed, even frazzled, about balancing all of her activities and assignments. There is just not enough time in the day, yet there is very little that she would give up or change at this point without feeling disappointed or defeated. This is not an unusual scene for many students.

Reflection Point 8.4: Too Much to Do with So Little Time to Do It

---

Can you identify situations similar to Suzie's, either involving yourself or other students you know? College provides many opportunities that are difficult to pass up, and it is quite easy to be overextended and feel overwhelmed. Are you able to resolve this dilemma by answering the following questions?

Do you use a tool for organizing your time such as a planner or to-do list? How efficiently does your organization of time and effort work toward accomplishing goals and commitments? Discuss the pluses and minuses of what you do.

Does your time management allow for flexibility? Does it balance the many aspects of your life or do you tend to work with intensive time periods where you churn out the most pressing task at the last minute because it is due?

Time and organizational management is a life skill that more often than not occurs as a matter of habit without conscious thought or a clearly defined system. You do things a certain way and by trial and error you find out what works (or not) and make some adaptations along the way. If you are lucky and have developed good organizing skills, you may have a system that now works well for you. However, since over half of all students are complaining about too many demands and pressure in their life, time management is clearly a problem for many students. As a peer educator, you are likely to encounter this as an issue with students in nearly any aspect of your service. Here is a brief overview of effective time and organization management.

1. *Prioritize.* There are only so many hours in the day (week/month) and so many things to do; how can they all get done? The first thing to do is prioritize what is on the list. Priorities are determined by levels of importance, urgency or time press,

and amount of time needed for accomplishment. Be aware, though, that urgency (deadline demands) might push back longer term but more important tasks until they become an urgency (and that paper that has been due for over a month becomes a crisis when you have only one day to complete it). A longer-term view is important to balance urgency and importance demands.

2. *Organize.* The way you tackle your "to do" list can make a big difference on how efficiently the task gets done. Here are a few ideas for organizing effectively: (a) break bigger tasks down into units with separate actions to be accomplished. For example, that paper that is due in four weeks can be broken down into finding a topic and doing background research; writing an outline and keying the main points to be covered; completing a draft that pulls the ideas together; and finally, editing the draft into a smooth, acceptable paper to be submitted. (b) Cluster your day and even week into blocks of time for activities that will be complementary to each other. For example, if you have two classes in the morning with an hour between classes, use that time for things that can be done in the one-hour break. (c) If you multitask, cluster activities that, when done together, are completed more efficiently. For example, if you need to run to the store because you ran out of bread and coffee, can you also complete a couple of other errands that can be done on the way?

3. *Customize.* Know when you do the best work for the time of day and the setting. For example, some people are most alert in the mornings and can do more concentrated and creative tasks at that time, whereas later in the day they might be better at doing more active things like exercise, running errands, or meeting with friends for a study group. Each person is different and should map out what works best and try to adapt to that type of schedule. Unfortunately, many students procrastinate their day away so

230

that all of their academic assignments are left until the late hours of the night (or morning) when the mind may be most fatigued. The other principle important to individualizing your activity planning and mapping is to leave some flexible time for those unexpected demands that come up. Also, remember that a plan is only a plan, so being able to adapt or be flexible is useful and necessary. Finally, balance, the art of mixing in all of the necessary ingredients—including sleep, food, social, recreation, and studying—will actually enhance the quality of your total experience.

4. *Execution.* The most important part of a plan is accomplishing that plan. Make sure that you have the resources and the opportunities to make your "to do's" become realities. A key to accomplishment is to remember the 3 Rs, *results, relief,* and *reward.* Results provide the intrinsic motivation to continue and be proud of what you have done. Cross out that action on the list, put a star on your daily planner, and reward yourself for achieving milestones by taking a break to do something you have been wanting to do for pleasure. Relief is another natural experience that comes from knowing the goal is accomplished, so take a sigh or relief and let yourself relax.

Learning Is Being Able to Self-Regulate

Self-regulation is the ability to consciously and intentionally manage personal resources to accomplish daily tasks. It means that an individual can integrate personal attributes (personality, learning style, and interests), work habits (managing time, organizing study, and self discipline), emotions (stress management, acknowledging and satisfying the "feeling rainbow"), support resources (electronic, people, and services), and meaningful self-direction (setting goals, directing actions, making adjustments, and achieving outcomes).

Students come to college after having been regulated by other people much of their life. Parents may have told you when to get up in the morning, taken care of most of your meals, and even influenced your decisions. High school filled your day with classes and monitored your attendance, while teachers made sure that you knew assignments were due or parents would be notified. For most students, the transition from high school to college is a major shift from a structured, more dependent lifestyle to an unstructured, more independent lifestyle. How well students function through this transition is dependent on how well they are able to assume self-regulation.

Are you able to organize your daily activities effectively? Do you maintain limits and boundaries? Do you address problem situations and have ways to implement solutions? Do you learn from mistakes and are you able to make corrections?

Exercise 8.1: A Week of Activity

Reflect upon the past week of your life as a student. Another option is to keep a log of typical daily activities throughout a given week. List all of the tasks that you perform, including academic, recreational, social, and physical, as well as daily maintenance, such as eating and sleeping. When you have completed your inventory, compile a summary of how much time you spent in the various categories.

How well balanced are these activities? Did you get plenty of sleep, exercise, and contact with friends? Did you eat regular meals? Did you have time to prepare for classes?

If you were to change your schedule in the next week, what would you do? In what areas do you feel a deficit? How would you change the activities to create the balance you desire?

NOW WHAT? A PROCESS MODEL TO HELP STUDENTS SUCCEED

This chapter has provided an overview of some of the important factors of students' academic success. We have emphasized how personal factors, including attitudes, motivations, behaviors, lifestyle, and emotion, are in many ways connected to achieving individual goals. The main focus has been on academic success, as it is obviously the main mission of higher education. However, learning is a part of all aspects of life and necessary if we want to adapt, grow, and maximize potentials to achieve any life goal. As a peer educator you may be involved with students in a specific area from residence life to health education, leadership training to service learning, or perhaps you are directly involved with academic progress as a tutor or learning center mentor. In the remainder of this chapter we describe a procedure for working with students toward the goal of improving their academic success. This process most certainly will be useful to those serving as academic tutors or working with freshmen orientation classes, special retention, or in academic enhancement centers. It will apply to other outcomes and serve as a model for intervention. An outline of the model is depicted in Figure 8.2.

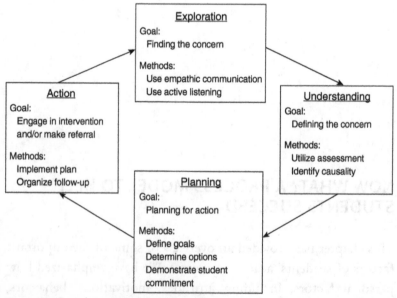

Figure 8.2. Academic Success Process

Exploration Stage

The peer educator's role during the exploration stage is to use a process of discussion, reflection, and discovery about how the educational experience is going and whether the student is achieving what was intended when starting the venture into college. When focusing on the educational experience, we usually assume that the student had academic goals such as going to class and preparing for assignments, tests, and papers. The exploration stage might also help with these types of issues: one's compatibility with courses, fitting in with classmates, meeting with instructors, utilizing help sessions, or just managing daily tasks of living. Of course, some students might indicate very minimal goals, saying something like, "Everybody expected me to go to college," or "I didn't have anything else to do." However, even these statements, no matter how minimal they may be, are a starting point for exploration.

If we go back to developmental theory described in Chapter Two, we know that college students are facing the challenge of becoming independent, developing a more individualized identity, forming interpersonal relationships, gaining a sense of purpose, and defining vocational interest. So these personal objectives themselves are learning experiences that may not seem as formal as classroom success but are nonetheless very important and certainly worthy of being explored and defined.

Recall the descriptive model you were first introduced to in Chapter One; this is the stage that we described as "what." You are essentially asking the student "what is going on in your life as a student?" "Where have you been?" "Where are you going?" "What does it mean to you?" It includes the listening and responding skills described in Chapter Four. These skills help you clarify beyond simple "yes" or "no" responses. But it also includes letting

235

the person being mentored describe strengths and weaknesses, highlights and pitfalls. Remember that you, as a facilitator, are not judging or evaluating the students but allowing them to clarify what is happening in their life, and you are using the conversation to allow them to make their own conclusions. Think of the process as an art that is similar to aikido, or the way of going with the energy of the subject to let its own momentum create the next action. In a true sense, having good communication with someone who understands, clarifies, and explores openly another's experience can proceed to a greater sense of direction and may prepare the student for the next stage of the process.

Exercise 8.2: Practice Interview with a Peer Partner

Now that you have an understanding of the personal factors that have an impact on student success, practice a developmental interview with a peer partner (either someone in your training group or another student you know who is willing to participate). This is an opportunity to use the interpersonal communication and problem-solving skills gained from Chapters Four and Five, as well as the information provided in this chapter. Here are example questions that may help stimulate the student to explore her or his role as a learner.

What have you enjoyed most about your experience here in college?
    What has been the most difficult part of being a student?
    (Note: It is often useful to use a strategy called bracketing, which asks opposite ends of a continuum such as best/worst, most enjoyable/least enjoyable.)

What has been a highlight for you this year?

236

What are three words that describe your learning style? Elaborate on how they describe you.

What habit would you most like to change?

What advice would you give a younger brother or sister about how to do well in class and still enjoy his or her college experience?

Remember, whatever questions you ask to start a conversation, the key to engaging the student partner is to use your active listening and responding skills from Chapter Four.

Exercise 8.2 is an example of the procedure being explained here for helping students improve and succeed toward academic achievement. The goal for this process is to provide the opportunity for students to achieve competence in special areas, do well in the classroom, complete a degree, attain employability skills, or enrich and expand knowledge and proficiency for its own sake. However, we also realize that there are many reasons that students change their goals and end up stopping or dropping out. Sometimes these are reasons they cannot control such as personal relationships, financial difficulties, family problems, or work opportunities. It is even true that not making "the grade" can channel a person toward a goal that better fits the student's interest and ability. Because it can help provide the student understanding of the circumstances that were experienced, this process can be useful when an academic goal is not reached or is changed. After all, setbacks can still lead to a different approach or new goals.

Understanding Stage

Exploration can clarify a focus for or direction of an area in which a student may desire more information and better self-realization. In a sense, this is the point at which students may gain from deepening the process to learn about themselves and receive some objectivity as well as insight. An initial direction established during the exploration stage could lead to a focus on a number of arenas of inquiry. These areas could include assessing compatibility with a major, looking at the way one studies for a course, clarifying motivation, looking at health and fitness behaviors, forming friendships and managing relationships, dealing with stress and the rigors of multiple demands, and determining time and self-management. Of course, this list could be extended to include many more areas. In this stage, understanding develops by being able to assess an area of life in more detail. It is much like getting a physical in order to know one's overall health status; we're measured on several dimensions, and we receive an objective reading. These measures and their subsequent feedback help students know where they are and what can be done about it.

Recommended during this stage is the use of inventories and assessments that can help map out a student's strengths and weaknesses. Become familiar with a variety of these inventories; they identify patterns and tendencies of an individual and can

238

provide useful feedback about where a student stands in regard to peers or in some cases established criterion considered to be a standard. These inventories are not meant to be used as medical tests or psychological diagnosis, but they have been developed from a theory base and tested with student samples to establish good reliability and validity of measurement. The following inventories are accessible either on-line or in written form. Typically, they can be accessed by the public for a relatively inexpensive fee and in some cases for no charge. If not available through a public Web site they are frequently available as resources at campus offices such as academic assistance centers, career centers, counseling services, and student health centers. Many of these inventories are self-assessments that can be readily used by the students themselves or during the peer-mentor program. In some cases, however, the peer mentors need to be trained on how to use the inventories and interpret the results, or they need to refer the students to professionals who can assist with debriefing.

- Study skills and learning assessments: LASSI (Learning and Study Strategies Inventory), CLEI (College Learning Effectiveness Inventory), SRI (Student Readiness Inventory)
- Career inventories and exploration programs: DISCOVER (ACT), SIGI–Plus career interactive
- Health appraisal and fitness testing: TestWell, HBA (Health Behaviors Assessment)
- Alcohol and drug appraisal: E-Chug, Alcohol 101, alcohol use inventories online
- Learning styles: VARK (Visual, Auditory, Read/Write and Kinesthetic)
- Personality style: Keirsey, Rotter Locus of Control

The outcome of the understanding stage is for students to gain enough information to accomplish the "so what" level of

239

understanding. In other words, they have explored some of the most important things going on in their own life (including thoughts, feelings, and achievements) and have received further information to assess how they stand in terms of specific factors whether they be academic, career, health, relationships, or personal development. At this point, they are ready to enter the planning stage.

Planning Stage

From the exploration and understanding stages, an individual brings to the planning stage information that identifies an area or areas that could be improved or adjusted. Recall Chapter Five's discussion about problem solving strategies and particularly the idea that a person may turn an area of need or deficiency into a goal and direction. The planning stage has also been referred to as the "now what" stage.

An important question to consider when working on a plan with a student is the student's readiness to develop and stay with a plan. Knowing how prepared a student may be to make a change is tracked by levels of readiness (Prochaska, Norcross, & DiClemente, 1994). The lowest level of readiness is precontemplation: there may seem to be a lack of concern, and the problem is addressed only because someone else identifies it. An example might be a student sent to the writing lab who thinks such assistance is unneeded and is there only because the teacher sent him. Level 2 is contemplation, characterized by awareness tempered with ambivalence. An example might be a student who says, "I would like to study more, but I really don't have enough time." Level 3 is preparation, which may include the experimentation and willingness to at least make small changes. An example might be a student who says, "I am willing to use a tutor for the next 3 weeks, just to see if it makes any difference." Level 4 is action: the student is ready and willing to directly take steps to correct a problem or deficit. This person should be ready to take reasonable action and stay with it in order to see results. Level 5 is described as maintenance: action and solutions have been addressed before; however, a need has been identified to continue and take further steps.

You will encounter some students who are only at precontemplation and show up to a referring service with little motivation; they desire to do nothing more than comply with a teacher, parent, or friend's recommendation. The goal at this level is mainly to raise awareness and provide opportunity for the student to improve readiness. At the contemplative level, a goal might be to develop a plan that lets the student try out new strategies or look at options without yet making a long-term commitment. If a person is at the planning stage, she is showing sufficient readiness to make a directed plan but will frequently need support to monitor and adapt and make changes, and will need some continued reinforcement of efforts to stay with the plan. At any of the three readiness levels, from precontemplative to planning, it is very important to make whatever plan that evolves very explicit and potentially in a contract-type format. Action- or maintenance-level students have strong enough commitment to carry out plans, but they may need the inputs and suggestions to help deal with hurdles or new interferences that might arise. Understanding and including readiness as a part of the planning initiative is crucial to success.

Action Stage

This is the point where a plan has been made and action has been specified. It is important at this stage for a plan not to end up like a New Year's resolution that sounded good but was never carried through. The four elements for maintaining action include (1) self-monitoring tools such as schedule sheets, to-do lists,

241

calendars with check-off items, and journals or logs; (2) monitoring and check-in points, including predetermined times to check in with a peer educator or a peer buddy system; (3) renegotiation points at which, based upon review, adaptations can be made; and (4) outcome evaluations in which progress can be objectively measured either against the specified goal or through measures such as improvements based upon the specified objective. When a plan is made to use referral to another resource, the referral itself can be monitored by scheduling a follow-up to determine how the referral has worked out and if there is a need for further input. In addition to the help you provide in supporting a student with a plan, the peer educator also receives feedback on the impact of a referral.

SUMMARY

This chapter describes college success as the most important outcome for all college students. Success is described in broad terms that include the institution's goal that students will develop knowledge and skills through educational contact from matriculation to graduation. It also can be very individualized because each student may have differing motivations and goals for being in a college environment. A major determinant for individual achievement of success involves the influence and impact of the personal variables including attitudes, dispositions, and behaviors. These personal variables are within the influence of students, who may make improvements and adapt in order to succeed with the talents and circumstances that they were given. Active learning as opposed to being a passive recipient is a key ingredient for success. Additional personal variables, including developing self-efficacy and self-regulation abilities and using resources, are ingredients for achieving optimum results. Peer educators are in a position to play influential roles in helping the students with whom they interact achieve success outcomes. A process model is useful for the peer mentor working with students to guide them from initial exploration to assessment and planning to final action and outcome evaluation.

CHAPTER EIGHT: SUMMARY QUESTIONS

1. Compare active with passive learning behavior.
2. Why are personal factors a key to student success?
3. What strategies can a peer educator use to help students explore their situations as a learner?
4. What resources and instruments are available to assist the process for finding and understanding the student's concern?
5. Define self-efficacy, self-regulation, and readiness for change.

CHAPTER 9

Using Campus Resources and Referral Techniques

LEARNING OBJECTIVES

After completing this chapter, you will be able to

1. List available campus and community resources.
2. Assess the appropriateness of campus and community resources available to students. Know whom to consult when assisting students.
3. Refer students to appropriate campus and community resources.
4. Understand and use appropriate knowledge resources and online support, such as virtual communities.
5. Offer postreferral follow-up and supports.

●

Sometimes called the "We Generation," students born between 1978 and 2000 are the youngest, largest, most diverse, best educated, and most powerful generation ever in America. They are global, wired, hopeful, responsible, and tolerant. They are activists ready to attack and solve the problems of environment, energy, economy, and war (Greenberg & Weber, 2008).

244

So what is needed for the "We Generation" to maintain themselves and function successfully as pioneers of the twenty-first century? Three important processes can help students face the challenges of this era. These processes include *adaptation to change, capacity to choose,* and *connection to people or resources.*

THE THREE CS: CHANGE, CHOICE, AND CONNECTION

Major discoveries throughout history have significantly impacted the lives of a given era's people. Examples include discovering how to use fire, learning to build tools from metal, creating means for mass industrial production, developing machines that fly, and using the microchip to make smaller computers with larger memories. In today's world, discoveries occur at a faster rate than ever before, with equally fast impact upon life situations. Literally, yesterday's discovery becomes outdated within months, and accumulation of knowledge and invention continues at a geometric rate. Peter Russell (2008) calls on this reality in his discussion about how we measure our age. Most of us measure our age in years. Calculating age in years reflects an assumption that a year is a significant mark of accomplishment or change or transition. However, given today's pace of accomplishment and change, a more accurate measure would be to describe your age in days. A lot happens in a day or over the course of days—as much now as what used to happen over the course of a year. To calculate your present age in this way go to the following link and recognize how fast your life may be moving relative to the changing world (http://www.peterrussell.com/Odds/WorldClock.php).

245

Adapting to change is a necessity if you want to be current with your contemporaries and prepared for personal and vocational viability. There is some concern that too much change and too many options has negative side effects such as increased stress, feelings of alienation, and short-sightedness by living only in the moment (Newton, 1998). The author of the book *Crazy Busy: Overstretched, Overbooked and About to Snap* captures the image of a stressed society, suggesting that the world has "gone ADD" (Hallowell, 2006). Living in a world of rapid change calls for many skills that vary from multitasking to learning to relax, from discriminating among options to learning to focus, from learning a particular job skill to transferring established abilities to new situations. Resources abound that can provide timely information, advice, and counsel; however, these resources must be accessed and utilized. As a peer educator, you can help students find appropriate resources.

Another result of a changing world is the more pressing need to make *choices*. We sometimes refer to our home location as a village, town, city, or other defined location within a geographic area. However, immediate access to information and resources from almost any corner of the world creates a figurative backyard of international opportunity, in which Internet communication, multinational businesses, and intercultural exchanges are a daily reality. The original village was relatively easy to define in terms of the rules and standards that were known and accepted as the way for life. Now, the rules and norms of society are in more flux than ever before, with myriad options for social contact and intimacy—the important areas where individuals receive support and security in their lives. The students of today have multiple life options as portrayed by media representation or actual contact with pluralistic possibilities. However, although the revolution of a changing society presents challenge, it also offers the opportunity for new solutions. A great portion of this opportunity resides with the potential of the peer group to influence themselves, each other, and the world around them (Newton, 2000).

As a peer educator, you are an example of students on a campus who may be well positioned to provide influence and suggest options during a period when others are looking for answers. Malcolm Gladwell in his book, *The Tipping Point*, (2000) suggested that a few people, the tippers, could have significant influence on peers by their ability to network a large number of contacts, be "tuned-in" as sensitive detectors of the interests and whims of others, and communicate in a manner that others will remember.

Beyond being able to adapt to change and make choices is the need for students to find connections. Connections begin with primary support networks of friends, family, and personal contact. Connections also may extend to those with whom interactions may be professional, recreational, or interest based. Even more broadly, connections might include those with knowledge, training, expertise, or other resource information. Students today face the paradox of striving to be more independent and self-reliant, on the one hand ("I can do it alone"), and, on the other hand, searching for personal support amid the pressures and demands that they experience. However, students sitting by themselves are typically not as alone as they appear. If they are near a computer, cell phone, or mobile device, they are connected as if they are in a room full of friends (Eberhardt, 2007). Connections are not limited to our immediate surroundings, as social networking via Facebook™, My Space™, and other online social networking locations are immediate and universal. For example, as an aftermath of the April 16, 2007, student shootings on the Virginia Tech campus, students used these means to build a sense of community, share important news separating fact from fiction, support each other while sharing grief, and, at the same time, inhibit attacking, derogatory, or

247

insensitive comments (MacEachran, 2007). Connecting is now possible through a multitude of channels. At the same time, with all of the possibilities for instant and wide range access to information worldwide, there is still a need for "high-touch," person-to-person contact, which cannot be replaced with high-tech (Milliron, Plinske, & Noonan-Terry, 2008).

A very important role for the peer educator is to assist students as they seek, find, and contact necessary resources outside their daily routine. As a peer educator, you must have a firm grasp of available campus and community resources and know their appropriate uses. In addition to knowledge of resources, you must learn how to direct students to these resources effectively.

RESOURCES AND REFERRAL

Campus and Community Resources

When any student strives to achieve a goal, whether it is academic success, overcoming a personal obstacle, or achieving a new skill, the effort will almost certainly entail the use of special resources. Every campus has in place an array of people and services with primary responsibility for providing this sort of assistance. Student affairs offices, various academic services, faculty members, community services, and even private businesses are potential sources for information and aid. Most of these forms of assistance will involve human resources, but there are also many physical facilities and technological resources. In today's world the reliance on digital media, high tech, and Web development will provide a rapidly expanding array of opportunities for information sharing that formerly were available only from face-to-face interviews or library searches. Online and telephone hot lines such as 800- (or 888- or 866-)

connections are additional sources. Knowing where to go for what becomes crucial information for effective peer helping.

Many students are unfamiliar with their campus and community resources and thus are unable to take advantage of them. Another problem students face when contemplating the use of campus resources is the misinformation and rumors that sometimes circulate about an office, service, or resource. Both lack of information and misinformation can quickly block use of a resource that could be a valuable asset in accomplishing personal goals.

At times, students may feel reluctant and even embarrassed to admit needing help. Even asking a question of a faculty member after class may be difficult for fear of appearing stupid. Therefore, peer educators can play a significant role in providing objective and reassuring information about the resources available. In your role, you may be called upon to share information about the existence of a resource or about its adequacy and quality, sometimes dispelling myths that might otherwise discourage students from taking advantage of available services.

It is also noteworthy that peer educators can often provide evaluative feedback to campus and community resources regarding students' perceptions of the services in question. This information gives the agency, program, or department the opportunity to clarify its role, improve publicity, and even improve the quality of its services and interactions with students.

Students will often hang back and avail themselves of support services and resource opportunities only when a situation has reached critical proportions. Peer educators can provide an important and advantageous service by getting a student to sources of assistance before the crisis breaks, when prevention and early intervention are possible. Ideally, campus resources are best used to help students achieve their personal and academic goals before those goals have been threatened by a developing problem.

Exercise 9.1: Locating Resources

Depending upon the goals and objectives of your mentoring program, devise a list of at least ten resources—sources of information, services, offices, or other support venues—that would be useful for referral. For example, if the goal of your program is to assist international students in their adjustment and orientation to your campus, the following might be considered important resources: language partners, bus and transportation systems, study and tutorial locations, food and eating options, emergency health care, setting up a bank account, reading a campus map, learning customs, or using the library.

Ten Potential Referral Resources

1.
2.
3.
4.
5.
6.
7.
8.
9.
10.

After this list has been developed, assign different individuals (or do this on your own if this is an independent study) to locate data about the specific resources, including telephone, location, Web page, the names of individuals to contact, hours of availability, and any other useful specific information important for the situation. This could be done by the individuals within a group as a "scavenger hunt"; it could result in a resource manual or a basic Question and Answer (Q&A) or Frequently Asked Questions (FAQ) resource for a Web page. This same exercise can be extended to similar resources available outside of a community by doing an online scavenger hunt. In this latter case it would be important to follow up by checking out the authority of the site for reputation and validity of information (see *caveat emptor* precautions described later in this chapter).

When to Refer

Frequently the beginning peer educator finds it difficult to determine when to refer a student to another resource. It is natural to want to help—that's what draws people into the peer educator role—but watch out if you find yourself feeling pressured to relieve and resolve the concern of the person requesting and needing assistance. This pressure can lead to giving quick advice, offering a solution by providing a suggestion out of your own repertoire of answers, or immediately directing the student to another resource that seems likely to hold the solution. Often your own solution may not be the answer to someone else's concerns, and a quick referral may feel like a brush-off or the beginning of a runaround. The following guidelines (adapted from Ender, Saunders-McCaffrey, & Miller, 1979) will help you make adequate and welcome referrals.

Listen Carefully   The first and often most important step is to listen carefully and clearly so as to understand what the individual needs in the way of assistance. Look back to Chapter Four for a discussion of the process of becoming an effective communicator. And remember, as a peer, you will probably be perceived as an approachable, friendly resource. Your support, encouragement, and guidance may be sufficient to help an individual figure out what to do, but there will be times when the student's concern is beyond your knowledge, greater than you wish to handle, or otherwise in need of professional attention. This is the point when you consider referral.

Know Your Limits   The second important item to address regarding referrals is to know your own limits for giving assistance. As a general rule, when in doubt, refer the student to a more

251

qualified resource. Trying to help a student with a serious problem when you possess only minimal skill and experience in that area may do more harm than good. Take, for example, the peer educator who, with little knowledge about the world of work, attempts to assist a student in clarifying a career decision. Such a student is apt to believe that the help received is the help needed in this area and may therefore be reluctant to seek additional assistance from a more qualified source. The student may waste valuable time following a course of action that does not fit her or his real needs, such as majoring in a field that proves to be without long-term interest to them, and this may eventually lead to frustration with the process.

Seek Consultation   Sometimes there may be an intermediate step between understanding a student's needs and setting up a referral. This step involves consulting with a knowledgeable resource person to find out what options exist for the student being helped. The student being assisted would first be informed that you, as a peer educator, would like to consult with another source who can assist in the process. Using the example of the career issue previously mentioned, you could say, "I would like to talk to a counselor at the Career Counseling Office and get suggestions for activities that might be helpful for the questions you are having. Would you mind if I call them and get back to you with their suggestions?" By clarifying what you are seeking from a consultation and getting the student's consent, you are enabling the student to be informed and in control of this process. Sometimes such a consultation can be made by phone with the student present; in other cases, it may be preferable for the peer educator to meet with a resource and then get back to the student in a timely manner. When seeking consultative assistance, it is important to have clear and complete information about the needs of the student you are representing.

While consultation may take place through a person with expertise in an area of assistance, you as a peer educator will also routinely seek consultation from the person who serves as your supervisor. It is important to regularly review the processes you are using as a helper and get feedback about the appropriateness of your interventions and referrals.

How to Refer

When you refer someone to another resource, whether a person, an office, a business, or even a telephone or Web site, you want the referral to be seen as welcome assistance and not some sort of brush-off. The following guidelines will help you accomplish effective referrals.

Be Honest   Be direct and straightforward in your recommendation. Explain in a clear and open manner why you feel it is desirable or necessary to make a referral.

Become Knowledgeable   Explain fully the services that can be obtained from the resource agency or person you are recommending. Provide confirming data about how the referral source can be useful and describe the source's qualifications or capabilities. This information can reassure the student that he or she will receive the help needed. It is preferable to avoid making a "shot in the dark" referral or providing information that might turn into a runaround because you do not know for sure that the agency has the assistance that matches the student's need. Check it out!

Demonstrate Respect   Allow the student to assume responsibility and control in making a contact or appointment. Student initiation and follow-up enhance commitment and promote a sense of autonomy in taking charge of the situation.

253

Personalize the Referral Process It can be useful to give the student the name of a particular person or persons who can be a direct contact at the resource organization. This will personalize and make the experience seem less intimidating. Be careful about this sort of referral, though. It may be best to not provide the name of anyone who may be hard to contact or may seem less available than a general referral.

Role Play or Practice Assist the student in formulating questions or approaches during an initial contact session. Some rehearsal or preparation can be reassuring.

Carefully Assess the Need In some cases, you may find a student resists or denies the need to go to a professional resource. You have several choices when you meet such resistance. You can accept the individual's decision to not take advantage of the referral. If you believe the individual simply needs more encouragement, you can provide more explicit reasons that you believe it is important for them to go. If the problem is uneasiness about approaching an office, you could consider more direct assistance such as offering to go with them to make an initial contact. Finally, if you believe there is the potential of danger to self or others, maybe because of reference to a suicidal threat, you should go to the professional resource on your campus on your own to get consultation and assistance for that individual.

Follow Up Encourage the student to get back in touch with you after visiting the recommended resource. In some cases, it would be appropriate to make the contact yourself if you don't hear back from the student in a reasonable time. This shows your concern and interest and provides continuity of the helping relationship. Also, this follow-up contact with the student provides additional incentive for the student to make contact with the referral source.

254

Think of a time that you personally have needed to find out about a campus resource or needed information:

What obstacles or difficulties did you encounter in trying to get your situation resolved?

What was the personal impact on you when dealing with these obstacles? Imagine someone else going through a similar situation to what you experienced.

Now what could you do to reduce the hassles and obstacles in getting what was needed?

ONLINE RESOURCES

As you know, the Internet offers users many more opportunities to reach out to peers and connect virtually. The potential of these socio-technical spaces is to have ever-present connectivity to others 24/7/365. Communicating online requires finesse because of the balance of electronic mediums and the public-private tensions.

Communications Tools

Text blogs and video blogs capture personalized expertise by defined authors or groups of authors; wikis capture collective knowledge around particular topics. Social networking sites enable users to create personal profiles, share information through text and multimedia, and interact with peers. Virtual communities have sprung up around mediated communications, with live audio and video chats and text messaging. Electronic mailing lists (known colloquially as "listservs") based on particular subjects unify groups or communities. Immersive 3D sites enable

255

human-embodied avatars to interact via a wide range of visual, sound, body language, and kinesthetic cues.

Current generation technologies have gone well beyond desktop devices to mobile ones such as smart cell phones and devices. RSS-feeds (Really Simple Syndication) allow easy collection of relevant information through subscriptions to "podcasts." People may stay in touch with pithy text messages via text messaging and mini-blogging "tweets." Devices now are also becoming more location-aware, which may mean real-time, real-space connections. These manifest in real-space games and geocaching (where rewards are hidden in public parks and on hiking trails and then indicated in terms of their geographical coordinates) and "flash mob" meet-ups in particular locations for predesigned "events." Anywhere there is wireless connectivity (or satellite), sophisticated mobile devices may access the World Wide Web.

Socio-Technical Tools

The convergence of socio-technical tools and applications means mash-ups of various capabilities and fast-changing Web-delivered resources. The global aspects of online resources may mean an increased divergence of opinions and insights. These Web 2.0 changes offer ways for peer educators to share information, connect around mutual concerns, and promote peer healthy behaviors. Students may connect more easily with each other. They may more easily and broadly explore aspects about their own identities; they may experiment with different selves. Ideally, these high-tech resources serve as a conduit to professional psychological support, as needed.

Web 3.0 is touted as a more personalized and customized Web, with clearer machine-awareness of the various individuals accessing the Web and artificially intelligent tailoring of Web services and contents to respective users.

Rich Digital Information Exchanges

The diversity of information and connectivity online will challenge peer educators to sift through information for accuracy, timeliness, originality, and appropriateness for peer use. In exploring online communities, you will have to see whether there is a caring and civil atmosphere; you will have to ensure that there are legal and policy protections for users of a site. You may explore whether a site's participants have listening and respectful attitudes and are savvy about the issues in order to promote strong synergies. Given the ever-changing nature of sites, continuing awareness will be important.

Human Facilitation

Human facilitation at various sites offers further value for peer educators. Individuals may form professional and personal relationships with others in mediated ways. By contrast, some sites use the presence of "intelligent agents" or robots that simulate human conversations using "natural language" interfaces. Some 3D immersive spaces have avatars that are so humanlike that some people may leave that space thinking that they had interacted with a live person (instead of computer scripting).

Caveat Emptor

Going online must involve some *caveat emptor* ("buyer beware") considerations. Peer educators need to remember that information is usually incomplete on most sites and in most relationship situations. In selecting sites to use you should consider the risks of "negative learning" or erroneous beliefs. A Web site service has many limitations: it is not therapeutic and not a substitute for professional care. Some virtual interactions may make some personal situations worse. How online sources are introduced

257

and used by people should be intelligently facilitated in the context of solid decision making.

Some other considerations in evaluating sites involve legal implications. Professional sites will have a policies section that addresses issues of privacy (and the use of site user information), copyright, interactivity guidelines, and other factors. These policies should be examined in depth. Sites also should be fully accessible, based on federal accessibility guidelines, to be as inclusive as possible of all users. Also, the site's commercials and business ties may result in e-mail spam and distracting advertising. Users of a site may be unwittingly signing over rights to their personal digital images and information. Seeing how responsive a site's webmaster is to legitimate queries will also be critical. Sites also develop reputations in cyberspace, and it may help to vet that information.

Technology has produced an extensive resource for gaining information and developing rapid and expansive communication systems, but face-to-face contact is still the most direct and personal way to respond to individual needs and circumstances.

Examples of Online Web Sources

Many resources for peer educators are unique to particular regions, circumstances (age groups, legal situations, and focuses), and institutions. Peer educator groups vary on social sites based on shared interests at a particular time. This is a partial listing of some resources available online.

Information Resources
National Association of Peer Programs (NAPP) (formerly the
    National Peer Helpers Association):
    http://www.peerprograms.org/

Peer Solutions Resources (The Arizona Department of Health Services):
http://www.peersolutions.org/help_resources.html

Substance Abuse and Mental Health Services Administration (U.S. Department of Health and Human Services):
http://www.samhsa.gov/

Ulifeline. A national online information and resource for mental health and emotional concerns of college students, including suicide prevention. It offers links, informative facts, suggestions for help, local referral sources, and e-mail response.
http://ulifeline.org

The University of Chicago Virtual Pamphlet Collection. Provides a variety of topical information resources on student concerns.
http://www.dr-bob.org/vpc

Social Resources

LiveWire: Peer Answers. Peer Support. Period.
http://www.golivewire.com/

National Empowerment Center, Inc.:
http://www.power2u.org/index.html

Daily Strength:
http://www.dailystrength.org/

University Life Café:
http://www.universitylifecafe.org

Canadian Resources

Youth Engagement Through Schools: Peer/Helper Programs:
http://www.safehealthyschools.org/youth/peer_helper
_programs.htm

Peer Resources:
http://www.peer.ca/peer.html

Reflection Point 9.3: The Online Experience

Think about your own time spent in online spaces and sites.

What resources can peer educators derive from substantive online resources?

What criteria will be important to use in deciding the validity of a site for peer use?

How can you encourage responsible use of online resources?

Tips for Evaluating Resources

The following tips (adapted from Ender, Saunders-McCaffrey, & Miller, 1979) will be helpful as you evaluate referral resources.

1. Visit the service. Meet with staff members of the resources most frequently used by the students with whom you work. This process is time consuming but provides many important benefits. It is easier to make an effective and reassuring referral if you know something about the beliefs and attributes of the persons at a particular office, as well as having knowledge of the services provided.

2. Tour the facility. Ask for a tour of facilities and material resources such as library, media collection, or computer lab. Familiarity with the physical facilities will also enable you to refer a student to the most appropriate resource available. Ask to be on any mailing list the office has for announcing special events or programs. Get a copy of any descriptive brochure—with extras to hand out if they're readily available.

3. Understand the agency's referral process. Ask specific questions regarding referral procedures, activities of the office, office hours, and even the philosophy or attitudes of the staff toward providing service. Discover the process a student goes through when seeking assistance, such as filling out forms and scheduling appointments. Find out if the agency has a policy regarding confidentiality.

4. Check out willingness to serve as consultants. Explore the possibilities of using agency resource persons as consultants

---

260

for helping you work with students. For example, if you are working with a student who has experienced a personal crisis, it would be very useful to know how to access a counseling psychologist or similar personal counselor to find out about dealing with crisis and referral.

Tips for the Evaluation of Online Resources
The following will help you evaluate online resources.

1. Evaluate the site's contents. Delve into all the parts of the sites to look at the approach. Evaluate the information to see how accurate it is. Look at how fresh the information is and how often it is updated. See whether there are negative or damaging messages that may be hurtful to your peers.
2. Get a sense of the other members on the site or in the virtual community. Interact with some of the individuals you meet on the site.
3. Develop a deeper sense of the interactivity on the site. See what tools there are for self-expression. Are the tools media rich, or are they constraining? Do the users seem to have wide degrees of freedom for self-expression albeit without intruding on others' spaces?
4. Examine the source of the site. Organizations, universities, companies, and government agencies may create sites that have value for peer educators. The reputation of each should be analyzed to see whether there are risky biases. Also, sites that have clear political agendas should be avoided.
5. Explore the policies and practices for the site. This may be a "Terms of Service" or an "End User License Agreement" or general policy and disclaimers. Look at how well users' rights to privacy are protected. Look at what happens to the intellectual property for the contents that users upload to the site. Consider how responsive the site owners are and how much oversight they provide to the goings-on there. These factors contribute to the quality of a site and the user experience.

Reflection Point 9.2: Determine Your Referral IQ

Think about your own work with other students and the limits of your skills:

What benefits can peer educators derive from having knowledge of campus and community resources?

What criteria does one use when deciding whether a referral is an appropriate strategy? Looking at the reverse standard, when would it be inappropriate to use referral?

What competencies and knowledge must you, the peer educator, possess to be an effective referral agent?

SUMMARY

Knowledge of available campus and community resources and of appropriate ways to make a referral will be an effective tool for a peer educator. The more you know about the purpose and function of various offices, the more effective you will be in helping students develop plans, solve problems, and achieve their goals. Online resources about your campus and well beyond are valuable resources; however, the caveat is even more important to make sure that these resources represent legitimate and authoritative content.

There are numerous services, facilities, and sources of information at your disposal as you work with other students. Timely, appropriate referrals to these services will become a significant aspect of your work. Take time to get to know and understand the substantial benefits these resources offer to students. Network with others who share your goal of assisting students as they maximize their college experience.

Scrutinize online resources carefully, and work with your fellow students to use the many online resources with savvy and appropriate content.

CHAPTER NINE: SUMMARY QUESTIONS

1. List two possible campus or community resources for each of the following student concerns: dating problems, parental problems, roommate problems, weight problems, financial problems, sexual harassment, difficulty with study, test anxiety, legal problems, sexually transmitted disease, conflict with a faculty member, and lack of social life.
2. What are some considerations to make when recommending an online source of information?
3. What are some general guidelines to follow when using another service or soliciting the advice of a person in a consulting capacity?

CHAPTER 10

Ethics and Strategies for Good Practice

LEARNING OBJECTIVES

After completing this chapter, you will be able to

1. Understand the need for standards of good practice and ethical behavior applied to peer helping relationships.
2. Recognize the importance of respect, privacy, and confidentiality in peer assistance work.
3. Describe ethical strategies for good practice in the peer educator's role.
4. Realize how to apply appropriate conduct to specific helping responsibilities.

●

> Let me give you the definition of ethics: it is good to maintain life and to further life. It is bad to damage and destroy life. And this ethic, profound and universal, has the significance of a religion.
>
> —ALBERT SCHWEITZER

As noted in Chapter One, you as a peer educator are entering into a relationship in which you are considered the person provid-

264

ing assistance. Even while you may be a peer in educational status, in this role you are the helper; you are the more knowing person in an area in which you provide service. Any service occupation recognizes the necessity for standards of good practice, including the appropriate behavior of those providing help. Such standards of good practice are referred to as codes of conduct and ethical standards. Typically, these rules may serve as guidelines that have been formulated through a consensus of practicing professionals. For example, the Association of College Student Educators International (ACPA) provides an ethical statement for professionals working in College Student Affairs positions. This document spells out competencies, responsibilities, and appropriate actions that serve as a guide for its professional membership (ACPA, 2006). This statement of ethical principles provides a useful overall template when working with college students.

Because peer helping falls outside of professional jurisdiction, you are not held to the mandated codes of a profession. However, the principles of conduct that apply to a professional helping relationships will in parallel ways enhance the peer helping relationship in that confidence, trust, and assurance of positive helping behaviors will help to produce beneficial outcomes. This chapter is designed to help you as peer educator explore what is meant by ethical behavior, understand how principles of helping can be identified, and recognize that clear expectations can be established for your practice. At the same time, you do not have a set rulebook regarding right or wrong behaviors in performance of your duties. Acceptable and effective practice requires good judgment, careful reflection of consequences, and a willingness to consult with knowledgeable others.

There are some limited published statements generated by professional associations to address standards for "interpersonal behaviors" of nonprofessionals in a helping role. The American Association of School Counselors (ASCA) has issued a statement for peer counseling in school settings including the responsibilities of those supervising peers (Tindall, 1996, pp. 255–258). The National Association of Peer Program Professionals (NAPPP), an organization with a focus on those supervising peer programs in K–12 (also including some colleges), has issued programmatic standards for professionals working with peer programs and a suggested code of ethics for peer helpers (National Association of Peer Program Professionals, 2009).

As a peer educator, your service activity may fall across a continuum of types of contact with students that may vary in content and delivery. For example, you may be providing information and education that is openly delivered in a classroom or group setting without accepting or revealing very personal individual information. Or on another level you could be attending to individuals who are talking about personal concerns that will require a regard for how to respond with privacy and appropriateness. Due to these variations in peer educator roles we have organized this chapter in a way that considers the topic of standards and ethics of practice from a broad base that can be useful in both the depth of content and the way assistance is delivered. We start by considering what areas might be included within a peer educator code of ethics. Some examples from a variety of peer education programs have been useful in order to define these possible options. This initial discussion is followed by providing a set of twelve guiding principles, specific examples that, adapted, would be useful as guidelines for any institutional program.

WHAT SHOULD BE INCLUDED IN A CODE OF ETHICAL PRACTICE FOR PEER EDUCATORS?

It is extremely important for you, as a peer educator, to understand and practice ethical behavior as you work with other students. The first step is to identify and understand certain content that underlies ethical behavior for peer educators. This awareness can be accomplished through a clear written statement that outlines standards of conduct, review and discussion in training, and working under the supervision of an adviser or professional mentor. We recommend that the content of an ethical statement consider at least the following points:

- Peer educators will have knowledge of and act consistently with any professional standards appropriate to the agency in which they are employed.
- Peer educators will respect the autonomy and individual dignity of the students they serve.
- Peer educators will avoid acting beyond the scope of service for which they were selected and trained and will not attempt to offer professional services requiring more extensive qualifications and training.
- Peer educators will maintain the right to privacy and confidentiality of the students they serve.
- Peer educators will act in their practice for the benefit and welfare of students, being careful to avoid issues in which conflict of interests, bias, or dual relationship could jeopardize this helping stance.

PRINCIPLES TO ENHANCE THE QUALITY OF PEER PRACTICE

The main points for ethical consideration listed in the preceding section will assist you, your institution, and outside agencies as all strive to promote high-quality, ethical services for students. These statements will also assist you as you implement your role in a competent manner. On a daily basis, you will be confronted with issues that have ethical implications: What if I am asked to respond to a situation that I know nothing about? What if my personal emotions interfere with understanding another person? What if I am feeling threatened, harassed, or seduced?

Although there is no blueprint for approaching the multitude of unique circumstances you will confront, we believe there are some principles for good practice that you can use as criteria for future decision making. These strategies can be sorted in regard to your skill level as determined by training, your relationship with your supervisor, your relationship with the students seeking your services, and your relationship with the university and community at large. The twelve principles suggested below are organized by those categories mentioned above.

Skills as Determined by Training

By far, your level of helping skills—determined by the training program designed to develop your ability to work with others, and past experiences or previous training—is the criterion that you should apply when making most decisions concerning what you are qualified for and capable of doing as you work with others.

> **Principle 1:** *Respond within the limits of your training and skill.*

When you receive requests for information, assistance, or support that require skills beyond your training, expertise, or jurisdiction, you must know your personal limits and not exceed the boundaries of your knowledge and skills by making suggestions or implying knowledge that may be lacking. If possible, you can briefly explain the reason or limits of your assistance without coming across as rejecting the student you are serving or withholding something you could provide if you chose. If you have knowledge of an appropriate referral source, that information should be shared and assistance offered in getting the person to the resource.

> **Principle 2:** Acknowledge your limits openly by saying that you do not know rather than providing false expertise.

Even within the limits of your role, you will be asked questions for which you do not have the answers. Do not play the role of expert. Saying, "I don't know" is much more helpful than faking it. When confronted with this situation, acknowledge your shortcomings and work with the person seeking help to find the right answer. This may involve consultation with other peer educators or your supervisor or making calls around campus to discover the information needed. In many cases, problem solving for how to find solutions is even more helpful than having the answer for someone. As the adage goes, "It is better to teach people to fish than to provide a fish," or "Teach a man to fish and feed him for a lifetime."

Relationship with Your Supervisor

Your supervisor is the most important contact you have in your role as a peer educator. Your supervisor will serve as your mentor, coach, employer, and guide in the area of helping others. This relationship is critical to your success.

> **Principle 3:** When in doubt—consult!

269

When you are confronted with a situation you are uncertain about or that may involve some conflict or dilemma, it is critical to consult with your supervisor. Use this person's expertise—as a professional in your service area who shares some responsibility for your success. Your supervisor can be your greatest resource. Many people are tempted to shield uncertainties from a supervisor out of fear that the supervisor will somehow think less of them for not having the answer. In reality, the moments you have questions or doubts are the most important times to get supervisory input. The need for consultation may vary based upon the urgency and resources needed. For example, a situation that requires immediate attention due to risk or time pressures warrants prompt consultation. The best situation is to know in advance the individual, system, or resource to consult in an emergency. Regularly scheduled consultation or supervision sessions may serve well the need for confirmation or suggestion of your service role. In other cases, where more detail or resource is necessary, the consultation might involve training, resource development, or referral.

> **Principle 4:** *Maintain client privacy and confidentiality as long as privacy protects the person being helped.*

Ideally, your relationship with students seeking your services is private and the helping agreement implies that you will not divulge personal data about them. This standard of conduct protects the privacy of the individual, and it also promotes a level of trust that makes self-disclosure of personal information possible.

But there are exceptions to the rule of confidentiality. First, if you are receiving supervision, it is both necessary and helpful to discuss with your supervisor aspects of your interactions with those you are helping. It is very important that a full disclosure be made to the student you are working with that you are being supervised and that you share information with that specific individual so as to improve your own service skills. The student then has the prerogative to agree to that condition or request an alternative. Another very important exception to maintaining a private and confidential stance with a student is when you have received information that reveals a potential danger to yourself, the peer-advised individual, or others. In these instances, you should consult with your supervisor or a responsible party at your institution, such as the dean of students, and determine an appropriate method for intervention by a resource of the campus or community. These exceptions are where the information stops. You should never gossip or otherwise casually reveal information received about another person you are working with. It is frequently a social norm to share information about others among friends. However, in a peer-educating situation, this norm is inappropriate and self-defeating to the helping relationship.

Relationships with Students Seeking Your Assistance

As in all helping situations, the interaction between two people—the quality of the relationship—is probably the most important factor in the success and helpfulness that occurs. The way in which a student requesting assistance perceives you and your skill is critical to the success that you will achieve.

Principle 5: *Show respect and dignity for other individuals.*

Tolerance and acceptance of both the individual student and his or her circumstances are important prerequisites for any assistance. No student with whom you work should be made to feel that you are condescending to him or her while you are serving in your role as helper. All contact—and information from that contact—should be maintained with respect and dignity. The exceptions to this rule are when the student agrees that sharing with others is appropriate or if the information learned puts you, the student, or the community in danger. Again, treat these matters as described in Principle Four.

Principle 6: Understand your own personal bias and avoid imposing this bias on others.

As a peer educator, you should be careful to not impose your personal bias on other students or to attempt to influence or prejudice the student's views or beliefs. This might include criticism of other individuals or authorities, disenchantment, or strong value judgments that ask the student to deal with personal agendas received from you, as a peer educator. Everyone has personal opinions and biases, but they should be stated with personal ownership and without a sense of pressuring or convincing another to accept that opinion. You are referred to Chapter Four for a more in-depth discussion of bias and discrimination issues based upon diversity of background, culture, and belief.

Principle 7: Continue to deal appropriately when working with persons for whom you feel some aversion.

You may find that in your role as a peer educator that you will meet and be asked to work with other students for whom you may feel some antagonism, dislike, or other strong emotional reaction. In these cases, you must consider why the aversion is being experienced and carefully assess whether these feelings will interfere with the role that you are to maintain. For example, you may feel irritated because the person acts a lot like someone you know who has hurt you in the past. In some instances, it may be best to admit the limitation and find a way that the individual can be served by another person. It is useful to consult your supervisor about ways to handle such personality difficulties.

> **Principle 8:** Act appropriately when working with persons for whom you feel attraction.

At times, you may meet students in your work whom you feel interest for or even attracted to. You may even recognize that you would like to date this person or be friends outside the activities of the job. These types of relationships can compromise your helping role and may set up problems of dual relationships. Avoidance of these dilemmas should be carefully discussed in peer training, emphasizing power differentials and influence involved in a helping role. You should consider, beforehand, how to avoid or deal with these dilemmas should they occur. And if an incident should occur, talk with your supervisor about it. The presence of online social networking sites and similar ways of public connection may create complicated situations beyond the peer working relationship when it is easy for you or the other person to be asked to become a "facebook friend."

> **Principle 9:** Knowing and managing your emotional response, while helping another, is crucial to your own well-being and to your ability to help.

273

As you serve, you may evoke emotionally charged reactions from students ranging from anger and irritation to grief and sorrow. Peer educators must be prepared to handle and even control emotional reactions by learning to set limits, accept but not absorb emotional output, and channel reactions through referral to appropriate resources on campus. On some occasions, a student reaction will stimulate parallel feelings from a peer educator's own experience. In these cases, a peer educator must know how to follow up and use personal resources of support to debrief from such encounters. Stress debriefing after crisis intervention is a common practice for disaster relief personnel and others who deal with emergency traumatic situations—there is no need to tough it out on your own, and you will not look any stronger or more competent if you try to do so. Maintaining good balance, support, and assistance in your own life only enhances your ability to be helpful to others.

Relationships with Your University Community and Beyond

As a peer educator working on a college campus, you work in a community setting that may include residence and full community services. It is important to note that you have obligations to this community both as a peer educator and as a community member.

> **Principle 10:** *Take responsible action if you learn about illegal behavior.*

In your role, you may become aware, from a student response, of behavior that is illegal or potentially unethical. In this instance, you may confront the behavior in a manner that points out the social norms and consequences in a manner that suggests that you are not the person to judge the behavior, but instead to point out the clear social expectations and laws that come with being a part of a community or society. When the information shared with you suggests a clear and present danger to others in the community, determine the appropriate course of action with your supervisor.

> **Principle 11:** *Remember that as a peer educator, you are a role model!*

As pointed out in Chapter One, peer educators are student role models, both on campus and in the community. This means you are obligated to maintain congruence between what you say to fellow students in your role and how you act in other facets of your life; remember, you will be seen (or heard) by those with whom you have worked. For example, if you help others with problems in the area of time management but you are the one who is always late to meetings, or if you are giving presentations on responsible drinking yet get picked up for a DUI, much of your credibility as a peer educator is quickly and decidedly undermined. Being a role model may require modeling of "good behavior," but it may also require demonstration of your own commitment to setting and achieving goals for your own improvement. As you are asked to set good examples it is also recognized that you, as a student, are subject to the same experimentation and social activity considered normal for the "college years." It is a challenge for all peer educators to use good judgment and not get caught up in the hypocritical "do as I say, not as I do" dilemma.

> **Principle 12:** *Maintain integrity and do not promote hearsay in commenting on professional relationships with others.*

In your role, students will ask for your opinion about the quality of other professionals, especially faculty on your campus and the type of classroom experience they offer. We believe you should refrain from giving negative opinions or at least limit any potentially critical comment to objective facts about a campus professional or agency. Everyone experiences other people differently. What may have been a poor experience for you could be quite excellent for others.

Exercise 10.1: Real-Life Ethics

Place yourself in the following situations:

- You are talking with a student who describes having taken part in an activity that, if caught, would probably be a felony. The person says this rather casually and even asserts rather boldly that nothing of consequence "happened."
- As a discussion leader of a group, you notice a student with whom you have had an unresolved conflict during the past year. You have some strong feelings and reactions to seeing this individual.
- You are very attracted to a person you have tutored in the past couple of weeks, and you would really like to ask that person out. You are looking for a "go between" friend to check out the situation for a "yes" or "no" interest without having to directly ask the other party.
- You have assisted a student with a personal improvement plan as part of a freshman wellness experience. Your role has mainly been to help design and monitor progress toward the goal. The student asks whether you would become his regular workout partner since that would really help motivate participation.
- You are interacting with a person who has a political or moral viewpoint that differs from yours. You find this viewpoint

276

reprehensible, although it could be understood as acceptable based upon this student's culture and value system. You want to argue a different point of view.

Using the discussion points below, consider the different reactions and actions that might occur with each of the situations stated above:

- Identify your reactions in each case.
- What are the consequences of possible follow-up actions?
- What are the implications for ethical conduct in each case?
- Describe some different ways for handling each of these situations.

VALUES PROMOTION BEYOND A CODE OF ETHICS

This final section of the chapter is included to suggest that students and all citizens of the campus community act in ways that enhance the college culture toward becoming more accepting, nurturing, and promoting of an overall value-based environment. Examples of topics and issues a person in this more activist role may need to embrace include the following:

1. An emphasis on the commitment to community-oriented values and integrity. The emphasis is placed on the process of examining core virtues that can be embraced as a basis for action rather than adaptation of any one system that merely becomes a dogmatic set of rights and wrongs. You might be asking questions such as: What constitutes a caring supportive community? What is an integrity honor system?
2. Support for sustainability that supports the maintenance and enhancement of a balance with nature and not a destruction of the resources. The "green" movement may focus on alternative sources for renewal energy, recycling of reusable

materials, reduction of pollutants, and conservation of our natural resources.

3. A promotion of safety and reduction of hostility so that harassment, "bullying," and practices that create unnecessary tensions and acts of violence are not condoned and may be prevented. These include but are not limited to acts based upon prejudice or intolerance by gender, ethnicity, religion, sexual preference, disability, or other markers of difference. Programs such as "safe zone" have been created to provide support for movements across many college campuses.

4. The utilization of a positive psychological focus to promote a good life. Positive psychology supports healthy living behaviors and their benefits rather than emphasizing scare tactics, or negative behaviors, such as smoking, drinking and drugs, and their detriments. Another example is the emphasis on positive response behaviors such as gratitude, thankfulness, and forgiveness as helpful and hopeful ways to overcome reactions of grief, anger, and unnecessary negative classifications that create victimization and self-diminishing labels.

For further information on this topic, consult the *Journal of College and Character*, which features discussion around the proactive movements on college campuses today. Margaret Wheatley (2002), a noted authority on community and organizational development, writes extensively concerning the ways to promote a community spirit of "oneness" during a time when fragmentation and separation has occurred in society. She indicates that the act of "listening through simple, honest, human conversation" is the key to connection (Wheatley, 2002, p. 3). This section is included in this chapter because many student and community-based organizations are using peer educators to have an impact on the development of a moral ethical climate and the promotion of an atmosphere that supports positive outcomes.

Exercise 10.2: Promoting Values Activity

As an individual or group ask the following questions:

- Are you aware of proactive movements on your campus today? What are examples?

- Does your group or organization promote enhancement of specific goals and objectives? If so, what would these be?

- How would you include a statement in your code of conduct that would communicate the peer organization's commitment to a proactive outcome?

Pledge for Quality Service

Our goal is to provide a helpful, user-friendly service to students. Our staff will strive to meet the following standards for a high-quality practice:

1. Privacy and confidentiality
2. Timely service
3. Courteous and helpful reception
4. Clear and specific goals for individual outcomes
5. Explanation of any strategy or procedure recommended
6. Information concerning referral options
7. Supervision from professional staff
8. Training of all staff prior to assuming position and continued weekly training
9. Sensitivity to cultural and lifestyle differences

If these standards are not being met to your satisfaction you have the right to make this concern or complaint known to the director and will receive a response within two days.

NOW WHAT? DESIGNING A PLEDGE FOR YOUR PEER EDUCATOR SERVICE

You have been provided with a structure for understanding, developing, and adhering to a code of ethics for peer practice. As a final activity for this chapter, look at the example Pledge for Quality Service in the box below. This Pledge was written for a peer counseling office and posted for clientele to view when they entered the service area. Read the sample pledge and design a similar statement that is adapted to your peer educator role.

CONCLUSION

To wind up your work in this training experience, we encourage you to collaborate with your fellow peer educators and your supervisor or advisor to develop a mutually acceptable statement of ethics. This may entail a series of statements of good practice to guide your work or a more formal statement of ethical practice. In either case, it is important that you have specific guidelines for evaluating your work and making decisions on a day-to-day basis.

CHAPTER TEN: SUMMARY QUESTIONS

1. Why do peer educators need ethical statements to guide their day-to-day practice?
2. Twelve principles for good practice were presented in this chapter. What are the five most important to your role as a peer educator? Why are these most important?

CHAPTER 11

Examples of Peer Education Programs in Higher Education

LEARNING OBJECTIVES

After completing this chapter you will be able to

1. Describe some real-world university and college programs using peer educators.
2. Identify practical benefits of using peer educators in various educational programs.
3. List some useful programmatic and organizational strategies in programs that use peer educators.
4. Summarize applied training strategies (both formal and informal) for peer educators.
5. Describe some real-world benefits to peer educators participating in various programs.

•

In Chapter One we noted that peer educators now serve in a large number of capacities. In this chapter we provide some examples of peer education programs that have been developed for a variety of educational services, and give you some ideas of the scope of students-helping-students service. We also offer a sampling of ways programs have been developed and strategies used to design, recruit, and train peer educators.

The examples in this chapter have come from several sources. These include programs familiar to us from our experience with several campuses. Other examples have been offered by a number of professional colleagues and from descriptions obtained through list-serves and other online sources. The programs are not exhaustive of all possibilities. They illustrate some innovations as well as tried and true methods well established in peer education practice.

Opportunities abound for extending peer education and the student-to-student mentoring process into a variety of educational and service activities. With funding sources diminishing and yet with growing needs for student-based services, peer educators have become more important and more prolific on most college campuses. In looking at the variety of applications within a number of institutions we found little evidence of any standard way to organize and classify the uses of peer educators. Figure 11.1 was designed to show that there is a thematic connectedness between the wide range of practices provided in this chapter. The examples that follow demonstrate the overlapping ways that peer educators now serve in many ways to impact the twin outcome qualities of personal enrichment and community enhancement.

RICH LEARNING: STUDY ABROAD AND SERVICE LEARNING

University learning extends well beyond the boundaries of a campus's geographical footprint. Students meet professors and other students from many regions of the world. They go abroad

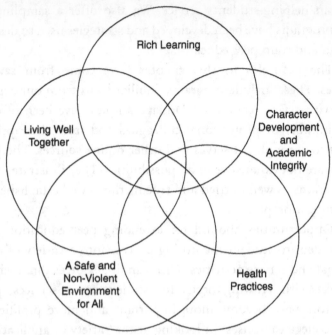

Figure 11.1. Exemplary Practices in Student Service Organizations with Peer Educators

themselves for short- to long-term study experiences. They co-design their study experiences in service learning and make contributions of service in both neighboring communities and around the world. You as peer educators can introduce these opportunities and experiences to your peers, helping them prepare and carry through with their creative learning plans. These endeavors promote a more global awareness as well as improved technology and learning diffusion.

Study Abroad Peer Programs

Peer mentor programs are offered by both study abroad offices on many college campuses and through private companies establishing study abroad connections. In these programs country-specific alumni are brought back to work as alumni "ambassadors" to introduce both study abroad and the destination countries.

These peer educators present basic information to prospective applicants for study abroad in their region of specialty; they may help those interested work through the application and planning process. They participate in predeparture orientations in classrooms and at events, such as study abroad fairs on their home campuses. Such returnees may capture broad attention with their experiences and observations. They also offer continuing analysis of the current generation of students' likes and dislikes, as well as of a program's strengths and weaknesses, in order to help administrators offer stronger service.

For their part, alumni peer mentors, sometimes called advisors, benefit by connecting with students who have similar interests. They will have venues through which to share their study abroad experiences. They may participate in social networks with others who are venturing abroad to a region of their knowledge and interest. In some cases, private companies organizing study abroad select alumni advisors from member institutions to help in the recruitment and preparation activities for a new study abroad group in the ensuing year.

The alumni peer advisor commitment usually extends for a full academic year. All prospective alumni peer advisors go through a competitive hiring process that focuses on their enthusiasm in promoting study abroad. Their background is represented through a transcript, a résumé, a letter of recommendation, and an essay about why they would be a positive representative for study abroad. Also, the program strives to increase "abroad participation" in underrepresented countries.

Those hired go through training for their role, including conflict resolution. Some training might involve job shadowing current alumni peer educators with a subsequent "reverse job shadowing" in which the staff will shadow the new peer educators for their training and skills development.

Marketing tools for this endeavor include fliers, posters, T-shirts, and publicity paraphernalia such as luggage tags. Others have used social media like Facebook™ to publicize study abroad. One study abroad program holds two annual study abroad fairs, one each semester. There are also invited fairs where this study abroad program has alumni peer advisors representing the program at information tables. Third-party representatives also conduct visits to the campus to showcase the program.

Alumni peer mentors may earn transfer credits for their work. They are also rewarded well—with an option of participating in a two-week intensive study abroad program at the end of the academic year or receiving a flight voucher to return abroad.

Benefits to the campus involve recruitment to the study abroad program. Other benefits involve lessened reentry shock by returning students, lessened culture shock by incoming international students, the maintenance of foreign language acquisition, and greater social integration of student groups on campus (with greater internationalization). Some international students even choose to do a double study abroad. Intercultural friendships have also originated from such contacts.

Community Service Program

Kansas State University Community Service Program (CSP) is a service-learning program dedicated to promoting service learning opportunities among university students and assisting communities with addressing vital issues both in Kansas and abroad. Through this program, students learn new skills in partnership with communities. CSP was started in 1987 and has continued to operate for over twenty years.

Local Service Programs   Students participate in programs such as Kansas Community Teams and Internships, International Summer Teams, America Reads / America Counts, CSP Tutors, Community Connections, Alternative Spring Breaks, and service learning support for faculty. Service learning continues throughout the year, with special intensive events. The Alternative Spring Break program supports student work domestically or abroad to address pressing social issues, such as homelessness or public health.

Community service is presently organized within a school for leadership studies. The educational goal for students participating in service learning falls within their overarching goals of developing knowledgeable, ethical, and caring leaders in a diverse and changing world. The experience uses hands-on experience and reflective learning.

For local service, four student coordinators run a volunteer service center that recruits volunteers, coordinates events, sponsors nonprofit activities, arranges club service projects, and conducts special day events such as Martin Luther King, Jr., Day, and Make a Difference Day. The experience of the student coordinators includes recruitment, promotion, online Web management, organizational liaison, and communication. It has become a way for students to develop a service philosophy, sense of purpose, and attitude of responsibility and care for their respective communities.

International Service Learning   The International program starts with an open recruitment and selection period during the fall semester. Screening may take thirty to thirty-five applicants that go through a careful process of group and individual interviews. Many factors are considered in selection, including interview and applicant statements, as well as skills in language, personal stability, and fit as a member of a team.

287

By late November, selection is completed, and a commitment to participate includes enrollment in a three-hour credit class during the spring semester. Although there is a permanent staff advisor, the class is coordinated by a previous alumni student of the program. The class members, divided into travel teams, are responsible to go through both personal readiness and project planning in a systematic reflective process, with the guidance of their facilitator.

In the early stages, they may reflect upon their own reasons for entering the experience and assess their own motives and reactions. They face issues such as how to form relationships with people from different cultures or backgrounds and how to deal with their own separation from and leaving of their comfort zone. Training proceeds to learning skills from basic CPR (cardiopulmonary resuscitation) training to language and communication.

All practical issues must be worked out during the spring for the summer project, including details of establishing contacts, housing and living arrangements, finding sponsors, having travel insurance, and designing program agreements and any details or problems that might arise. The students must complete their process reflections throughout the course and have a viable plan for their experience. The student team members carry out the trip with their own leadership without a chaperone or supervisor.

After the eight to ten week service project, the students return in late summer and by the end of August, all teams meet with the coordinator and faculty sponsor to debrief their experience.

Students in past years have had projects in Mexico, Guatemala, Turkey, Kenya, and Botswana, conducting projects in response to difficult problems and with low-income and otherwise challenging conditions. Most students find that the experience is transforming to their learning, their outlook, and even the direction of their life. The experience enhances the ability to problem solve, cope with difficulty, adjust to differences, and confront their own fears and attitudes.

Of course, these experiences have not been without difficulties and setbacks. There have been incidents of team conflict, member illness, and other personal difficulties with coping or managing change. However, the program has continued to be one of the best learning experiences encountered by the students who have completed this service. The peer role continues the process as last year's experienced service learners become coordinators for new volunteers.

CHARACTER DEVELOPMENT AND ACADEMIC INTEGRITY

Traditional-aged students are working through crucial developmental stages and personal choices in their college years that will affect their lives. They are also working to establish academic integrity to earn valid college credits and degrees and to truly strengthen their education and professional skill sets. Peer educators help each other in these endeavors by offering support and upholding academic integrity standards.

Honor and Integrity System (Honor Council and Honor and Integrity Peer Educator)

Peer student educators play a central role in supporting one campus's efforts in upholding the university's modified honor code and school pledge: "On my honor, as a student, I have neither given nor received unauthorized aid on this academic work." Here, student volunteers have the responsibility to hold their peers accountable for their actions; they also uphold the dignity of the university's degrees and certificates. The rationale has been summarized colloquially as: "Hey, we're working hard for a degree. Why aren't you?"

Students serve as the majority on the five-member Honor Council that determines whether a fellow student is responsible for a violation of the honor pledge. Here, students may serve in any role—case investigator, hearing panelist, or chair. The various colleges nominate two to three students each (based on the size of the college) to serve on the Honor Council for a two-year term. (Approximately 120 cases are handled through the Honor Council every year.)

Students also serve as Honor and Integrity Peer Educator (HIPE) members. They serve two main purposes: to educate the university community about issues of academic integrity to create a culture of integrity, and also to assist students (alleged violators) going through the hearing (or appeals) process.

Approximately half of HIPE members have committed an academic violation but have addressed that issue, and many of these students are some of the best HIPE members. HIPE members go through an application process. Currently, the Honor Council pool has thirty-four faculty and twenty student members, and there are eight HIPE members.

Honor Council members attend a series of professional development activities with faculty members to understand the system and their roles within it. They also train on how to conduct the sessions and on how to ask questions in a noninflammatory way, such as "Can you explain what you saw?" instead of "Are you sure you saw that?" The chairperson role rotates between faculty and students. Peer educators on the Honor Council also work to address all members of the group by honorifics (Mr., Ms., or Dr.) or all by first name—for consistency.

HIPE members train with the assistant director of the Honor and Integrity Office regarding the Honor and Integrity System, presentation skills (to make the presentations their own), contacts for presentations, and strategies to support the alleged violators.

Both Honor Council and HIPE members train intensively on maintaining confidentiality and respect for all those involved in this process. The seating of an Honor Council is done by purposefully not drawing from the student's own department in order to protect his or her privacy and also so as not to be punitive. Part of the training is done through online modules.

HIPE has also reached out to local high schools to begin education about academic integrity at earlier levels, beginning with ninth grade.

Recruitment into HIPE is a challenge because there is not one major area of study to recruit from. There are no financial incentives. Students also do not earn credit for their service. However, they benefit through getting to know others outside their own major. This focus on academic integrity may work as a résumé builder.

The Honor and Integrity Office has a small budget for office needs and to send one of its members to a national conference on academic integrity. HIPE was recently registered as a student organization and is thereby able to apply for student government funding for some activities, such as an annual "Integrity Week"; a mock hearing performance on a branch campus; "chalking" the campus for awareness raising; and sponsoring a related movie.

HEALTH AND WELLNESS PRACTICES

All college students, young and old, are confronted with decisions and behaviors about their health and fitness that affect their life currently and will have an impact in the future. Eating behaviors, physical activity, drinking and drug use, and sexual activity are significant aspects of the college experience. Body image, eating disorders, overweightedness and obesity, binge drinking, sexually transmitted diseases, and alcohol violations are identified as problems on a campus. Although health behaviors have universal applicability to all students, it is frequently the problem behaviors that grab the headlines and attention of college policy and formal intervention.

The problem emphasis communicates that this important facet of college life is private and quietly disregarded as behavior related only to the closeted bedroom, party antics, or intimate relationships—except when something goes wrong. Yet it is extremely important for students to have access to solid educational information, frank discussions, and personal values clarification as they confront these issues. The role of trained and capable peer educators provides a great opportunity for helping students gain important information and make more deliberate choices regarding health and wellness practices. Student-to-student dialogue can offer a forum for sharing information, bringing up concerns, raising issues, and promoting appropriate referrals to services. The following synopsis of peer health programs on one campus illustrates some of these possibilities.

SHAPE: Sexual Health Awareness Peer Educators

The Sexual Health Awareness Peer Educators (SHAPE) program aims to help students make informed choices concerning their sexual behavior. The intent is to promote positive attitudes, maintain awareness of safer sex practices, and share knowledge about sexually transmitted diseases (STDs).

SHAPE is an official student organization under the supervision of a professional health educator who works for student health services.

Students who are prospective SHAPE members must apply and interview for membership. They must complete a three-hour credit peer education class, which includes modules from a Red Cross training manual and use of *Students Helping Students* as a text.

These peer educators deliver services through presentations to various groups including student residence halls, Greek houses, campus organizations, and classrooms. They also participate in a variety of health fairs and table displays around the campus commons areas.

This student organization has its own officers, in charge of carrying out meeting and program responsibilities. All peer mentors need to complete at least five presentations a semester. Organizationally, SHAPE offers about fifty presentations a year with contact numbers of over 3,000 (including contact that occurs through presentations and promotional tables) annually. They also distribute 8,000 condoms a year.

This student organization receives limited funding from the student senate, specific allocations from residence hall programming, and supplies from the health center. They conduct fundraisers through sales of T-shirts with catchy slogans (such as "in case spooning leads to forking"). The edgy promos often mean that they cannot use any official school logo or mascot identification, but such messages result in T-shirt sell-outs.

SHAPE has been in existence for twenty years. Alumni of the program have gone through medical school or work in other health-related areas; they often credit their peer education experience as part of their career commitments. Contact for current and former group members is maintained through a Facebook™ page.

SNAC: Sensible Nutrition and Body Image Choices

Sensible Nutrition and Body Image Choices (known by the catchy acronym SNAC) focuses on providing accurate information about healthy eating behaviors and promoting positive body image.

This student organization began as the result of a graduate student project in 2001 and was maintained under the supervision of a registered dietician and nutrition counselor employed as part of the Health Education office of the Student Health Center. SNAC is affiliated with the BACCHUS Network.

To be considered for leadership in SNAC, students must complete an online application and provide a personal reference from a professional source.

Once accepted, they go through an online training and an on-campus orientation for new members. The online modules are constantly updated to reflect changes in dietary and exercise guidelines. The emphasis in the course is on solid, evidence-based information. The advisor is considering offering more ongoing, supplemental training outside regular meetings that would address topics such as body image and disordered eating.

Many of the students in this group come from nutrition, kinesiology, and pre-med fields of study. Some of them join to fulfill work hours for their respective academic programs.

SNAC members meet twice a month to plan their activities, including presentations to groups, campus organizations, and classes. They sponsor Eating Disorders Awareness Week, which features a nationally known keynote speaker, highlights themes such as "Be Healthy! Be Confident! Be YOU!!!," and attracts hundreds of participants. They also participate in health fairs, featuring laptops with interactive online assessments. Each member is required to offer at least one presentation per semester and collect audience feedback for continual improvement.

This group strives to reach people who really need the help—those at highest risk of disordered eating—through various types of outreaches. They have expanded to the international student population by coordinating with the International Student Center on campus. Most recently, they offered a peer presentation on adapting to American foods and preventing weight gain. Also, they conduct an eating disorders prevention program for sixth graders in an after-school event that runs for eight weeks. In turn, these sixth graders become peer trainers to fourth graders.

Peer educators in SNAC are trained to recognize eating disorder symptoms and how and when to refer students to campus and community resources for professional consultation. Early professional intervention is linked to better outcomes for those affected.

Member communication is enhanced via a SNAC listserv, Web site, and Facebook™ group. Peers are required to proactively encourage campus groups to host a presentation. They also use the on-campus learning system to share meeting minutes, communicate, and coordinate a calendar.

The numbers of students reached annually via formal presentations range from 100 to 400 contacts. Approximately 300 or more students are reached through SNAC exhibits at various campuswide events throughout the year. SNAC is looking to evaluate their impact more formally in the near-term, such as through a pre- and post-assessment at presentations.

This organization has been successful in obtaining funding from student government to support nationally recognized guest speakers for its annual Eating Disorders Awareness Week. Other fund-raising efforts (product sales such as Tupperware™, T-shirts, and jewelry) have had limited success. Members recently opted for annual membership dues (approximately $20/year) to help underwrite expenses. In the future, healthy bake sales may also be hosted.

Healthy Decisions

This is a program that was developed under the umbrella of student activities to coordinate and promote various offerings

295

of student services, organizations, and activities that provide "healthy choices" for students. The main goal of this initiative is to "get the word out" and communicate about a variety of programs. Communication includes special events that are held in the Student Union center such as "Health Decisions Week," where organizations staff booths with information, guest speaker and media activities, a printed directory, and online Web site to inform students what is available to them on campus.

Healthy Decisions (HD) was formed by the university's vice president of student affairs to promote the "healthy decisions" theme, especially with incoming freshmen students. This is a well funded endeavor which includes full-time staff, office space and supplies, printing, and funding for special events. This endeavor has been in existence for a year and so is still exploring and developing many options.

The student involvement includes a student advisory board with officers and special events designees. While this program supports an overarching and broad based approach to "healthy decisions," the following student-run panels exemplify the topical range. These include "Making the Transition to College," "Managing Time and Stress," and "Getting Ready for Internships or Summer Experience Abroad." The students are responsible for coordination, developing content, publicizing, and marketing of the program. Healthy Decisions has involved the development of a Web site and a live online question and answer resource known as "Ask Willie" (with the university's mascot responding).

Members are selected from application and screening by the previous year's board. Training includes a preservice retreat that focuses on member team building, orientation to activities, and doing simulations and mock practice

296

Healthy PAC-CATS

PAC-CATS, an acronym for Personal Assessment Challenge—Choosing Activities for Today's Success, is a peer-facilitated intervention for incoming college freshmen cooperatively developed by three offices (Counseling, Health, and Recreation) to reach students through their First Year Experience class. This FYE course provides a semester of orientation with the goal of preparing freshmen to utilize resources and establish behaviors that can help them achieve success in college.

This program received development and implementation support by a grant from a state health foundation with the overall goal that students be introduced to and then attain healthy behaviors such as good eating, physical activity, and personal management skills, including sleep, stress, problem solving, and time management. Established in 2004, the program was implemented over the next four years with over 2,000 students completing a personal assessment and over 500 students going through an eight-week program for personal change.

The start-up development included the creation of a criterion-based online survey of health behaviors, a systematic self-assessment profile, an information based Web site of wellness resources, promotion and publicity packages, a training package for peer mentors to serve as personal coaches and facilitators for freshman participants, and a student workbook for students to implement a personal program of change.

Each year the program starts with the training of twelve to eighteen peer mentors that are selected through an application and screening process. Training occurs before the first week of classes in the fall with eight training sessions that include listening and facilitations skills, information modules, and use of the PAC-CATS assessment and personal program of change workbook. Peer mentors continue to meet bi-weekly for group supervision and program progress reports throughout the semester.

One of the most significant aspects of this program is the systematic research activity that has been used to validate the outcomes of the PAC-CATS intervention. Using the inventory of health behaviors, data are collected before and after intervention on all participants. Individual goal attainment is also recorded by self- and mentor-confirmed activity logs. Finally, focus groups are used as follow-up to receive qualitative examples of student engagement with the program. Four years of data have confirmed the effectiveness of the intervention, showing significant student improvements on thirteen out of seventeen wellness categories (Newton, Kim, & Newton, 2006). The program has been used as a model demonstration of how a student service can provide student-learning outcomes, outcomes that satisfy the requests by national accreditation agencies to provide value-added evidence.

The University Life Café

One example of a peer-to-peer helping Web site is the University Life Café (www.universitylifecafe.org), originated and maintained by Kansas State University and originally funded by Substance Abuse and Mental Health Services Administration (SAMHSA); this site launched in early 2009 to promote emotional well-being for college students.

It was built on a technology substructure that allows site users to share writings, multimedia, audio recordings, music, and videos and comment on each other's ideas in the Student Brew area. This site purposefully connects novices with experts in a community of college students.

Professional mental health professionals created contents on a different part of the site (the Bookshelf) on relevant topics

Figure 11.2. The University Life Café

about stress management, study tips, problem solving, developing a support system, conflict resolution, financial management, substance abuse, and other relevant topics. They purposefully seeded the site pre-launch to create a culture of decorum and mutual care. Wellness topics addressed on the site include those linked to a variety of topics such as anxiety, depression, nutrition, suicide, PTSD (posttraumatic stress disorder), relationships, and sleep disorders.

Campus mental health professionals are present on the site to respond to and moderate questions on topics such as drug use (mental health professionals such as Dr. Bill, the "Drug Czar"). The AI (artificial intelligence) provides warnings if particular

299

threats of self-harm are posted by the university's students, thus warranting live human intervention.

Site visitors from around the world may view all contents, but only those who are authenticated members of the host university community with an active electronic identification may post to the site. Students may also create anonymous identities as their online "selves," but they are still identifiable by site administrators on the back-end via artificial intelligence in case of the need for a potential crisis intervention.

A blog encourages users to share ideas and mutual support. An Events tab helps localize the community by listing local campus and community events. There is an atmosphere of caring and sharing in the interactions. An art contest was launched in Spring 2009 to encourage the sharing of various types of art (captured digitally) that then created an online gallery show, with a correlating physical art show on campus. Site "heuristics" and surveys that are self-administered are available through this site for users to gain some self-perspectives.

The University Life Café partners with various student support services and campus entities to provide rich information on the site. The mix of live human oversight and machine-driven AI protections keep the site fairly safe from "griefers" and digital vandals. A solid legal policy was put into place on inception to ensure that user privacy would not be infringed upon, that intellectual property be upheld, that people uphold "civility and care," and that liabilities not be incurred. The policies also clearly encourage professional help-seeking in various circumstances, in particular those of "dire" need, and explain the limits of the online anonymity on the site.

Site originators who consider the various informational, support, communications, and other needs of users, and who are responsive to their evolving needs, support the interests of student peers in reaching out to each other.

300

AN ENVIRONMENT OF SAFETY AND NONVIOLENCE FOR ALL

Academic environments require safety as a core element. Safety refers to physical security and comfort; it also refers to the protection of all learners against a sense of threat or harm in any form (physical, emotional, and others). A critical element in creating this environment involves educating students about the importance of understanding, empathizing with, and respecting others. Peer educators in various programs reach out to fellow students to support these endeavors of creating a more civil society but also a safer campus, in every sense of "safety."

Safe Zone: A Social Action Movement Utilizing Peers

For over thirty years, Safe Zone programs have existed across the country to provide a safe place and support for gay, lesbian, bisexual, trans-sexual (GLBT) students. Some institutions have extended the Safe Zone program to include a broader perspective on community safety; it has become part of a social justice movement aimed at creating a safe and equitable campus and promoting an atmosphere of nonviolence for everyone. This program recognizes that any one of us can be affected by emotional, verbal, or physical violence. In particular, individuals who differ from the majority in areas such as religious beliefs, ethnic identity, sexual orientation and sexual identity, culture, or other issues may encounter actions that discriminate, intimidate, harass, or emotionally violate them. On a large campus it can be difficult to know about or access resources that can help in such situations. Safe Zone is a community-based way of uniting to make resources more visible on campus and to support each other.

301

The Safe Zone program trains faculty, staff, and students to become Safe Zone "allies." Initial training for ally status promotes active listening, helpful support, and knowledge of resources and referral opportunities. It is helpful that students are also trained as allies because often students will first talk with other students about their concerns. By including this peer education approach for students as well as faculty and staff, Safe Zone helps provide accommodation, adjustment, and safety for those who might otherwise feel alienation. The completion of the initial training allows an ally to post the Safe Zone emblem on an office door or to wear the emblem on a button as a sign of commitment to being a place of acceptance. Allies also become part of a network of those sharing responsibility to provide the elements of nonviolence and care in the community. Advanced training workshops, offered as continuing education to allies, are also made available to the campus community; these educational sessions could include training on conflict management, nonviolent advocacy, respectful and assertive communication skills, and other topics that may be determined by the needs of the campus.

Because Safe Zone is a movement and a network of those advocating a similar philosophy, it may take many different structures on a given campus. It may have an office connected to a multicultural center, a women's center, GLBT center, or even its own identified space. Funding may come from student allocations or as a special grant from the institution. Typically, a coordinator serves to provide continuity, but the main activities depend upon people networked from all facets of the campus community. In reality, a part of its strength comes from the collaboration, which may avoid the separate or "silo" mentality of a given office or campus agency.

Safe Zone symbols are unique to a campus but frequently include elements such as the triangle and circle above or include rainbows and the words "safe zone" as a representation easily recognized on any campus.

LIVING WELL TOGETHER

Aligning with the concept of safety is the idea of communal living, which promotes harmony and mutual well-being. The integration of many types of individuals living together in a shared space occurs on residential campuses (versus commuter ones). Here, peer educators working in and around residence halls provide enriching programs to their peers on a variety of issues, including getting along with roommates, dealing with diversity issues, problem-solving, and living in community. These are life lessons that have long-term benefits.

Residence Hall Peer Education

Residence Life programs have a long and rich history of using peers as personnel for a variety of service duties. In many ways residence halls represent a microcosm of the greater campus community, providing peer support personnel in the traditional role as live-in residence assistance (RAs). Students also serve as peer educators promoting diversity, academic assistance, student judicial boards, health, fitness, and nutrition consultation, hall programming, and more. In one institution we noted that peer educators in various roles represented about 10 percent of the resident population. The intent for including residence halls in this sampler of programs of peers helping peers is to recognize the breadth of responsibility and important services peer educators provide in the living situation.

Describing residence halls as living learning environments acknowledges that students will spend the largest amount of

303

their daily time interacting in the place they live. One's living environment undoubtedly and significantly impacts personal development. Residence halls are the "mixing bowl" or "melting pot" for social interactions, which include communication and relationship with other students from diverse backgrounds and extend the student living experience far beyond the norms of the original family. Students will learn to deal with crisis and problems in the community, maintain self-governance, and provide recreational and social outlets; also, service routine responsibilities such as staffing the reception desk and working the dining halls are often roles fulfilled by students.

Many institutions today promote a residence environment emphasizing individual responsibility through personal self-regulation and community citizenship. This in turn requires a balanced inclusion of both professional staff and student leaders: professional staff need to provide experience, continuity, and skills in overseeing the general operations of residence halls, and student-leader participation is needed in much of the day-to-day assistance of other students.

The following list includes examples of some of the peer educating and mentoring roles now available. The resident assistant (RA) is the traditional student assistant selected and trained to live on a floor, section, or wing of the hall and provide a variety of administrative, liaison, support, and control functions as defined by the permanent hall staff. Multicultural assistants (MAs) are a newer feature of staff charged with providing understanding and education for diversity, programs on topics such as cultural awareness, acceptance and mediation, and building community. Community assistants (CAs) are trained as hall reception desk and information resources. They become a major front line for providing information and even emergency contact to residents twenty-four hours a day. They also check out sports and kitchen equipment, report on necessary repairs, and even provide wake-up calls. Academic resource coordinators (ARCs) are available for staffing residence hall centers for academic assistance including tutoring, computer labs, and special study seminars. Hall governing boards and judicial boards are composed of elected or appointed student residents responsible for establishing activities, self-governance, and adjudication or sanctions for hall violations. The self-governing board will typically have a budget based upon a residence fee that provides the support for the social and programming activity within the hall.

Selection and training are important to the success of residence hall peer training programs. The following features are found in many successful training programs.

1. Selection is based upon application, interviewing, and screening committees' recommendations and usually occurs in the spring semester before the following service year. Typically, but not universally, applicants are recruited from student residence halls.

2. Training is frequently offered in a credit course either in the semester prior to assuming duties or concurrent to job entry. The advantage of the credit experience is having a blocked time schedule to cover in-depth training. Training covers the content of procedures and duties but also trains in facilitation communication, triage of problem situations, and referral and use of resources. A difficulty with credit courses is the fact that an elective course, outside of the student's major, adds additional student cost.

3. Preservice training usually takes place in the week (or weeks) immediately before the beginning of the academic term. Preservice training is an intensive, usually all-day, activity that includes a range of experiences from staff team-building to orientation to policies and procedures to introduction to campus resources and workshops on topics that may range

305

widely from identifying mental health problems and referral to hall evacuation during an emergency.

4. Continuing training and supervision is a standard practice in most settings as regular meetings are used as opportunities for discussing situations, adding information, and providing ongoing education.

SUMMARY

These ten programs highlight some real-world university and college programs that employ peer educators in a student-centered way. These were designed to support students as well as the development of the peer educators themselves. The leadership behind these programs has demonstrated foresight in their programmatic and organizational strategies. The applied training strategies focus on enhancing peer seducators' knowledge bases and skill sets, as well as on providing excellent paraprofessional services to students. These cases demonstrate many real-world benefits of using peer educators in academic programs; these also show the educational and career enhancements that peer educators may achieve in their work of helping their fellow students.

The examples offered in this chapter to illustrate the variety of possibilities for effective uses of peer educators were based upon actual programs. Example programs illustrate some of the main issues involved in the development of peer education programs, including sponsorship, funding, recruitment, training, promotion, service ideas, and outcome evaluation. It is understood that a reader may wish to follow up and find out more about a given program. We have intentionally not included information permitting this as contact people and programs will change over time, and URL-locator data may quickly become out-of-date. A longer-term solution to idea sharing would include the use of an online site to promote the sharing of information and connections about programs and people throughout the world. One example of this is the BACCHUS network focusing on health and safety initiatives (http://www.bacchusgamma.org).

GLOSSARY

Ability factor (n): Factors such as grades and other measures of previous academic performance used to determine one's compatibility with or likelihood for success at an academic institution

Advice (n): Guidance

Aggressor (n): An individual who will create disturbance in a group, often through bullying behavior

Assessment (n): Appraisal as in a systematic pulling together of data to provide basis for diagnosis and clearer understanding

Atmosphere (n): The surrounding mood or environment

Attending (v): Being emotionally and physically present

Authority (n): A specific power or authorization

Backsliding (v): In terms of goal-setting, a description of behavior if you were to fall back or do worse

Behavioral observation (n): Observing behaviors for the sake of learning about and then improving strengths and weaknesses

Bias (n): A perspective that is tilted in favor of or against a group of people

Brainstorm (v): Creatively and open-mindedly produce ideas and solve problems

Challenge (n): The presence of a crisis, through an event, decision moment, or particular concern

Circumstance factor (n): Factors such as socioeconomic status, ethnicity, geographic location, family background, or job situation used to determine one's compatibility with or likelihood for success at an academic institution

Cohesive (adj): Unified and integrated

Color blindness (n): Denial that one is influenced by racial prejudice

Comfort zone (n): A place or situation where one feels at ease

Competence (n): Having the required knowledge and skill base

Conformity (n): Aligning or agreeing with a standard

Congruent (adj): In agreement

Consultation (n): A discussion or conference; meeting with another for advisement

Crisis (n): A time of intense difficulty, trouble, or danger

Culture (n): That which makes an individual who he or she is

Cultural advocacy (n): Actions that support or argue in favor of a culture

Cultural awareness (n): Knowledge and awareness of other cultures

Cultural blindness (n): Being aware of a cultural issue but choosing to ignore it

Cultural fluency (n): Knowledge that enables learning and collegiality between and within diverse cultures

Cultural programming (n): The various ways in which culture affects people and helps them make sense of the world

Cultural sabotage (n): Means by which individuals or institutions cause damage to cultures

Cultural tolerance (n): The act of being aware and accepting of other cultures

Cumulative (adj): Consisting of a totality of a range of factors, formed by the addition of successive parts

Customize (v): In terms of time management, the act of aligning tasks with performance conditions, such as when one is most alert during the day

Delegation (n): The act of assigning and entrusting tasks to others

Demographic (n): A vital statistic of a human population

Denial (n): As it relates to multiculturalism, hesitation to admit prejudice toward another group

Discrimination (n): The expression of prejudice or a stereotype

Dissonance (n): Inconsistency between beliefs, or between actions and beliefs, creates tension

Distracter (n): An individual who leads a group off task by being disruptive or clowning around

Diversity (n): Variety, a range of differences; respect for differences

Empathy (n): Intellectual and emotional understanding of another person from that person's frame of reference

Engagement (n): Emotionally and mentally invested behavior

Equilibrium (n): A state of balance or stasis

Equity (n): Quality of being fair and impartial

Externship (n): Supervised practice done away from campus but in a particular professional field of study

Extrinsic motivation (n): Activation of goal-oriented behavior from sources external to oneself

Facilitate (v): To assist or help progress

Fellowship (n): Friendly relationship or companionship

Force-field analysis (n): A theory by Kurt Lewin that may be applied to the analysis of an organization or a group situation (or dynamic) and that examines the competing factors that led to a particular situation

Formative (adj): Supporting development or formation, contributing to a developmental stage in learning

Gate-keeping (n): The act of controlling access to something

Goal attainment (n): The achievement of particular aims or objectives

Gratification (n): Satisfaction, reward

Harmonizer (n): An individual who tries to please others so much that it glosses over actual conflicts

Human relations (n): Relations with or between people, particularly the treatment of people in a professional context

Implement (v): To perform or fulfill

Individual discrimination (n): When one person treats others differently, based on group identity rather than personal characteristics

In-group (n): Insiders to an exclusive group, possibly with shared interests and a sense of community

Institutional discrimination (n): When an imbalance of control emerges inside an organization, such as a government, school, business, or even a family

Integrity (n): Sound moral character, honesty

Interchangeable (adj): Able to be used in the place of another

Intercultural (adj): Occurring between two or more cultures

Interdependent (adj): Reliant or mutually dependent on each other

Intermural (adj): Involving students from different institutions of higher education

Internship (n): A formal educational and training program to provide practical learning experiences

Interpersonal (adj): Relating between individuals to the relationships

Intramural (adj): Involving students at the same college or university

Intrinsic motivation (n): Internal activation of goal-oriented behavior

Leadership (n): The ability to guide and direct

Learner packet (n): A self-contained learning module developed by peer educators for use with students as they work to overcome particular skill deficits

Learning style (n): Various approaches to or ways of learning, including visual, aural, read/write, and kinesthetic preferences

Majority culture (n): Culture that is the most common

Manipulator (n): An individual who draws attention from others by pretending to be interested or acting in an alluring way, especially by communicating a dependency on others and a need for rescue and support

Maturation (n): The act of growth and development

Mentor (n): A trusted and influential supporter and guide, often in a particular aspect of learning

Mind map (n): Diagram used to represent words, ideas, tasks, or other items linked to and arranged around a central key word or idea; used to generate creative problem-solving ideas

Minority culture (n): Culture unlike the majority culture

Monopolizer (n): An individual in a group setting who tends to dominate verbally and draw undue attention to himself or herself

Motivation (n): Something that offers an incentive or inducement

Motivational interviewing (n): A strategy to help individuals deal with ambivalence and sometimes resistance to make changes

Multiculturalism (n): The acceptance of multiple ethnic cultures, for practical reasons and/or for the sake of diversity

Neutralize (v): To counteract or make harmless or ineffectual

Normative (adj): Acceptable and agreed upon behavior in a group

Out-group (adj): People outside a particular group, perceived as "other"; people considered inferior

Parameter (n): A characteristic or aspect helping to define a system

Paraprofessional (n): An individual trained to assist a professional but not licensed to practice in the profession

313

Peer (n): A person equal to another in background and qualifications

Peer educator (n): A trained fellow student who works with other students to offer educational or personal services that assist in the adaptation and management of some aspects of the college experience

Practicum (n): A part of a course that focuses on practical work in a particular field

Prejudice (n): Preconceived opinion that is not based on reason or actual experience

Privilege (n): A special right or immunity

Rationalization (n): As it relates to prejudice, acknowledgment of a prejudice, and subsequent justification without analyzing true and perhaps subconscious motives

Readiness (n): A person's stage of preparation for a transition or shift in life

Reflection (n): Deep consideration or study

Resolution (n): A determination to take a particular course of action

Rich learning (n): Information that is accurate and useful, applied especially to what is found on the Internet

Self-efficacy (n): The belief that one is capable of performing in a certain manner to attain certain goals

Self-regulation (n): The ability to modify attitudes and behavior when current ones are in some way detrimental to you or others

Self-reliant (adj): Relying on the self, not dependent on others

Service learning (n): Attaining knowledge and personal understanding for self while providing service to others

Simulation (n): An enactment or imitation

Skill deficiency (n): The lack of a particular skill, or the lower standard of a particular skill

Social influence (n): The idea that one's friends have an effect over the attitudes and behaviors of those in their social network

Sociocultural (adj): The interaction of social and cultural elements in a particular phenomena or situation

Sociotechnical (adj): The interaction of social and technological elements, often in an online space

Stagnate (v): To stop growing or advancing

Stereotyping (n): To characterize another person or group with particular descriptors that are not founded in fact

Summative (adj): Something that summarizes cumulatively

Sympathy (n): Understanding, but from one's own perspective rather than that of the other person

System (n): Any group is a system, a complex set of interactive variables that may vary from healthy to unhealthy, growth enhancing to growth inhibiting

Tolerance (n): A fair attitude toward those with different ideas or backgrounds

Transition (n): A change between one developmental state to another

Universalization (n): An attitude that focuses on how people are similar to others and have shared experiences

Variable (n): A factor

Zeitgeist (n): A general trend that represents a particular age or period of time; the "spirit of the age"

REFERENCES

ACT, Inc. (2002). *Return/Graduation Rate Data for 2002.* Retrieved October 10, 2009, from http://www.act.org/news/releases/2002/11-15-02 .html#1

American College Health Association. (2009). National College Health Assessment Spring 2008 Reference Group Data Report. *Journal of American College Health, 57*(5), 477–488.

Association of College Student Educators International. (2006). *Statement of Ethical Principles and Standards.* Retrieved October 13, 2009, from http://www.2.myacpa.org/ethics/statement.php

Astin, A. (1993). *What Matters in College? Four Critical Years Revisited.* San Francisco: Jossey-Bass.

Astin, A. W. (1999). Student involvement: A developmental theory for higher education. *Journal of College Student Development, 54,* 208–225.

Bandura, A. (1997). *Self-Efficacy: The Exercise of Control.* New York: Freeman.

Birchard, K. (2009, June 30). Campus shooting led to widespread depression. *Chronicle of Higher Education.*

Bong, M. (2004). Academic motivation in self-efficacy, task value, achievement goal orientations, and attributional beliefs. *Journal of Educational Research, 93*(1), 287–297.

Borton, T. (1970). *Reach, Touch, and Teach.* New York: McGraw-Hill.

Brack, A. B., Millard, M., & Shah, K. (2008). Are peer educators really peers. *Journal of American College Health, 56,* 566–568.

Brislin, R. (1993). *Understanding Culture's Influence on Behavior.* Orlando, FL: Harcourt Brace.

Burns, J. M. (1978). *Leadership*. New York: HarperCollins.

Buzan, T. (2002). *How to Mind Map: The Thinking Tool That Will Change Your Life*. ThorSons.com.

Carkhuff, R. R. (1969). *Helping and Human Relations*. Austin, TX: Holt, Rinehart and Winston.

Carns, A. W., Carns, M. R., & Wright, J. (1993). Students as para-professionals in four-year colleges and universities: Current practice compared to prior practice. *Journal of College Student Development, 34*, 358–363.

Cartwright, D., & Zander, A. (1968). Issues and basic assumptions. In D. Cartwright and A. Zander (eds.), *Group Dynamics*. New York: HarperCollins.

Chemers, M. M., Hu, L., & Garcia, B. F. (2001). Academic self-efficacy and first-year college student performance and adjustment. *Journal of Educational Psychology, 93*(1), 55–64.

Chickering, A. W., & Reisser, L. (1993). *Education and Identity*. (2nd ed.) San Francisco: Jossey-Bass.

Daniels, T., & Ivey, A. (2007). *Microcounseling: Making Skills Training Work in a Multicultural World*. Springfield, IL: Charles C. Thomas.

Davidson, W. B., & Beck, H. P. (2006). Using the survey of academic orientations to predict undergraduate stress levels. *NACADA Journal, 26*(2), 13–20.

De Bono, E. (1970). *Lateral Thinking: Creativity Step by Step*. New York: Harper & Row.

De Bono, E. (1971). *New Think*. New York: Avon Books.

DiTiberio, J. K., & Hammer, A. L. (1993). *Introduction to Type and College*. Palo Alto, CA: CPP, Inc.

Dunning, D. (2003). *Introduction to Type and Communication*. Mountain View, CA: CPP, Inc.

Eberhardt, D. M. (2007). Facing up to Facebook. *About Campus, 12* (4), 18–26.

Egan, G. (2009). *The Skilled Helper: A Problem-Management and Opportunity-Development Approach to Helping* (9th ed.). Belmont, CA: Brooks/Cole.

Ender, S. C., Saunders-McCaffrey, S., & Miller, T. K. (1979). *Students Helping Students: A Training Manual for Peer Helpers on the College Campus*. Athens, GA.: Student Development Associates.

Ender, S. C., & Winston, R. B., Jr. (eds.) (1984). *Students as Paraprofessional Staff*. San Francisco: Jossey-Bass.

Feldman, K. A., & Newcomb, T. M. (1970). *The Impact of College on Students: An Analysis of Four Decades of Research*, vol. 1. San Francisco: Jossey-Bass.

Fiedler, R. (1967). *A Theory of Leadership Effectiveness*. New York: McGraw-Hill.

Friedlander, L. J., Reid, G. J., Shupak, N., & Cribbie, R. (2007). Social support, self-esteem, and stress as predictors of adjustment to university among first-year undergraduates. *Journal of College Student Development, 48*(3), 259–274.

Fuhriman, A. J., & Burlingame, G. M. (1990). Consistency of matter: A comparative analysis of individual and group process variables. *Counseling Psychologists, 18*(1), 6–63.

Gardner, H. (2006). *Multiple Intelligences: New Horizons in Theory and Practice*. New York: Basic Books.

Gazda, G. M., Asbury, F., Balzer, F. J., Childers, W. C., & Walters, R. P. (1977). *Human Relations Development: A Manual for Educators*. (2nd ed.) Needham Heights, MA: Allyn & Bacon.

Gellin, A. (2003). The effect of undergraduate student involvement on critical thinking: A meta-analysis of the literature 1991–2000. *Journal of College Student Development, 44*, 746–762.

Gilligan, C. A. (1982). *In a Different Voice*. Cambridge, MA: Harvard University Press.

Gladwell, M. (2000). *The Tipping Point: How Little Things Can Make a Big Difference*. New York: Little, Brown.

Good, J. M., Halpin, G., & Halpin, G. (2000). A promising prospect for minority retention: Students becoming peer mentors. *Journal of Negro Education, 69*(4), 375–383.

Greenberg, E., & Weber, K. (2008). *Generation We: How Millennial Youth Are Taking over America and Changing Our World Forever*. Emeryville, CA: Pachatusan.

Guttman, H. M. (2009). The accountable leader. *Leader to Leader Journal*, *51*, 47–51.

Hallowell, E. M. (2006). *Waking Up in Time: Finding Inner Peace in Times of Accelerating Change*. Novato, CA: Origin Press.

Hershey, P., & Blanchard, K. (1977). *Management of Organizational Behavior: Utilizing Human Resources*. Upper Saddle River, N.J.: Prentice Hall.

Herzberg, F. (1968). One more time: How do you motivate employees? *Harvard Business Review*, *46*(1), 53–62.

Hesselbein, F., Goldsmith, M., & Beckhard, R. (1996). *The Leader of the Future: New Visions, Strategies, and Practices for the Next Era*. San Francisco: Jossey-Bass.

Hill, C. (2009). *Helping Skills: Facilitation, Exploration, Insight and Action* (3rd ed.). Washington, D.C.: American Psychological Association.

Hirsh, E., Hirsh, K. W., & Hirsh, S. K. (2003). *Introduction to Type and Teams*. Mountain View, California: CPP, Inc.

House, J., & Mitchell, T. R. (1974). Path-goal theory of leadership. *Journal of Contemporary Business*, *3*(4), 81–98.

Ivey, A. E., Bradford-Ivey, M., & Zalaquett, C. O. (2010). *Intentional Interviewing and Counseling: Facilitating Client Development in a Multicultural Society* (7th edition). Belmont, CA: Brooks/Cole.

Komives, S. R., Lucas, N., & McMahon, T. R. (2007). *Exploring Leadership* (2nd ed.). San Francisco: Jossey-Bass.

Kouzes, J. M., & Posner, B. (2002). *The Leadership Challenge* (3rd ed.). San Francisco: Jossey-Bass.

Kuh, G. D. (1996). Guiding principles for creating seamless learning environments for university undergraduates. *Journal of College Student Development*, *37*(2), 135–148.

Kuh, G. D. (2003). What we're learning about student engagement from NSSE. *Change*, *35*, 24–32.

Kuh, G. D., Cruce, T. M., Shoup, R., Kinzie, J., & Gonyea, R. M. (2008). Unmasking the effects of student engagement on first-year college grades and persistence. *Journal of Higher Education*, *79*(5), 540–563.

Kuh, G. D., Hu, S., & Vestper, N. (2000). They shall be known by what they do: An activities-based typology of college student. *Journal of College Student Development*, *41*, 228–244.

Lahmers, A. G., & Zulauf, C. R. (2000). Factors associated with academic time use and academic performance of college students: A recursive approach. *Journal of College Student Development, 41*(5), 544–556.

Lewin, K. (1951). *Field Theory in Social Sciences*. New York: HarperCollins.

Light, R. J. *Making the Most of College: Students Speak Their Minds*. Cambridge, MA: Harvard University Press, 2001.

Lockspeiser, T. M., O'Sullivan, P., Teherani, A., & Muller, J. (2008). Understanding the experience of being taught by peers: The value of social and cognitive congruence. *Advancement in Health Science, 12*, 123–134.

MacEachran, B. (2007). Commentary. *About Campus, 12*(4), 25.

Marson, S. M., Wei, G., & Wasserman, D. (2009). A reliability analysis of Goal Attainment Scaling (GAS) weights. *American Journal of Evaluation, 30*(2), 203–216.

Materniak, G. (1984). Student paraprofessionals in the learning skills center. In S. C. Ender & R. B. Winston Jr. (eds.), *Students as Paraprofessional Staff*. San Francisco: Jossey-Bass.

Mellanby, A. R., Rees, J. B., & Tripp, J. H. (2000). Peer-led and adult-led school health education: A critical review of available comparative research. *Health Education Research, 15*, 533–545.

Miller, W. R., & Rollnick, S. (2002). *Motivational Interviewing: Preparing People for Change* (2nd ed.). New York: Guilford Press.

Milliron, M. D., Plinske, K., & Noonan-Terry, C. (2008). Building for a new generation of learning: Conversations to catalyze our construction. *Planning for Higher Education, 37*(1), 7–14.

Myers, I. B., & Myers, P. B. (1995). *Gifts Differing*. Palo Alto, CA: Davies-Black.

National Association of Peer Program Professionals. (2009). *National Association of Peer Program Professionals Code of Ethics for Peer Helpers*. Retrieved October 9, 2009, from http://www.peerprogramprofessionals.org/publications/standards/2010.doc

National Center for Higher Education Management Systems. (2009). *Progress and Completion: Graduation Rates*. Retrieved January 2010 from http://www.higheredinfo.org

National Center for Education Statistics. (2007). *Persistence and Attainment of 2003-2004 Begining Postsecondary Students: After Three Years.* Retrieved October 2, 2009, from http://nces.ed.gov/publsearch

Newton, F. B. (1974) The effect of systematic communication skill training on residence hall paraprofessionals. *Journal of College Student Personnel, 15*(5), 366-375.

Newton, F. B. (1998). The stressed student: How can we help? *About Campus, 3*(2), 4-10.

Newton, F. B. (2000). The new student. *About Campus, 5*(5): 8-15.

Newton, F. B., & Kim, E. (2009). *Health Behaviors Predicting Student Success Outcome.* Retrieved October 2, 2009, from http://www.k-cat.org

Newton, F. B., Kim, E., & Newton, D. W. (2006) A program to establish healthy life-style behaviors with freshmen students. *NASPA Journal, 43*(3), 497-517.

Newton, F. B., & Newton, D. W. (2001). Marketing good student behavior: What the tipping point can teach us. *About Campus, 6*(5), 26-28.

Newton, F. B., & Rieman, A. J. (1978). Improving the functioning of college groups, or doctor can you keep the patient healthy? *Southern College Personnel Association Journal, 1*(1), 27-36.

Newton, F. B., & Wilson, M. W. (1991). The presence and function of metaphor in supervision sessions: An intensive case study using process methodology. *Journal of College Student Development, 32*(5), 455-465.

Nonis, S. A., & Hudson, G. I. (2006). Academic performance of college students: Influence of time spent studying and working. *Journal of Education for Business, 81*(3), 151-159.

Owens, H. (1997). *Open-Space Technology: User's Guide.* San Francisco: Berrett-Koehler.

Pascarella, E. T. (2006). How college affects students: Ten directions for future research. *Journal of College Student Development, 47,* 508-520.

Pascarella, E. T., & Terenzini, P. T. (1991). *How College Affects Students: Findings and Insights from Twenty Years of Research.* San Francisco: Jossey-Bass.

Pike, G. R., & Kuh, G. D. (2005). A typology of student engagement for American colleges and universities. *Research in Higher Education, 46,* 185–209.

Porter, O. E. (1990). *Undergraduate Completion and Persistence at Four-Year Colleges and Universities.* Washington, D.C.: National Institute of Independent Colleges and Universities.

Porter, S. R., & Umbach, P. D. (2006). College major choice: An analysis of person-environment fit. *Research in Higher Education, 47,* 429–449.

Posthuma, B. W. (1996). *Small Groups in Counseling and Therapy.* Needham Heights, MA: Allyn & Bacon.

Powell, J. R., Pyler, S. A., Dickerson, B. A., & McClellan, S. D. (1969). *The Personnel Assistant in College Resident Halls.* Boston: Houghton Mifflin.

Prince, G. M. (1971). The operational mechanisms of synectics. In G. A. Davis and J. A. Scott (eds.), *Training Creative Thinking.* Austin, TX: Holt, Rinehart and Winston.

Pritchard, M. E., & Wilson, G. S. (2003). Using emotional and social factors to predict student success. *Journal of College Student Development, 44*(1), 18–28.

Prochaska, J. O., & Norcross, J. D. (2002). *Systems of Psychotherapy: A Transtheoretical Analysis* (5th ed.). Pacific Grove, CA: Brooks-Cole.

Prochaska, J. O., Norcross, J., & DiClemente, C. C. (1994). *Changing for Good: The Revolutionary Program That Explains the Six Stages of Change and Teaches You How to Free Yourself from Bad Habits.* New York: William Morrow & Co.

Robbins, S. B., Lauver, K., Le, H., Davis, D., Langley, R., & Carlstrom, A. (2004). Do psychosocial and study factors predict college out-comes? *Psychological Bulletin, 130*(2), 261–288.

Robins, K. N., Lindsey, R. B., Lindsey, D. B., & Terrell, R. D. (2006). *Culturally Proficient Instruction: A Guide for People Who Teach* (2nd ed.). Thousand Oaks, CA: Corwin Press.

Rogers, C. R. (1951). *Client-Centered Therapy: Its Current Practices, Implications, and Theory.* Boston: Houghton Mifflin.

323

Rosen, C. S. (2000). Is the sequencing of change processes by stage consistent across health problems? A meta-analysis. *Health Psychology,* *19,* 593–604.

Russell, P. (2008). *Waking Up in Time: Finding Inner Peace in Times of Accelerating Change.* Novato, CA: Origin Press.

Sawyer, R. G., Pinciaro, P., & Bedwell, D. (1997). How peer education changed peer sexuality educators' self-esteem, personal development, and sexual behavior. *Journal of American College Health, 45,* 211–217.

Sax, L. J., Astin, A. W., Korn, W. S., & Mahoney, K. M. (2000). *The American Freshman: National Norms for Fall 2009.* Los Angeles: Higher Education Research Institute, UCLA.

Terrion, J. L., & Leonard, D. (2007). A taxonomy of the characteristics of student peer mentors in higher education: Findings from a literature review. *Mentoring and Tutoring, 15,* 149–164.

Tindall, J. A. (1996). *Peer Programs: An In-depth Look at Peer Helping, Planning, Implementation, and Administration.* Bristol, PA: Accelerated Development.

Tinto, V. (1999). Taking retention seriously: Rethinking the first year of college. *NACADA Journal, 19*(2), 5–9.

Tracey, T. J., & Robbins, S. B. (2006). The interest-major congruence and college success relation: A longitudinal study. *Journal of Vocational Behavior, 69,* 64–89.

Upcraft, M. L., Gardner, J., & Associates. (1989). *The Freshman Year Experience.* San Francisco: Jossey-Bass.

U.S. Department of Education (2003). *Remedial Education at Degree-Granting Postsecondary Institutions in Fall 2000, NCES 2004–010, by Basmat Parsad and Laurie Lewis. Project Officer: Bernard Greene.* Washington, D.C.: U.S. Department of Education.

VanZile-Tamsen, C. (2001). The predictive power of expectancy of success and task value for college students' self-regulated strategy use. *Journal of College Student Development, 42*(3), 233–241.

Velasquez, M. M., Gaddy-Maurer, G. G., Crouch, C., & DiClemente, C. C. (2001). *Group Treatment for Substance Abuse: A Stages of Change Therapy Manual*. New York: Guilford.

von Oech, R. (1986). *A Kick in the Seat of the Pants*. New York: HarperCollins.

Wheatley, M. (2002). *Turning to One Another: Simple Conversations to Restore Hope to the Future*. San Francisco: Berrett-Koehler.

Wheatley, M. (2006). *Leadership and the New Science* (3rd ed.). San Francisco: Berrett-Koehler.

White, R., & Lippitt, R. (1968). Leader behavior and member reactions in three social climates. In D. Cartwright & A. Zander (eds.), *Group Dynamics: Research and Theory*. New York: HarperCollins.

Wolniak, G. C., & Pascarella, E. T. (2005). The effects of college major and job field congruence on job satisfaction. *Journal of Vocational Behavior, 67*, 233–251.

Yalom, I. D., & Leszcz, M. (2005). *The Theory and Practice of Group Psychotherapy* (5th ed.). New York: Basic Books.

Yamauchi, G. (1986). Students helping students: The emergence of para-professionals in campus activities. *Campus Activities Programming, 25*, 430–436.

Zhao, C., & Kuh, G. D. (2004). Adding value: Learning communities and student engagement. *Research in Higher Education, 45*, 115–138.

INDEX